T0214408

Computer Communications and Networks

For further volumes:
www.springer.com/series/4198

The Computer Communications and Networks series is a range of textbooks, monographs and handbooks. It sets out to provide students, researchers and non-specialists alike with a sure grounding in current knowledge, together with comprehensible access to the latest developments in computer communications and networking.

Emphasis is placed on clear and explanatory styles that support a tutorial approach, so that even the most complex of topics is presented in a lucid and intelligible manner.

Bogdan Ciubotaru · Gabriel-Miro Muntean

Advanced Network Programming – Principles and Techniques

Network Application Programming with Java

 Springer

Bogdan Ciubotaru
School of Electronic Engineering
Dublin City University
Dublin, Ireland

Gabriel-Miro Muntean
School of Electronic Engineering
Dublin City University
Dublin, Ireland

Series Editor
A.J. Sammes
Centre for Forensic Computing
Cranfield University
Shrivenham campus
Swindon, UK

ISSN 1617-7975   Computer Communications and Networks
ISBN 978-1-4471-6036-6   ISBN 978-1-4471-5292-7 (eBook)
DOI 10.1007/978-1-4471-5292-7
Springer London Heidelberg New York Dordrecht

Springer is part of Springer Science+Business Media (www.springer.com)

Bogdan Ciubotaru:
*This book is dedicated to my wonderful daughter **Ilinca-Meda** and my lovely wife **Madalina** who have supported me throughout this effort, encouraged me, and blessed me with their love.*

Gabriel-Miro Muntean:
*This book is dedicated to my wonderful children **Daniel-Sasha** and **Alexandra-Nadia** who are smart, playful and happy, and make me feel very proud being their father, to my parents **Dora-Aurelia** and **Ivo** who gave me the most important gifts of wisdom and knowledge and are always encouraging me, and last, but not least, to my lovely wife **Cristina**, a true life partner of mine.*
Thank you very much!

Preface

This book on Advanced Network Programming Principles and Techniques covers in detail network architectures, including the latest wireless heterogeneous networks, communication protocol models, and protocols and support for communication-based services. Network programming techniques are introduced in this book, including server-side and client-side programming solutions, advanced client–server communication models (i.e., socket-based, Remote Method Invocation, applet–servlet communication), network-based data storage, and multimedia transfer.

Advanced Network Programming Principles and Techniques is a useful asset for any reader interested in computer networking whether they are interested in understanding the underlying architectures and paradigms or are application developers looking for useful examples to build communication-based programs. Additionally, this book is an excellent companion to any network programming module taught at the third level institutions worldwide.

To all the readers of this book, the authors hope it will be of great help and wish them "happy reading".

Dublin
Ireland
March 2013

Bogdan Ciubotaru
Gabriel-Miro Muntean

Acknowledgements

Many thanks to Irina Tal and Cristina Muntean who have extensively contributed with their comments which helped make this book better.

Authors

Bogdan Ciubotaru received his Ph.D. degree from Dublin City University, Ireland in 2011 for research in the area of quality-oriented mobility management for multimedia applications and B.Eng. and M.Sc. degrees from "Politehnica" University of Timisoara, Romania in 2004 and 2005, respectively. Dr. Bogdan Ciubotaru was an IRC Postdoctoral research fellow with the Performance Engineering Laboratory, School of Electronic Engineering, Dublin City University (DCU), Ireland. Currently he is with Everseen Ltd, Ireland. His research interests include wireless mobile networks, multimedia streaming over wireless access networks as well as wireless sensor networks and embedded systems. He is a member of IEEE and ACM Institute, Ireland.

Gabriel-Miro Muntean received his Ph.D. degree from Dublin City University (DCU), Ireland in 2003 for research in the area of quality-oriented adaptive multimedia streaming and B.Eng. and M.Eng. degrees from "Politehnica" University of Timisoara, Romania in 1996 and 1997, respectively. He is Senior Lecturer with the School of Electronic Engineering at Dublin City University, Ireland, co-Director of the DCU Performance Engineering Laboratory, Director of the Network Innovations Centre, RINCE Institute, Ireland, and Consultant Professor with Beijing University of Posts and Telecommunications, China. His research interests include quality-oriented and performance-related issues of adaptive multimedia delivery, performance of wired and wireless communications, energy-aware networking and personalised e-learning. Dr. Gabriel-Miro Muntean has published over 180 papers in prestigious international journals and conferences, has authored two other books and 12 book chapters and has edited four other books. Dr. Muntean is an Associate Editor of the IEEE Transactions on Broadcasting, Associate Editor of the IEEE Communications Surveys and Tutorials, and reviewer for other important international journals, conferences and funding agencies. He is a member of ACM, ACM SIGMOBILE, IEEE, and IEEE Broadcast Technology Society.

Contents

Chapter 1
Introduction

Abstract Currently, computer networking has already become ubiquitous, the number of diverse devices is increasing constantly, as are also their capabilities, the range of applications and network-based services is expanding, and user expectations are rapidly evolving. This is the context in which the authors set the scene for this network programming book in its introductory chapter.

The past decades have seen an unprecedented evolution in computer networks. If originally a network has interconnected few computers in a research lab and then has linked computing machines across several university campuses, nowadays the Internet interconnects network devices worldwide. In the developed world, wired broadband Internet access is available in most homes and office buildings and diverse wireless broadband and cellular network technologies enable network access anywhere and anytime, in private and public places alike. Although lagging behind in developing countries or rural areas, network connectivity is becoming available in wireless forms (terrestrial or satellite) to an increasing population, even in the most remote places.

Due to the wide availability of the Internet access, both the range and popularity of communicating network applications has increased dramatically. Applications such as simple Web browsing or file transfer, although still used today, have been shadowed by the increasingly popular rich-media-based applications, ranging from video conferencing to video on demand, IP television, and online gaming.

Services such as electronic mail, online data storage, virtual servers, and workstations, as well as a wide range of utility and entertainment applications, are also growing in popularity among the Internet users.

Furthermore, mobile and hand-held devices are becoming increasingly capable both in terms of computational power and communication capabilities. Smartphones and light portable PCs such as netbooks are highly attractive to all users, including very young ones. As these devices are usually equipped with multiple technology wireless interfaces, they can easily communicate over the Internet, opening the door for a wide range of applications.

This book approaches the very active field of computer networks and network application programming. This field is extremely vast from both theoretical and practical points of view. The amount of information available to a reader willing to

B. Ciubotaru, G.-M. Muntean, *Advanced Network Programming – Principles and Techniques*, Computer Communications and Networks, DOI 10.1007/978-1-4471-5292-7_1, © Springer-Verlag London 2013

explore this field of computer networks and network programming is overwhelming and any help in filtering or organizing the information is highly useful.

This is the context in which this book proposes a novel practical approach in which the reader is introduced gradually to basic and more advanced computer networking concepts. Side-by-side there are theoretical descriptions of these concepts and practical examples and step-by-step discussions.

An extensive and comprehensive set of practical code examples are presented with detailed comments and explanations. The reader benefits from a well organized approach to teaching computer network concepts and network programming techniques which is useful for both readers with a more theoretical interest and readers mostly interested in practical aspects.

The authors have a vast research and development experience in the area of wired and wireless networking. They have been involved in various research projects in the area of wired and wireless networks with focus from low power wireless sensor networks to high performance state-of-the-art wireless heterogeneous environments. The authors have almost 200 top international publications, including books, book chapters, and journal and conference papers addressing various aspects of networking starting from low layer protocol design to high layer application development. They have also been involved in application development projects using both wireless and wired network infrastructure for communication.

Noteworthy is that the authors are teaching various courses in the area of computer networks to both undergraduate and postgraduate students. They have designed this book in order to act as a significant reference to network programming modules taught at their university, and also at other third level institutions worldwide.

Advanced Network Programming Principles and Techniques introduce you to the most up-to-date network architectures, protocols, and paradigms, as well as network programming techniques. This book discusses basic and advanced principles of computer networking, including architectures, communication protocols, and network programming techniques and models. The code examples are extremely useful for understanding the practical aspects of computer networking and of communication services offered by various operating systems, and for learning how to develop network-based applications.

Chapter 2
Network Architectures

Abstract The networks have evolved significantly since the first network architecture has been proposed. Lately, the architecture is seen more as a framework which specifies not only the network topology, network type, network components, and their functionality, but also presents data communication protocols, data formats used, and supported services. This chapter introduces network topologies, network types, and network components, and discusses several network communication technologies.

2.1 Introduction

Designing network architectures and proposing or improving various data communication protocols were at the center of extensive research and development interest. Various network architectures have been proposed since 1950s when the first architecture involving several communication links only used to connect central processors to remote peripherals (e.g., printers). The networks have evolved significantly since, and currently a network architecture is seen as a framework which specifies not only network topology, network type, network components, and their functionality, but also presents data communication protocols available, data formats employed, and a set of services supported. Often billing aspects are also considered.

The first two chapters of this book discuss network architectures and data communication protocols focusing on two directions. This chapter details network topologies, types, components, and communications technologies, and the next chapter presents communication protocols and services, respectively.

Network components include many network devices which enable data exchange between different network parts alongside end-user devices. *Network topologies* indicate how network devices are interconnected by links and how all these are arranged to form a functional communication network. When discussing *network types,* one refers to the classification of networks based on various aspects, including size, communication technology, etc., and when mentioning *network components,* the focus is on both network links and network devices. *Communication technologies* are concerned with the mechanisms employed to exchange data between interconnected network or user devices via the communication links, whereas *protocols* are seen as formal mechanisms to exchange messages between network compo-

B. Ciubotaru, G.-M. Muntean, *Advanced Network Programming – Principles and Techniques*, Computer Communications and Networks, DOI 10.1007/978-1-4471-5292-7_2, © Springer-Verlag London 2013

nents. A protocol architecture includes all the protocols used to transport messages over a certain network infrastructure and indicates the way these protocols interact with each other. Although there is a thin line separating *services* from protocols, the latter are seen mostly application-linked and related to the network interface with end-users or devices.

All these aspects are of extreme importance for application developers, especially when performance constraints are involved. This chapter introduces network architectures' major aspects with the focus on existing and future network technologies.

2.2 Network Topologies

A network topology refers to the arrangement of nodes (i.e., network devices, servers, and host machines) and links between them to form a computer network. Nowadays, various types of topologies have been proposed and are in use. Among these topologies, most known are *ring*, *star*, *bus*, *tree*, *mesh*, and *ad-hoc*. These will be discussed in detail next.

2.2.1 Ring Topology

In a ring topology, each node is connected with exactly two other nodes forming a single data path in a form of a ring. Such a network arrangement is presented in Fig. 2.1.

In the basic ring network topology, the messages (data bits) travel in one direction only. Each node has a dual role, as a host and as a relay. As a host, each node will send data messages to other nodes and will receive messages addressed to it. As a relay, each node forwards messages addressed to other nodes to the next node on the ring.

The main issue concerning ring networks is their reliability. If a single link is broken, the communication between certain nodes is impeded. Dual ring solutions, where communication is possible both clockwise and anticlockwise, have been proposed to improve reliability through redundancy. The increase in redundancy comes with higher deployment and maintenance costs.

Standardization related to the ring topology includes the Token Ring protocol (IEEE 802.5), initially proposed by IBM. Apart from the specifications of the protocol, IEEE 802.5 also includes details on the data formats.

2.2.2 Star Topology

In a star topology, every host is connected to a central network component (denoted as *hub*), which may be a network hub, a switch, or a router, as illustrated in Fig. 2.2.

Fig. 2.1 Ring topology

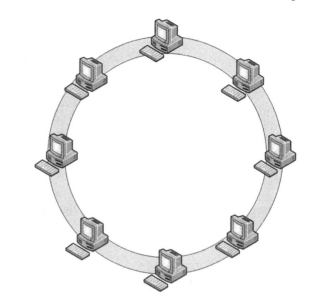

Fig. 2.2 Star topology

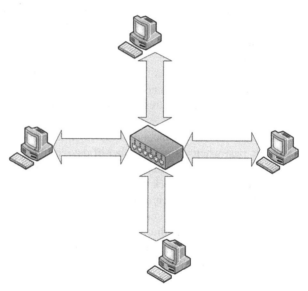

This topology is very popular for home networks where various devices such as desktop PCs, laptops, and mobile devices are connected to a local router, which is further connected to the broadband modem.

In terms of link failure, star topologies are more robust. If a certain link fails, only the hosts using those links will be disconnected from the network, while all the other hosts will not experience any disruptions in communications. The negative aspects of a star topology include the existence of a single point of failure and increased

Fig. 2.3 Bus topology

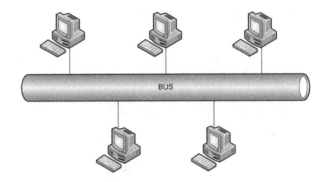

deployment costs. The latter has been mitigated with the latest advancements in wireless networking.

2.2.3 Bus Topology

In a bus topology, a common backbone link is used to connect all the devices in the network with each other, as presented in Fig. 2.3. The hosts compete for accessing the backbone (a single cable) for data transmissions, which is a common communication medium.

When a host gains access to the medium, it sends data messages which are then received by all the hosts connected to the same backbone. However, only the host to which the messages are addressed will react to these messages, while the rest of the hosts will discard them.

The bus-based interconnection of hosts in a local network has been highly popular in the past when a small number of devices have required wired network connectivity. Today there are many diverse devices in need for network connectivity. However, bus networks work the best when a limited number of hosts are connected to the common bus and their efficiency is affected severely when a large number of stations require network access. This is mainly determined by the contention-based access to the common medium. As a consequence, bus topologies are less popular nowadays, in the context of the increasing demand for network connectivity and large growth of data traffic.

Standardization efforts related to the bus topology include the Token Bus protocol (IEEE 802.4) and the Fiber Distributed Data Interface (RFC 1188), which extends the token bus approach.

2.2.4 Tree Topology

The tree topology consists of a combination of bus and star topologies. As it can be seen in Fig. 2.4, the hosts are connected to a network hub which is further connected

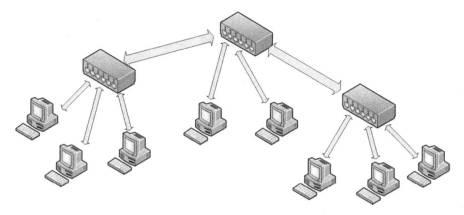

Fig. 2.4 Tree topology

to other hubs in a tree-like structure. Each hub acts as a root and router for a tree of hosts.

Routing messages in ring, bus, and star topologies is performed by broadcasting the messages to all hosts connected in the network. When tree topologies are used, messages originating at a host travel up the tree as far as necessary and then down the structure towards the destination host. Routing solutions become more important when tree topologies are involved, as efficiency is of high importance. In general, tree topologies support more scalable networks than bus and ring topologies. However, their maintenance may incur higher costs.

2.2.5 Mesh Topology

In a full mesh network topology, each host or network device is directly connected to any other device or host within that network. Although extremely robust, in general mesh topologies are very expensive, as they involve a high level of redundancy. This makes them less used for wired connectivity.

However, mesh topologies are most popular for wireless networks, as wireless links can be easily and cost effectively established and maintained. Full mesh topologies are also used for backbone networks.

Using partial mesh topologies is a more cost effective option. In such a topology, some of the devices are connected in a full mesh manner, while others are only connected to one or two devices.

There are several advantages brought by mesh topologies. Mesh networks can withstand high data traffic, as multiple independent paths can be formed to connect different devices within the network. Robustness is another advantage of mesh networks. Expansion and modification of the networks can also be done with minimum traffic disruption.

Fig. 2.5 Mesh topology

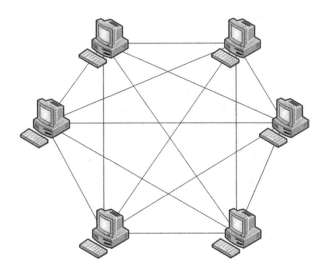

However, as already mentioned, the main disadvantage of the mesh networks is related to the high redundancy which leads to high costs of deployment and maintenance.

A full mesh topology is presented in Fig. 2.5.

2.2.6 Ad-Hoc Topology

Lately there is an increased effort put on providing support for user mobility, and wireless connectivity already enables this. A step further is performed by wireless ad-hoc networks in which each node (potentially mobile in this case) dynamically establishes a communication link with the devices in its proximity. Each mobile node has a dual role, both as a mobile host and as a mobile router.

Ad-hoc networks do not rely on any infrastructure. Remote hosts communicate over dynamically formed paths based on links established between neighboring nodes. The messages travel over multiple links in an multi-hop manner in order to reach their destination. Such a network is graphically depicted in Fig. 2.6, but its topology is dynamically changing.

The main advantage of this type of network is its ease of deployment, low cost, and flexibility. As there is no previously deployed infrastructure, the network is formed on the go, as mobile hosts come and go. As each host in the network also acts as a router, the network range is also variable, adding scalability to the list of advantages.

Despite the advantages, ad-hoc networks suffer from unpredictable routes and data throughput. Due to host/router mobility, each route can be broken at any time due to a mobile device on the route moving away or going off-line.

Fig. 2.6 Ad-hoc topology

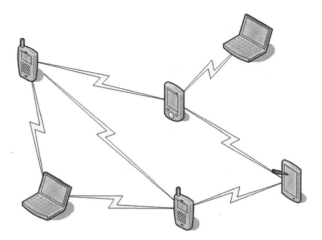

Furthermore, host mobility complicates paths formation, maintenance, and routing messages between senders and receivers, affecting both delivery efficiency and performance.

2.3 Network Components

Regardless of the network architecture employed, the major network components are their nodes and the inter-connecting links.

Based on the physical media used for data transmission between devices, the networks links may use: twisted pair, coaxial cable, fiber optics, as well as wireless media such as radio waves, microwaves, infra-red, and even visible light waves. Note that all these media have different characteristics which highly influence the communication properties and consequently determine their usage.

A twisted pairs cable consists of two insulated copper wires twisted together in a helical form. This cable was at the base of the first widely distributed network which enabled both telephony and later on basic data communications at very low bitrates.

A coaxial cable consists of a stiff copper core covered in a insulating material. The insulator is further surrounded by a cylindrical conductor, usually in the form of a mesh. This outer conductor is further protected by a plastic insulator. By making use of coaxial cables, the data transmission rate was improved, the interference was reduced and networks offering richer services such as cable TV were supported.

Fiber communications are very popular mainly due to their large bandwidth and low effect of interferences. They are performed over fiber optic cables which consist of three elements: a glass core, a glass cladding and some plastic cover. The glass core is the main light propagation medium and is at the center of the fiber cable. The plastic cover is like a shell and is used to protect the fiber. The glass cladding has a lower refraction index and is introduced to keep the light within the core and the plastic cover.

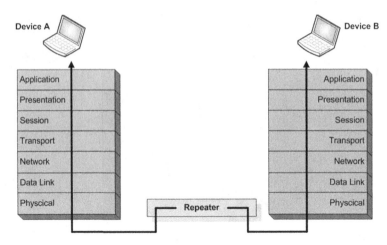

Fig. 2.7 Repeaters operate at physical layer

Wireless communication networks use modulated electromagnetic waves to send messages between directly linked devices. These devices can communicate directly among themselves in a distributed manner, forming ad-hoc networks or rely on a centralized network device to handle inter-end-device communication in the infrastructure mode. Among wireless networks, some use line-of-sight, others non-line-of-sight transmissions; some use low-latency channels (e.g., satellite communications), others fast communication channels; some use low frequency channels, despite the low bandwidth (e.g., military use), others high frequency-high bandwidth, etc.

In terms of network nodes, most visible are the end-user devices which range from smartphones, netbooks, and laptops to desktops and even servers. Lately, diverse consumer devices have also been enabled to exchange data via the networks. This is in the context of smart homes, but the trend is set to continue, supporting also networked device control.

The classic network nodes, also known as inter-networking devices, consist of intermediate devices which provide various support for data exchange and enable networking. Each type of inter-networking device is deployed at different network layers and provides different services. The most known are repeaters, bridges, routers, and gateways.

A repeater is a network device which amplifies, reshapes, and/or retimes the input signal in order to increase the distance, improve the signal quality, and boost efficiency of transmitted data. As repeaters do not attempt to make sense of the content of the data transmitted in any way, performing on the physical signal only, they are seen as operating at the physical network layer, as shown in Fig. 2.7. Repeaters' reshaping function is illustrated in Fig. 2.8.

A bridge is a network device which reduces the amount of traffic on a LAN by dividing it into two segments or enables communication between two LANs by inter-connecting them. Bridges filter data traffic at network boundary and take

Fig. 2.8 Repeaters operate at physical layer

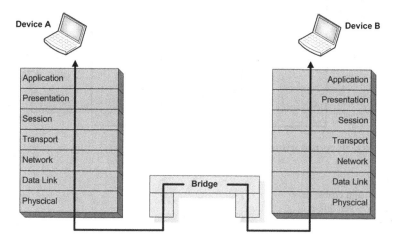

Fig. 2.9 Bridges operate at data link layer

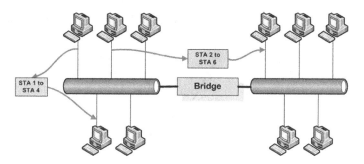

Fig. 2.10 Bridges filter the traffic between network segments

decisions whether or not to allow traffic passage. As bridges require some network-related information, they operate at the level of frames at the data link network layer, as illustrated in Fig. 2.9. A very important task bridges do when dividing networks into segments is confining local traffic to the various network segments, supporting overall network scalability and increasing communication efficiency. An equally important task bridges do when enabling inter-LAN communication is accommodating data exchange despite having different frame formats, payload sizes, data rates, bit order of addresses, usage of priority bits, existence of acknowledgments or negative acknowledgments (ACK/NACK), etc. The principle of bridges performing traffic

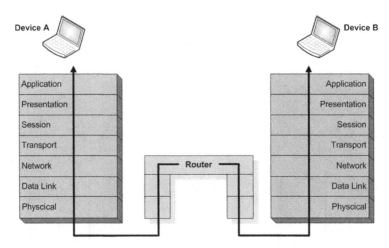

Fig. 2.11 Routers operate at network layer

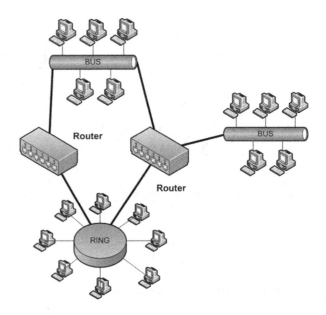

Fig. 2.12 Routers interconnect and enable data exchange between different networks

filtering and reducing the amount of data exchanged across two network segments is shown in Fig. 2.10.

A router is a network device which inter-connects different networks and relays packets from a network to another according to their destination address. Routers communicate with each other and are involved in network information collection which they store in forwarding tables. Based on this information, the routers run routing algorithms to determine the best path between any two hosts and forward the data packets on those paths. Routers are active at the network layer as shown in Fig. 2.11 and are deployed as illustrated in Fig. 2.12.

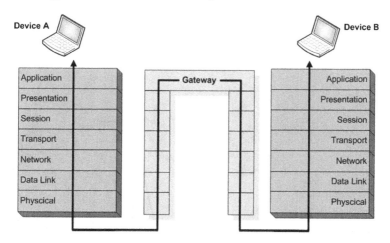

Fig. 2.13 Gateways operate at application layer

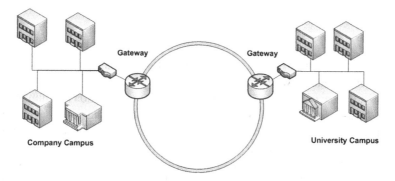

Fig. 2.14 Gateways interconnect and control data exchange between different networks

A gateway is a network device which extends the functionality of a router to include the application layer as illustrated in Fig. 2.13. Modifications of the data packets could include filtering or blocking certain type of traffic, changing values in the header and/or trailer fields, adjustments of data rates, modifications in the size of packets, applying security, etc. An example of gateway deployment is presented in Fig. 2.14.

2.4 Network Types and Communication Technologies

Networks differ in many aspects, not only in their topology, from communication technology to range. In this context, there are many criteria which can be used to classify the networks.

Fig. 2.15 Broadcast
networks

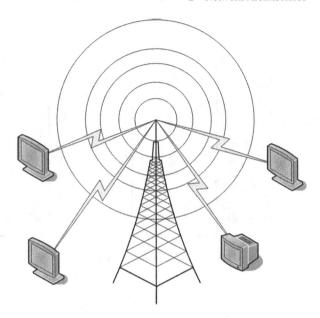

Based on their *transmission technology*, the networks can be classified as broadcast or point-to-point networks.

In a broadcast network, all nodes share the same communication medium. A message sent by a node is heard by all other nodes connected to the network. This constitutes a major advantage of the broadcast networks as it allows the possibility to send the same message to all receivers attached to the network in the most efficient manner. A well known example of a broadcast network is the television network as presented in Fig. 2.15. The same content (TV channels) is delivered to all devices attached to the network, a mechanism suitable for distribution of highly popular non-interactive services.

As opposed to broadcast networks, point-to-point networks use many connections to link individual pairs of devices. A message travels from the source to its destination by traversing multiple interconnected devices. All these intermediate devices and the links connecting them form a communication route. A source node may be connected to a destination node by multiple routes, as presented in Fig. 2.16. Choosing the right route for message transportation is very important in point-to-point networks. These networks are suitable for delivering differentiated content based on various requests.

However, potentially the most important criterion for classifying networks is their scale. In general, the network scale dictates the transmission technology used and often the corresponding communication protocols.

Based on their scale, networks can be classified as personal area networks, local area networks, metropolitan area networks, wide area networks, and the Internet. Next these network categories are discussed in detail.

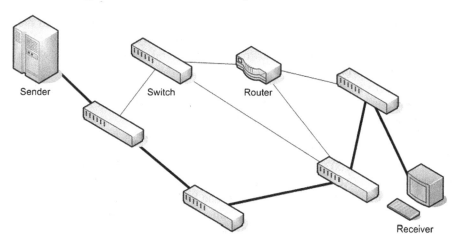

Fig. 2.16   Point-to-point networks

Fig. 2.17   Personal area
network

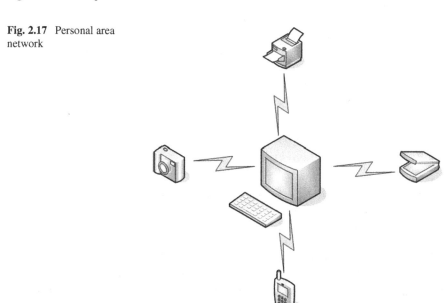

2.4.1 Personal Area Networks

Personal Area Networks, or PANs, use short range transmission technologies (1 m)
and are usually intended to serve one person, hence their name.

An example of a PAN is presented in Fig. 2.17. In this case, wireless communication technology is used to link various peripherals, such as a printer, scanner, as well
as keyboard and mouse with the computer. Moreover, devices such as smartphones
and video cameras can also be connected to computers forming PANs.

Wireless Personal Area Networks (WPANs) are increasingly popular, and the IEEE 802.15 Working Group has been established especially in order to standardize WPAN technologies. Their work has resulted in several standards, among which most important are briefly introduced next.

IEEE 802.15.1 (2002, 2005) standardizes the well known Bluetooth wireless communication technologies used by many portable devices to interconnect or communicate with peripherals or personal computers.

IEEE 802.15.2 (2003) address the coexistence of WPANs with other wireless networks such as wireless local area networks.

IEEE 802.15.3 (2003), IEEE 802.15.3b (2005), IEEE 802.15.3c (2009) address the physical and MAC layers for high-rate WPANs.

IEEE 802.15.4 (2011) specifies the MAC and PHY layer for low-rate, low-range, and low-power wireless network communications. Based on this standard, protocols such as Zigbee and 6LoWPAN define the network layer specialized on ad-hoc networking and the application layer targeting WPAN networks.

IEEE 802.15.5 (2009) provides an architectural framework for mesh networks deployed on low-power wireless communication technologies.

IEEE 802.15.6 (2012) is focused on low-power and short-range wireless technologies to be used around the human body or even in the human body for specific medical applications.

IEEE 802.15.7 (2011) targets the standardization of short-range wireless optical communication based on visible light.

2.4.2 Local Area Networks

Local area networks (LANs) are usually contained within a single building, campus or geographical area, up to a few kilometers in size. LANs are usually privately owned and their main purpose is to interconnect computers and resources such as printers and data storage units belonging to a single functional unit such as an office building, factory, school or university.

LANs are usually small in size, and LAN communications benefit from short delays and reduced error rates. Typical data transmission rates range between 10 and 100 Mbps with newer technologies reaching transmission speeds of up to 10 Gbps.

The most popular technology for LANs is Ethernet, standardized as IEEE 802.3. Other technologies such as token ring, token bus, and FDDI can also be used.

Often Ethernet uses a star topology, where multiple computers are interconnected using wires (usually twisted pairs) or fiber optics to a central active network device.

Fast, Gigabit, and 10 Gigabit Ethernet refer to Ethernet networks capable of reaching transmission speeds of up to 100 Mbps, 1 Gbps, and 10 Gbps, respectively, over twisted wired cables or fiber optics.

Figure 2.18 illustrates three typical LAN topologies.

Wireless Local Area Networks (WLANs) are increasingly popular, mostly due to the reduced cost of deployment and maintenance and their support for mobility.

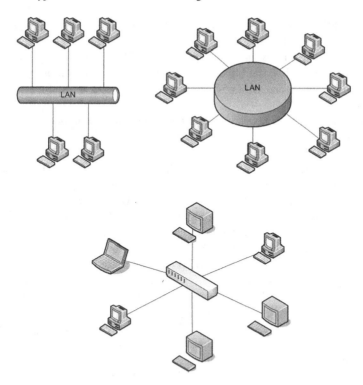

Fig. 2.18 Local area network

Currently, the IEEE 802.11 family of standards has been widely adopted and is being heavily used worldwide for WLANs. This family (also known as WiFi) includes the original standard and various extensions which address different issues including higher bit rates, QoS support, security, etc.

The standards for wireless access networks usually cover the physical layer and the medium access control protocol (MAC) sub-layer. The original IEEE 802.11 standard first released in 1997 [1] supports data rates up to 2 Mbps and was initially developed for best effort traffic only.

Each host connected to a certain IEEE 802.11 access point shares the wireless medium with the other mobile hosts associated with the same access point. This leads to race conditions for medium access which determine high collision rates and consequently low data rates, especially when the number of mobile hosts involved in simultaneous data communications increases.

The IEEE 802.11 MAC layer provides mechanisms for medium access coordination, including the Distributed Coordination Function (DCF) and the partially centralized Point Coordination Function (PCF).

A group of mobile stations connected to a single Access Point (AP) form the basic building block defined by this standard as a Basic Service Set (BSS). The geographical area covered by a BSS is called a Basic Service Area (BSA). Connecting several BSSs through a Distribution System (DS) determines the creation of an Extended Service Set (ESS).

The first IEEE 802.11 extension, IEEE 802.11b [2] increased the maximum data rate to 11 Mbps, which was a huge step forward. Following additional efforts, the data rate was further increased to 54 Mbps in the IEEE 802.11a and IEEE 802.11g standard extensions [3, 4].

Maintaining high QoS levels by using the two coordination methods, DCF and PCF, is difficult, thus novel QoS enhancements for IEEE 802.11 MAC layer were standardized by IEEE 802.11e [5].

Consequently, two new mechanisms are described by the new standard, namely the Hybrid Coordination Function (HCF) and the Enhanced Distributed Coordination Function (EDCF). HCF is based on PCF, and EDCF relies on its implementation on DCF. Further enhancements brought by this standard extension are block acknowledgments which allows acknowledging more then one MAC frame by sending only one acknowledgment packet and *No Ack* which allows time critical data frames not to be acknowledged. To enhance QoS provisioning for time sensitive and bandwidth hungry applications, traffic prioritization was proposed for IEEE 802.11 [6]. Four traffic categories are defined: voice, video, best effort, and background, and in this order, IEEE 802.11e offers prioritization support.

The emerging IEEE 802.11n standard [7] aims at providing even higher bitrates, of up to 600 Mbps. The data rate enhancement approach of IEEE 802.11n is oriented on improving MAC layer techniques, unlike other IEEE 802.11 which aim at increasing the data rates at the physical layer. IEEE 802.11n uses the same QoS support techniques proposed for IEEE 802.11e.

The currently under study IEEE 802.11 VHT (Very High Throughput) [8] aims at offering data rates of up to 1 Gbps for low velocity mobile hosts.

The IEEE 802.11 family supports limited host mobility except for the IEEE 802.11s standard [9, 10] which specifies support for wireless mesh networks and which addresses host mobility within the wider range mesh network.

IEEE 802.11p standardizes wireless access in vehicular environments which represents a short to medium range communication service providing high data transfer rates for roadside-to-vehicle or vehicle-to-vehicle data communications.

The IEEE 802.11 family groups several other standards addressing various aspects of wireless data networks, including security, management, and compatibility. A more detailed overview of IEEE 802.11 family of standards can be found in [11].

Tables 2.1 and 2.2 summarize the characteristics of the most important IEEE 802.11 standards and extensions, including maximum data rates and frequencies.

2.4.3 Metropolitan Area Networks

Metropolitan Area Networks (MANs) usually cover an area the size of a city. Figure 2.19 graphically depicts a MAN interconnecting various areas of a city. Originally, MANs have been developed to distribute television services over the cable TV

Table 2.1 IEEE 802.11 family of standards

Standard	Bitrate	Frequency	Description
802.11	1 Mb/s (2 Mb/s)	2.4 GHz	Initial standard
802.11b	11 Mb/s	2.4 GHz	Data rate enhancement
802.11a	54 Mb/s	5 GHz	Data rate enhancement
802.11g	54 Mb/s	2.4 GHz	Backward compatibility
802.11n	600 Mb/s	2.4 and 5 GHz	Data rate enhancement
802.11p	27 Mb/s	5.9 GHz	Vehicular communication
802.11ac (VHT)	1 Gb/s	<6 GHz	Data rate enhancement
802.11ad (VHT)	1 Gb/s	60 GHz	Data rate enhancement

Table 2.2 IEEE 802.11 family of standards

Standard	Description
802.11e	Extension for QoS support
802.11aa	Extension for audio/video streaming
802.11r	Handoff support
802.11s	Transparent multi-hop operation (Mesh)
802.11u	Interworking with external networks (cellular)

network. The development and increased popularity of the Internet has determined the operators to adapt the cable TV network for the delivery of Internet services.

Several technologies have been used for implementing MANs. These technologies include Asynchronous Transfer Mode (ATM), Fiber Distributed Data Interface (FDDI), and Switched Multi-megabit Data Service (SMDS). These technologies are currently in the process of being replaced by Ethernet-based solutions.

Wireless MAN links interconnecting local area networks have been built based on either microwave, radio, or infra-red laser communication technologies.

Distributed Queue Dual Bus (DQDB), standardized as IEEE 802.6, has been developed specifically for MANs. This technology offers communication infrastructure over long distances, up to 160 km. The operating speed ranges from 34 to 155 Mbps.

Wireless Metropolitan Area Networks (WMANs) were developed to cover whole cities and to interconnect LANs or WLANs as well as individual users, both static and mobile. WMANs use two types of connectivity: *line of sight*, when there is a requirement for communication success such as no obstacles between senders and receivers can exist, and *non-line of sight,* when senders and receivers are not required to see each other in a straight line for communications.

Companies producing equipment for WMANs have formed the Worldwide Interoperability for Microwave Access (WiMAX) forum concerned with the standardization and technology development in this area of wireless communications.

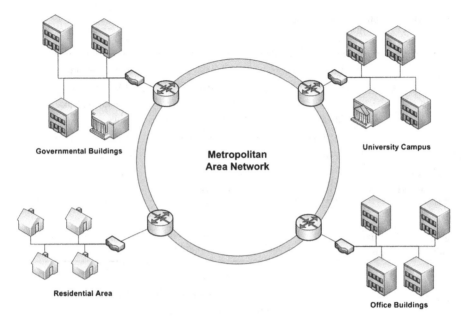

Fig. 2.19 Metropolitan area network

Specific to WMANs is the IEEE 802.16 family of standards. The IEEE 802.16 is based on two systems: the Multichannel Multipoint Distribution System (MMDS) and Local Multipoint Distribution System (LMDS) [12].

The MMDS system offers better coverage (i.e., typical cell radius is 50 km), but the throughput is quite low, between 0.5 and 30 Mbps. LMDS has lower coverage (e.g., 3 to 5 km radius), but provides higher bandwidth (e.g., 34 to 38 Mbps with an increase to 36 Gbps for the newer versions).

IEEE 802.16 provides QoS provisioning support. This is achieved mainly trough connections, service flows, and service scheduling. QoS provisioning is negotiated at the initiation of the session, and QoS requirements are mapped on the QoS parameters in the IEEE 802.16 MAC layer. Mobility is supported in the new IEEE 802.16e standard which permits mobile hosts to change their base station while the data connection is still active. Both soft and hard handover mechanisms are supported, while several enhancement solutions are being proposed [13].

WiMAx is relatively popular as a wireless broadband solution, with several types of mobile devices already having WiMAX interfaces. However, new technologies are already threatening WiMAX.

High Performance Radio Access (HiperACCESS) standardized by ETSI offers non-line of sight broadband wireless access using frequencies between 11 and 43.5 GHz. The typical cell radius is 5 km, and the data rates per cell ranges between 25 and 100 Mbps [14].

High Performance Radio Metropolitan Access Network (HiperMAN), also standardized by ETSI, offers broadband connectivity targeting residential and small office areas. HiperMAN works in the frequency bands below 11 GHz and offers non-line of sight connectivity with aggregated data rates of up to 25 Mbps [15].

WiBro is another WMAN solution developed in Korea which offers broadband connectivity to both stationary and mobile users. WiBro operates in the 2.3–2.4 GHz frequency band offering data rates of up to 50 Mbps [16]. The major advantage of WiBro over the other WMAN technologies is the mobility feature which is very well developed.

High Altitude Platforms (HAP) [17] use a quasi-stationary aerial platform equipped with wireless transceivers offering broadband wireless access with data rates of 120 Mbps or up to 10 Gbps in some configurations. This type of wireless technology offers good coverage with better line of sight connections.

IEEE 802.22 Wireless Regional Area Network (WRAN) offers data rates up to 18 Mbps for rural and remote areas using the unoccupied TV channels between 54 and 862 MHz [18].

Cellular networks which initially offered only voice services are already offering broadband Internet access through the current third generation (3G) and the future fourth generation (4G) networks.

The first to provide mobile communication services were the first generation (1G) cellular networks which supported only analog voice calls and very limited data applications. This technology was replaced by the second generation cellular networks (2G) which is entirely digital and apart from voice communication also supports low bit rate data communication in the form of Short Message Service, Multimedia Message Service.

The current cellular network technologies can be grouped in two main families: Global System for Mobile Communications (GSM) based on time division, multiple access (TDMA), and code division multiple access (CDMA) [19].

The maximum bit rate in GSM was 9.6 kbps; however, throughput enhancement solutions have been developed for this standard including the 2.5G General Packet Radio Service (GPRS) and the 2.75G Enhanced Data Rates for GSM Evolution (EDGE).

GPRS supports theoretical data rates around 114 kbps, but in reality the throughput reaches values around 40 kbps only. EDGE is the first to open the door for multimedia applications over cellular networks. It supports theoretical throughputs around 400 kbps.

The third generation cellular network (3G) supports voice and continues the improvement of the data communication rates.

In the GSM category, the Universal Mobile Telecommunications System (UMTS) makes use of wideband CDMA (WCDMA) and High-Speed Packet Access (HSPA) technologies in order to support bit rates of up to 2 Mbps.

The CDMA-based standards for 3G networks include the CDMA2000 family among which CDMA 1xRTT, supports average data rate of 40–80 kbps with peak data rate of 150 kbps. CDMA 2000 1xEV-DO supports only data communications with maximum data rates of 2.4 Mbps.

As the demand for higher bandwidth and QoS support is increasing with the increased popularity of bandwidth-hungry, real-time applications, the forth generation network (4G) is in the process of being defined and standardized.

The technologies which are principal candidates for 4G networks are Long-Term Evolution (LTE), Ultra Mobile Broadband (UMB), and 802.16m (WiMAX II) [19].

LTE is developed based on the GSM technology with data rates around 250 Mbps. LTE will support QoS provisioning for real-time applications like multimedia streaming [20].

UMB is developed based on the CDMA technology and provides data rates up to 288 Mbps. UMB incorporates control mechanisms which optimize data transmission in order to meet the QoS requirements of various user applications [21]. UBM also supports inter-technology handover with CDMA2000 standards [21].

IEEE 802.16m (WiMAX II) is developed based on the WiMAX standard with adaptation for cellular networks. 802.11m aims at supporting higher data rates and QoS support for various multimedia services. The data rate is expected to reach 100 Mbps for mobile users and 1 Gbps for static users.

2.4.4 Wide Area Networks

Wide Area Networks (WANs) usually cover larger geographical areas such as a whole country or even a continent. The biggest WAN known today is the Internet, spanning the whole globe. However, a typical WAN may interconnect several LANs, MANs, or even other WANs, providing the backbone infrastructure to transport data between the interconnected networks.

As it can be seen in Fig. 2.20, a WAN may use several technologies for the communication subsystem.

Wired infrastructure, including fiber optics or telephone lines, as well as wireless technologies, including terrestrial or satellite-based communication systems, can be used for data transfer within a WAN.

In general, a WAN consists of two basic elements: communication lines (i.e., copper wires, optical fibers, radio links) and switching elements (i.e., routers).

The switching element connects two or more communications lines. Whenever data is received by the switching element on a communication line, it decides on which line the data should be forwarded and transmits the messages on that particular line.

For long distance communications over wired links, WANs tend to use technologies such as Multiprotocol Label Switching (MPLS), Asynchronous Transfer Mode (ATM), Frame Relay, and X.25.

Similar to the wired WANs, the Wireless Wide Area Networks have the largest coverage area among the wireless networks. WWANs can be used as separate networks or as interconnection backbones for MANs.

WWANs are usually satellite networks, but terrestrial versions are also considered. A terrestrial WWAN is standardized by the IEEE 802.20 [22]. This standard targets high mobility users with speeds of up to 250 km/h. QoS preservation methods as well as handover management schemes are supported by this technology.

Satellite WWANs have the advantages of global coverage, high mobility support and broadcast capabilities [12]. Initially satellite networks had only broadcast

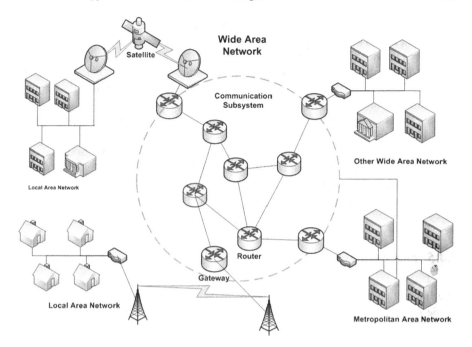

Fig. 2.20 Wide area network

capabilities, but within the Next Generation Satellite System (NGSS) unicast and multicast is also provided.

The Digital Video Broadcasting (DVB) standard family started first by supporting digital video and data broadcasting through the satellite networks. DVB-S (satellite) enables down-link data transfer with rates of up to 45 Mbps only. The newer DVB-S2 increases the downlink rate to 60 Mbps. For uplink DVB-RCS (return channel satellite) standard was developed supporting rates of up to 2 Mbps.

Apart from the satellite versions (DVB-S) DVB has also standardized a terrestrial wireless data service through the DVB-T, and more recently DVB-T2.

DVB-T offers much flexibility in terms of data rates. Depending on the particular configuration of the various parameters specific to the wireless transmission it offers a wide range of bitrates starting from 3.7 up to 31 Mbps [23].

Although DVB-T broadcasts multimedia content to static and mobile users, including vehicular receivers, it is not optimized for highly mobile handheld devices.

Consequently, DVB team has developed DVB-H (handheld) [24] for multimedia content delivery to mobile devices. DVB-H is developed based on the DVB-T (terrestrial), whose infrastructure it uses. Similar to DVB-T, DVB-H offers one way (downlink) point-to-multipoint data communication over wireless links with indoor and outdoor coverage. Considering the limited radio capabilities of a mobile handheld device as well as the higher error rates due to device mobility, DVB-H incorporates powerful error correction mechanisms. Time-multiplexing technologies are used to improve power consumption to cope with the energy constraints of battery powered handheld devices. Seamless handover between base stations is also supported, and loss is highly reduced due to the time-slicing techniques used for power efficiency even with only one radio interface [25].

DVB-H supports mainly downlink communication, interactivity being achieved through separate backward point-to-point channels using other wireless data communication technologies like GPRS or UMTS. Supporting mainly broadcast services, DVB-H scales well offering downlink data rates between 3.3 and 31.6 Mbps. DVB-H specifies only the protocol layers below the network layer.

DVB-H provides an Internet Protocol (IP) interface for higher transport layers which is defined by the IP-based Data Broadcast (IP Datacast) specification. IP Datacast also offers the option of accessing an external cellular network for the backward channels and to create the so-called hybrid networks [26].

2.4.5 The Internet

The Internet can be best described as a network of networks. The Internet is not a single network, but instead a collection of a vast diversity of networks in terms of topologies and communication technologies which use, however, a common set of protocols to offer certain services.

Figure 2.21 schematically presents an overview of the Internet structure. As it can be seen in the figure, networks such as LANs owned by universities or small communities, regional Internet Service Provider (ISP) distribution networks, cellular networks, offering also data services, can be interconnected via backbones allowing for the creation of a global inter-network.

To describe how user hosts are interconnected and are allowed to communicate over the Internet, we will start from the client location. The client PC or home LAN router will be connected to the ISP modem/router which is designed to interconnect the user's LAN with the ISP Point of Presence (PoP) over the telephone lines or cable network. At the PoP level, the signals originating at the home are sent to the ISP's regional network.

Often, the local telecommunication company or the cable TV operator is also the ISP, so the telephone or cable networks and ISP regional networks are overlapping.

Except for the cable and telephone lines, home users my be offered access to the ISP core network using fiber or wireless links such as WiMAX or cellular.

The ISP's regional network consists of interconnected routers and links spread across the area served the ISP. The ISP regional network is further connected to the backbone network owned by a backbone operator. Backbone operators are companies owning and operating large international networks consisting of thousands of routers interconnected by high-bandwidth fiber optical links. These backbone networks can transport huge amounts of traffic and usually link countries and even continents.

The end user usually does not get direct access to a backbone. The ISP regional networks or distribution networks are connected to the backbones. However, large

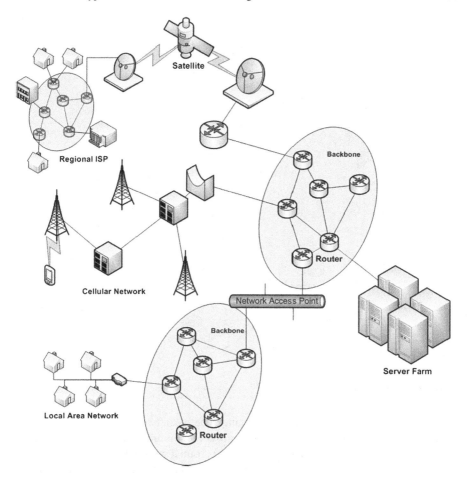

Fig. 2.21 Overview schematic of the Internet

corporations may be connected directly to the backbone, especially those operating high capacity server farms capable of handling millions of service requests and high amount of data traffic.

Various backbones exist, interconnecting all regions of the world, and being operated by various companies. In order to reach a global coverage, all these backbones are interconnect at Network Access Points (NAP). These NAPs basically consist of a high speed LAN interconnecting routers corresponding to different backbones.

Moreover, NAPs are not the only technique to interconnect backbones. Private peering is a well known technique where various routers belonging to distinct backbones have direct links between them allowing data packets to be exchanged between distinct backbones.

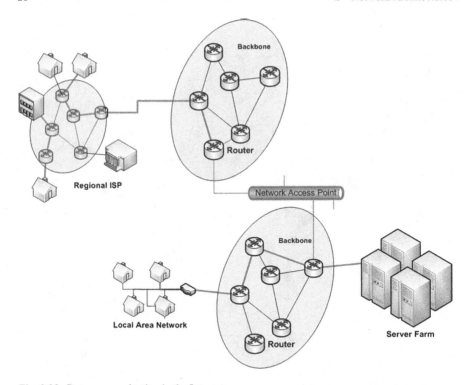

Fig. 2.22 Data communication in the Internet

Figure 2.22 describes how data is exchanged between two hosts over the Internet. As it can be observed in the figure, if two hosts communicate and are connected to the same ISP regional network then the traffic is routed within the ISP network only.

If, for example, a host accesses a service (e.g., a website) located on a server farm, the traffic will be routed from the ISP's network to the corresponding backbone and then through the farm's local network to the destination server.

If two hosts are connected to distinct ISP networks which are further connected to distinct backbones, the data packets will travel from the ISP regional network to the backbone, and then over the NAP to the other backbone and further to the destination ISP's regional network.

2.5 Conclusions

This chapter introduced the various network topologies used today, presented the major network components, and discussed various criteria used to classify the networks. Among the criteria identified, coverage area is accepted as one of the most relevant and with the greatest impact on network cost, complexity, and performance. Various network types identified based on size have been discussed along with the specific communication technologies used by each type of network.

Although the technologies and network characteristics discussed so far represent the foundation of any network, there is still a need for additional support to provide robust and performance-oriented network communications.

There is a need for a set of protocols to govern the way data is produced, formatted, transported, and consumed by various interconnected nodes communicating to each other and a set of services to be offered to the end-users.

The next chapter introduces these protocols and presents major network-based services.

References

1. IEEE (June 1999) IEEE standard for local and metropolitan area networks specfic requirements—Part 11: Wireless LAN medium access control (MAC) and physical layer (PHY) specfications
2. IEEE (September 1999) IEEE standard for local and metropolitan area networks specfic requirements—Part 11: Wireless LAN medium access control (MAC) and physical layer (PHY) specfications high speed physical layer extension in the 2.4 GHz band
3. IEEE (1999) IEEE standard for local and metropolitan area networks specific requirements— Part 11: Wireless LAN medium access control (MAC) and physical layer (PHY) specifications high speed physical layer in the 5 GHz band
4. IEEE (June 2003) IEEE standard for local and metropolitan area networks specific requirements—Part 11: Wireless LAN medium access control (MAC) and physical layer (PHY) specifications amendment 4: further higher data rate extension in the 2.4 GHz band
5. IEEE (2005) IEEE standard for local and metropolitan area networks specific requirements— Part 11: Wireless LAN medium access control (MAC) and physical layer (PHY) specifications MAC enhancements for QoS
6. Xiao Y (2005) Performance analysis of priority schemes for IEEE 802.11 and IEEE 802.11e wireless LANs. IEEE Trans Wirel Commun 4(4):1506–1515
7. IEEE (September 2008) IEEE draft standard for local and metropolitan area network-specific requirements—Part 11: Wireless LAN medium access control (MAC) and physical layer (PHY) specifications mendment 5: enhancements for higher throughput
8. Eastwood L, Migaldi S, Xie Q, Gupta V (2008) Mobility using IEEE 802.21 in a heterogeneous IEEE 802.16/802.11-based, IMT-advanced (4G) network. IEEE Wirel Commun 15(2):26–34
9. IEEE (December 2009) IEEE draft standard for information technology—telecommunications and information exchange between system—LAN/MAN specific requirements—Part 11: Wireless medium access control (MAC) and physical layer (PHY) specifications: amendment 10: mesh networking
10. Hiertz G, Denteneer D, Max S, Taori R, Cardona J, Berlemann L, Walke B (2010) IEEE 802.11s: the WLAN mesh standard. IEEE Wirel Commun 17(1):104–111
11. Hiertz G, Denteneer D, Stibor L, Zang Y, Costa X, Walke B (2010) The IEEE 802.11 universe. IEEE Commun Mag 48(1):62–70
12. Kuran MS, Tugcu T (2007) A survey on emerging broadband wireless access technologies. Comput Netw 51(11):3013–3046
13. Lee DH, Kyamakya K, Umondi J (2006) Fast handover algorithm for IEEE 802.16e broadband wireless access system. 6 pp
14. ETSI (March 2002) Broadband radio access net-works (BRAN) HIPERACCESS system overview
15. ETSI (March 2001) Broadband radio access networks (BRAN); Functional requirements for fixed wireless access systems below 11 GHz: HIPERMAN

16. Kim D (2005) Wibro overview and tta activities. Technical report, TTA
17. Cianca E, Prasad R, De Sanctis M, De Luise A, Antonini M, Teotino D, Ruggieri M (2005) Integrated satellite-hap systems. IEEE Commun Mag 43(supl 12):33–39
18. Chouinard G (2005) Status of work in the IEEE 802.22 WG. Technical report
19. Ortiz S (2007) 4G wireless begins to take shape. Computer 40(11):18–21
20. Anas M, Rosa C, Calabrese F, Michaelsen P, Pedersen K, Mogensen P (2008) Qos-aware single cell admission control for utran LTE uplink, pp 2487–2491
21. Gozalvez J (2007) Ultra mobile broadband [mobile radio]. IEEE Veh Technol Mag 2(1):51–55
22. Bolton W, Xiao Y, Guizani M (2007) IEEE 802.20: mobile broadband wireless access. IEEE Wirel Commun 14(1):84–95
23. Ladebusch U, Liss C (2006) Terrestrial DVB (DVB-T): a broadcast technology for stationary portable and mobile use. Proc IEEE 94(1):183–193
24. DVB (November 2004) Transmission system for handheld terminals (DVB-H), ETSI EN 302304 v1.1.1
25. Kornfeld M, Daoud K (2008) The DVB-H mobile broadcast standard [standards in a nutshell]. IEEE Signal Process Mag 25(4):118–122, 127
26. Kornfeld M, May G (2007) DVB-H and IP datacast mdash; broadcast to handheld devices. IEEE Trans Broadcast 53(1):161–170

Chapter 3
Network Communications Protocols and Services

Abstract As the previous chapter has introduced network topologies, types, components, and major communication technologies, this chapter completes the network architecture description by presenting network protocols and various services supported by the current networks. The hierarchical organization of network protocols is detailed focusing on the most known reference models and the layered communication paradigm. Furthermore, the various protocol layers are detailed, especially at transport and application layers which involve protocols and services mostly detailed in this book. Last, but not least, the principles of the most popular network-based services are summarized, including electronic mail, Web, and the increasingly popular multimedia-based services.

3.1 Introduction

The previous chapter has introduced existing network topologies and communication technologies used to enable data exchange between network-interconnected remote hosts. Although communication technologies and network infrastructures are at the basis for message exchange between nodes, in order to fully support data exchange, a set of protocols has to govern the way messages are sent, routed, received, and interpreted by the communicating parties and the network devices. This chapter presents some of the most important communication protocols and discusses major network services.

3.2 Protocol Hierarchy

3.2.1 Network Reference Models

In order to reduce design complexity and allow for a better standardization process, network protocols are organized in layers (or levels), each layer providing a set of services to the layer immediately above and relying on services from the layer below.

B. Ciubotaru, G.-M. Muntean, *Advanced Network Programming – Principles and Techniques*, Computer Communications and Networks, DOI 10.1007/978-1-4471-5292-7_3, © Springer-Verlag London 2013

Fig. 3.1 OSI and TCP/IP
reference models

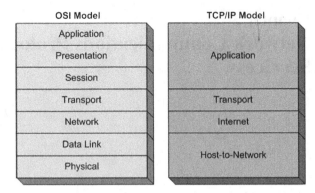

The layered network architecture is organized in reference models; among these the most well known are the ISO Open System Interconnection (OSI) reference model and the TCP/IP reference model.

The OSI model is a theoretical model, and the protocols associated with its layers are rarely used. However, the model itself is widely used to present the concepts used in networking.

As opposed to the OSI, the TCP/IP model is less used for theoretical purposes, but the protocols associated with it are widely used in practice.

Figure 3.1 graphically shows the layers included in each reference model.

The OSI reference model includes seven layers: Physical, Data Link, Network, Transport, Session, Presentation, and Application. There layers are briefly introduced next.

- The *Physical layer* is responsible for transmitting raw bits over a communication channel.
- The *Data Link layer* is in charge of several tasks such as reliability, flow control, and medium access control for point-to-point data communication.
- The *Network layer* is mainly in charge of routing packets through sub-nets.
- The *Transport layer* offers end-to-end data communication services to upper layers.
- The *Session layer* allows users to establish sessions between them, each session offering services such as dialog control and synchronization.
- The *Presentation layer* is concerned with the syntax and semantics of the information (data) exchanged.
- The *Application layer* contains a variety of protocols specific to user applications.

Unlike OSI, the TCP/IP reference model has only four layers: Host-to-Network, Internet, Transport, and Application.

- The *Host-to-Network layer* corresponds to the Data Link and Physical layers from the OSI model, but the TCP/IP reference model does not detail this layer. However, the protocols used at this layer are specific to the network technology used to interconnect the physical user devices and network devices.
- The *Internet layer* corresponds to the Network Layer of the OSI reference model and similar to it, it is in charge of routing data packets through the sub-nets to

Fig. 3.2 A more realistic
TCP/IP reference model

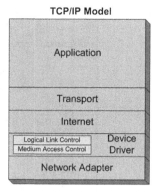

their destination. The widest used protocol residing at this layer is the Internet
Protocol (IP).

- The *Transport layer* of the TCP/IP reference model corresponds with the same
  layer of the OSI model and offers similar services. The protocols residing at this
  layer are the Transmission Control Protocol (TCP) and User Datagram Protocol
  (UDP).
- The *Application layer* of the TCP/IP model is similar to the corresponding layer
  of the OSI model. Protocols residing at this layer include but are not limited
  to File Transport Protocol (FTP), electronic mail protocols (SMTP, IMAP, POP),
  Hypertext Transfer Protocol (HTTP), Domain Name System (DNS), Secure Shell
  (SSH), etc.

A more realistic reference model for TCP/IP is presented in Fig. 3.2. Although
controversial, the host-to-network layer of the initial TCP/IP reference model has
been split in two by some network specialists. These sub-layers are the Device
Driver and Network Adapter sub-layers.

The Network Adapter layer corresponds to the physical layer of the OSI reference
model and mainly consists of the hardware implementation of network interfaces.

The Device Driver layer contains two sub-layers, namely the Logical Link Control and the Medium Access Control. The Logical Link Control (LLC) offers the
upper layers and the operating system access to the device driver. The Medium
Access Control (MAC) is responsible for reporting and setting the device status,
package outgoing data received from LLC in the format required by the network
adapter, sending outgoing data at the appropriate time, receiving incoming data and
unpacking it before verifying its integrity, and delivering it to the LLC sub-layer.

Figure 3.3 schematically presents the structure of the TCP/IP reference model
and some of the network technologies and protocols involved.

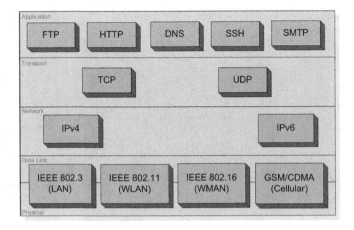

Fig. 3.3 Protocols and Networks specific to TCP/IP reference models

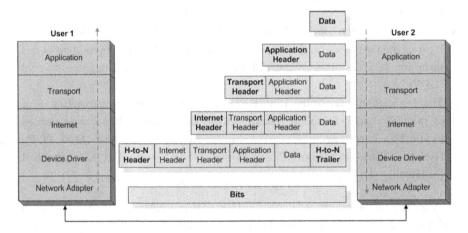

Fig. 3.4 TCP/IP reference model, data flow diagram

3.2.2 Layered Communication Paradigm

As mentioned in the previous sections, the layers of any reference model, including the TCP/IP model, rely on the services provided by the layers above and provide a set of services to the upper layer.

For example, the application layer protocols such as FTP use transport layer protocols such as TCP to carry the content of the files being transferred. The interaction between layers is done using dedicated interfaces which advertise the services provided by the particular layer.

Figure 3.4 schematically presents the data flow through the TCP/IP protocol hierarchy.

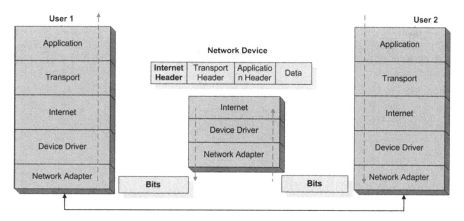

Fig. 3.5   TCP/IP reference model, data flow diagram through network devices

To exemplify, we consider two users, User 1 and User 2, exchange files using FTP. We assume that User 2 has an FTP server and the file repositories and User 1 has an FTP client and requests a certain file to be retrieved.

Figure 3.4 illustrates the file transfer process. The content of the file represents the Data. It is handed over to the application layer FTP protocol which adds its specific headers (Application Header). The FTP protocol may split the original file into chunks for transmission. FTP then hands over the data including the FTP headers to the transport protocol (i.e., TCP). The transport protocol splits the application data into packets, adds its own headers (transport layer headers) and hands over the packets to the Internet Protocol (i.e., IP). The Internet Protocol further adds its specific headers and injects the packets in the network, where the packets are routed towards the destination. The packets are sent via the network by being handed over to the Host-to-Network layer. This layer further adds its headers and trailers and manages the transmission of the raw bits representing the data packets to the next neighbor machine. The next neighbor machine is usually a network device mainly the LAN router. At the router level, the TCP/IP reference model is deployed up to the Internet level. As it can be seen in Fig. 3.5, at the network device level, the raw bits are decoded up to the Internet protocol level where routing is performed. The Internet layer changes the headers accordingly and re-injects the packets in the network by sending them to the next hop on the path towards the destination. At the receiver side, as it is presented in Fig. 3.4, the raw bits are received and are delivered from the physical layer across the layers to the user application. It can be seen that each layer removes its own headers before sending the data to the immediate upper layer.

From an application network programming perspective, all the details concerning layers below the application layer are hidden. For example, as it can be seen in Fig. 3.6, applications can use Sockets for accessing the data transport services offered by the transport layer. In these circumstances, next we discuss application and transport layer issues, ignoring the lower layers.

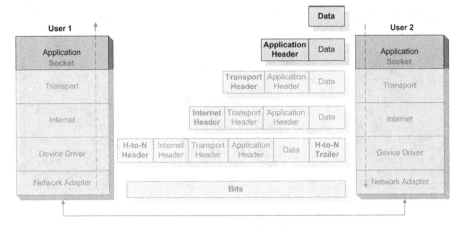

Fig. 3.6 TCP/IP reference model, transport layer programming interface

Fig. 3.7 TCP packet
structure

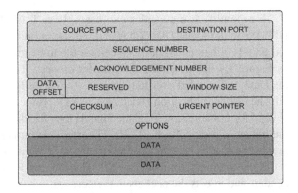

3.2.3 Transport Layer

Transport layer protocols provide end-to-end data transmission and optionally provide functions such as congestion avoidance, reliability and flow control. Transport
Control Protocol (TCP) [1] and User Datagram Protocol (UDP) [2] are two de-facto
protocols employed at the TCP/IP transport layer. These two protocols are designed
and widely deployed in wired network communication environments.

3.2.3.1 Transport Control Protocol

Transport Control Protocol (TCP) [1, 3] is a reliable, connection-oriented, congestion controlled byte stream data transfer protocol. A TCP packet consists of a 20
byte header followed by a payload as illustrated in Fig. 3.7.

The header includes a number of fields that enable the provision of key services.
TCP uses 16 bit source and destination port number fields for multiplexing data to

various sending and receiving processes. The 32 bit sequence number field identifies the byte in the stream that the first byte of data in the segment represents. This field enables the reordering of out-of-order packets. The 32 bit acknowledgment field contains the sequence number of the next data segment the receiver expects to receive. This allows the sender to identify packets that have not been received, yet. These two fields are essential for providing a reliable delivery service. The 4 bit data offset/header length field specifies the length of the header. The 6 bit field is reserved for future use. Next, there are 6 flag bits. URG (U) is used to determine if the value in the urgent pointer field is valid. If set, the urgent pointer contains a sequence number offset, which corresponds to a TCP segment that contains urgent data and it should be expedited to its destination. ACK indicates if the acknowledgment number field is significant. It is used to by the receiver to inform the server that the packets it received are in order and intact. PSH is used to minimize the amount of buffering used before passing the data in this packet to the receiving process. The RST flag used to reset the connection, while the SYN and FIN flags are used for establishing and closing the TCP connection. The 16 bit window size field specifies the number of bytes each end of the connection is willing to accept, beginning with the one specified by the acknowledgment number. This field enables connection flow control. Finally, a checksum field covers the header and payload of the TCP segment.

Flow control is achieved by TCP using the window size field. This field identifies the number of bytes, starting with the byte acknowledged, that the receiver is willing to accept. If a receiver is busy or does not want to receive more data from the sender, this value can be set to 0. In addition to the flow control based on the window size, the current TCP standard (RFC 2581 [4]) uses a complex congestion control mechanism which involves four algorithms: Slow Start, Congestion Avoidance, Fast Retransmit, and Fast Recovery. The slow start algorithm employed by TCP tries to avoid congestion by starting the transmission at a low rate and fast increasing the rate until there is the first indication that the available bandwidth limit is being reached. Congestion avoidance further increases the rate gradually to a level acceptable given the existing bandwidth resources. Both slow start and congestion avoidance employ an Additive Increase Multiplicative Decrease (AIMD) approach, enabling the rate of transmitted data to increase incrementally, while the network is still capable of sustaining the current rate (i.e., no packet loss occurs). As soon as this rate exceeds the available network bandwidth (i.e., lost packets are detected), the sender dramatically reduces the data rate. Fast retransmit and fast recovery algorithms were introduced in order to speed up data delivery following loss and the consequent TCP drastic reduction in transmission rate.

TCP is used for a number of best effort applications, which rely on application-layer protocols such as the Hypertext Transfer Protocol (HTTP) for Web browsing and File Transfer Protocol (FTP) for file transfer. These applications are not time critical, but require guarantees that the integrity of the received data is maintained. For this reason TCP is not the preferred choice for streaming media. Streaming media requires video to be delivered in a timely manner and maintain relatively stable throughput, while also tolerate some loss. Some researchers proposed using

Fig. 3.8 Datagram structure

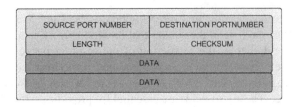

TCP for streaming media more than 10 years ago [5], but did not receive great attention at the time. However, the latest developments in network technologies have made TCP to be considered again for streaming multimedia, including as part of commercial implementations such as Apple's HTTP Live Streaming (HLS) [6] or the latest standard on Dynamic Adaptive Streaming over HTTP (DASH) [7].

3.2.3.2 User Datagram Protocol

User Datagram Protocol (UDP) [2] is a connectionless transport protocol. It provides the basic functionality required for applications to send encapsulated IP datagrams without having to establish a connection. A UDP datagram (see Fig. 3.8) consists of an 8 byte header followed by a payload.

The header consists of four 2 byte fields: source port, destination port, length, and checksum. The source and destination port fields provide required information to allow transport layer daemon processes to route packets to their correct destination application. This multiplexing/demultiplexing feature is the main benefit UDP has over raw IP datagrams. The 16-bit length field specifies the length of the datagram in bytes of the entire datagram (header and data). The field size sets a theoretical limit of 65,527 bytes for the data carried by a single UDP datagram. Finally, a 16-bit checksum field is used for error-checking of the header and data. UDP does not provide any reliability or congestion control features. As a result applications using this protocol must generally be willing to accept or deal with loss, duplication or out-of-order delivery and rely on network-based mechanisms to minimize potential of congestion collapse. The majority of applications using UDP often do not require reliability mechanisms and may even be hindered by them. Applications requiring high degrees of reliability should use a reliable protocol (e.g., TCP). These characteristics make UDP well suited for real-time multimedia streaming applications.

3.2.3.3 TCP/IP and Wireless Networks

As opposed to wired communications where packets not acknowledged by recipient within the expected deadline are supposed to be lost due to network congestion and buffer overflow, packet loss in wireless communications may be caused by interference, noisy channel, etc., which does not necessarily imply congestion.

UDP is a datagram-oriented protocol that provides no delivery guarantee to upper layers, and does not provide any support mechanism for congestion detection or reliability control. This is why UDP is not suitable for use for services requiring transport reliability such as e-mail or file transfer applications.

Several studies [8–10] on the performance evaluation of these two protocols have shown that there are various performance issues when using them for data transport over wireless communication networks.

Several variants of TCP have been proposed, each making improvements in terms of energy consumption, network throughput, and reliability.

TCP Tahoe [4, 11] mainly contributes in the design of slow start, congestion avoidance, and fast retransmission, and is the first protocol to include congestion control and thus is energy efficient for bursty error which happens quite often in wireless sensor networks. TCP Reno [12] implements the three functions of Tahoe and adds additional fast recovery mechanism. TCP New-Reno [13] modifies the fast recovery scheme. The fast recovery function detects packet loss and initiates retransmission without the timeout signal required by traditional retransmission policies. In this case, it provides shorter delay and better quality for multimedia streaming applications. SACK [14] uses selective ACK instead of cumulative ACK to indicate successful transmission of specific packet, thus the sender is able to figure out which packets are lost and save the energy for redundant retransmission; and simulation results show that incorporating SACK in TCP achieves better performance in terms of packet delay and throughput [15]. SACK is supposed to be energy efficient as it decreases the number of unnecessary retransmissions; however, the study in [16] points out that the energy gain is neutralized by the extra overhead. Vegas [17] modifies the congestion control scheme and adapts the transmission rate at the sender side according to the observed Round Trip Time (RTT), and WestwoodNR [18] differentiates the causes of packet loss, i.e., traffic congestion or error-prone wireless channel, and adapts the congestion window size at the sender side accordingly.

3.2.4 Application Layer

The application layer provides most of the functionality required by the user in terms of its direct interaction with the network-based services. The lower layers, including the transport layer, provide data transport services to the application layer. Although the transport layer protocols support data exchange services, their functionality is still too basic for the applications layer. As a consequence various protocols have been developed and deployed at the application layer in order to support the requirements of the highly diverse user applications. Some of these protocols will be discussed in this section.

3.2.4.1 The Domain Name System

In order to initiate a TCP connection or to send UDP datagrams to a host in the network, one needs to know the host's IP address. The main disadvantages of addressing a host by its IP address include the less user-friendly format of IP addresses

Fig. 3.9 DNS resource
record structure

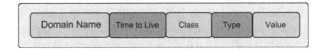

(i.e., numerical form) and the possibility that a host will have its address changed by the network administrator.

To solve this issue, textual names (i.e., domain names) have been introduced to decouple the name of a host from its IP address. Consequently, user applications will address a specific host by its name and not its IP address. However, the underling network still uses IP addresses to exchange and route data packets.

The Domain Name System, best known as DNS, is a distributed system storing records about domain names and host machines. A standard DNS resource record contains the fields presented in Fig. 3.9, which are briefly introduced next.

The *Domain Name* represents the domain the record refers to and is the main query parameter when a DNS server is interrogated for particular records.

The *Time to Live* parameter is an indicator of how stable the record is expected to be. This is mainly relevant for cached records which may soon become outdated.

Class is usually "IN" for Internet information. Other codes can be used for non-Internet information.

The *Type* denotes the king of recorder, among other one of the most important is "A" which represents the IP address.

The *Value* can be a number, a domain name, or an ASCII string.

The following is an example of a DNS record specifying the IP of the host to which the domain *pel.eeng.dcu.ie* refers to. The time to live for this record is 86400 seconds which represents 24 hours. This is a stable record. For less stable records, the time to live field may be set to 60 seconds.

pel.eeng.dcu.ie 86400 IN A 10.10.105.189

Theoretically, a single server could store the DNS records for the whole Internet. In reality, this would quickly lead to this server being overloaded by a huge amount of requests and eventually fail. Moreover, having one single server delivering DNS service poses significant reliability problems risking to bring the whole Internet activity to a halt.

As a consequence, the DNS space is organized in a tree-like structure as illustrated in Fig. 3.10.

The top-level contains generic domains such as .com, .edu, .net, etc., and country domains such as .us, .fr, .ie, .de, etc. Each of the top-level domains is the root of a tree of sub-domains. A leaf domain is a domain that does not have any sub-domains and may represent a host or a organization with hundreds of hosts.

The domain name tree is organized in zones and each of these zones is served by a primary name server and several secondary ones.

There are two types of queries supported by named servers. To exemplify, we consider the host in Fig. 3.10, running a client application willing to initiate a TCP connection with a server running on the host represented by the domain name

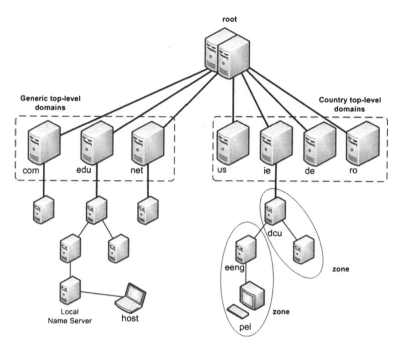

Fig. 3.10 DNS space

pel.eeng.dcu.ie. The client application will call a resolver procedure passing the domain name as a parameter. The resolver will use UDP to send local name server a request for the IP corresponding to *pel.eeng.dcu.ie*. Assuming this domain has never been accessed from the host machine before, the local name server will not have any records of it.

Depending on the type of query (recursive or non-recursive) the local name server will forward the query to the top-level name server (i.e., ie) or will reply with the address of the top-level name server.

For the rest of the example will assume the query is recursive. The local name server forwards the query to the *.ie* name server. The top-level server does not have records of the leaf domains but has records of the next level sub-domains. Consequently, it forwards the request to *dcu* domain server which further forwards the request to *eeng* name server. The *eeng* name server retrieves the authoritative record from its database and forwards it to the originator of the query which further returns the record towards the local name server of the client host. The local name server sends the record to the resolver of client application. The authoritative record comes from the server that manages the domain (i.e., *eeng* name server) is always up to date. In the context of the presented example, the client host's local name server caches the record for quick future name resolution (the cached record will be kept for as long as the Time to Live parameter specifies, in order to avoid stalled data).

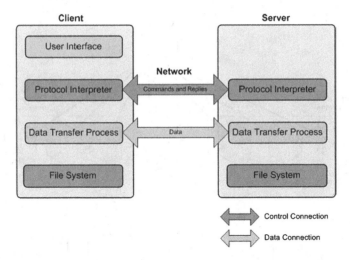

Fig. 3.11 FTP session

3.2.4.2 File Transfer Protocol

File transfers account for large amounts of data exchange over the Internet. File transfers involve clients transferring file content in a reliable manner and efficiently to and from servers, but also data exchange between peers in peer-to-peer settings. In general, file transfers are performed using the File Transfer Protocol (FTP).

FTP was developed in 1985 and is still widely used today. The protocol has been first defined in RFC 959, but then several extensions have been proposed to enhance flexibility and security (RFC 1579, RFC 2228) [19–21]. FTP works on top of TCP and in general uses port 21; however, the administrator may choose to use different ports.

The client connects to the server and sends commands, and the server responds with command status messages. In general, each session involves at least one file transfer. The basic principle of file transfers using FTP is outlined in Fig. 3.11.

FTP involves two connections: control and data connections. FTP commands and replies are exchanged via the control connection, while data is exchanged over the data connection. Control connection must be working when the data is transferred. In practice, a single connection is used for both data and control.

Commands can be grouped in three categories.

- Access control commands include:

    - USER—indicates the user;
    - PASS—indicates the password;
    - CWD—change directory;
    - CDUP—change directory to parent;
    - QUIT—logout.

- Transfer parameter commands include:
  - PORT—publish local data port;
  - PASV—server passive (listen);
  - TYPE—indicate data representation (A-ASCII, E-EBCDIC, I-Image, L-Local);
  - MODE—indicate transfer mode (S-Stream, B-Block, C-Compressed);
  - STRU—establish file structure (F-FILE, R-RECORD, P-PAGE).
- Service commands include:
  - RETR—retrieve file;
  - STOR—send and store the file remotely;
  - APPE—send file and append;
  - DELE—delete the file;
  - MKD—make a new directory;
  - RMD—remove a directory;
  - PWD—print working directory;
  - LIST—list files.

Every command must generate at least one reply from the server. This enables the synchronization of requests sent by clients and actions performed by the server and also allows the clients to know the server status. In general, the reply is a single line; however, multiple lines are also accepted. The reply must contain a three digit status code which enables machines to assess server status and a text message which describes the server status in human language.

There are several issues when using FTP for file transfers. Security is an important issue for many companies that have installed firewalls. Firewalls prevent unauthorized users from getting access to the networks. However, firewalls may also inadvertently prevent valid users from accessing some resources. When FTP is involved the network administrators must design rules for classes of FTP connections which may be a costly and error prone process.

Another issue is standardization. There are many FTP client applications with different interpretations of the FTP protocol. Consequently, FTP server administrators must know how to support all of these different client classes.

An alternative to FTP is Web-based file transfer. A Web-based file transfer client runs within the Web browser. There is no need for any software to install, license to purchase or software to maintain. Additionally, there is no need to set-up firewall rules for each user class.

3.3 Services

3.3.1 Electronic Mail

Nowadays, the e-mail service is one of the most used means of electronic communications. It involves users sending messages to other users via the network. In

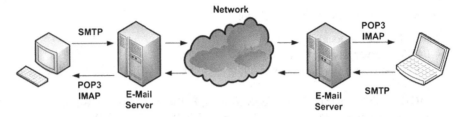

Fig. 3.12 E-mail message exchange

Fig. 3.13 E-mail message format

practice, client machines enable messages to be written and sent to local e-mail hosts (e-mail servers), which communicate with remote clients' e-mail hosts. Remote clients enable the contact with the remote e-mail servers for the messages to be retrieved and then read by the remote users.

The e-mail system is composed of a User Agent (UA) and a Message Transfer Agent (MTA). The UA allows users to send and retrieve messages and may also provide a graphical user interface. The MTA transfers the messages from the source to the destination.

The e-mail system requires several services to be provided by the two agent components: UA and MTA. Composition is provided by UA and refers to the creation of messages and reply messages. Transfer is ensured by MTA and refers to delivering the messages from source to destination. Reporting, also provided by MTA, involves informing the sender about the status of the messages sent. Displaying is provided by UA through the user interface and involves displaying the message so that it can be accessed by the user. Depending on the type of content, sometimes the messages need to be converted before displaying. Often another program is invoked, such as plug-in (embedded in the mail client application) or application (independent from the mail client application). Disposition, managed by the UA, refers to what the remote user does with the message (e.g., save, delete, etc.).

Figure 3.12 shows the basic principle of the e-mail service.

The e-mail message structure involves an envelope, a header, and a body, as outlined in Fig. 3.13 and is formalized in RFC 822 and RFC 2822. The envelope encapsulates the message and contains all info required to transport the message such as destination address, priority, and security level. The header contains the control information required to display the message (e.g., date, subject). The body represents the content useful to the human user.

Multipurpose Internet Mail Extensions (MIME) is a standard (RFC 1341, RFC 2045-2049) that extends the format (RFC 822) of the e-mail messages to support extra features and encoding rules for non-ASCII messages. These features include characters with accents (e.g., in French, German, etc.), text in non-Latin alphabets (e.g., Cyrilic, Hebrew, etc.), text in non-alphabetic languages (e.g., Chinese, Japanese), non-text data (e.g., multimedia, images, audio).

MIME defines five new message headers. The new headers include:

- MIME-Version—Indicates MIME version;
- Content-Description—String describing the content;
- Content-Id—Unique identifier;
- Content-Transfer-Encoding—How body is wrapped for transmission (e.g., 7-bit ASCII, 8-bit codes, base64 binary, etc.);
- Content-Type—Type and format of content, RFC 2045 defines 7 types, including Text (Plain, Enriched), Image(Gif, Jpeg), Audio (Basic), Video (Mpeg) Application, Message (RFC 822, Partial, External-body), Multipart.

Messages not including MIME-Version header are assumed to be in English plain text.

Simple Mail Transfer Protocol (SMTP), standardized in RFC 821, allows messages to be sent from UA to MTA. SMTP works on top of TCP and in general uses port 25.

The client initiates the TCP connection with the server and waits for the server to state it is ready. After the server confirms it is ready, the communication sequence commences. The client sends commands and the server responds with command status messages. Status messages include ASCII encoded numeric codes and details in text. The order of the commands is very important for the success of the message sending operation.

The SMTP commands include:

- HELO—identifies client;
- MAIL FROM:—starts a mail transfer session and identifies the mail sender;
- RCPT TO:—identifies one recipient; there may be multiple RCPT TO: commands;
- DATA—sender ready to transmit a series of lines of text, each ending with CR&LF. A line containing only a period "." indicates the end of the data;
- QUIT—request to finish the session and close the connection.

Extended SMTP (ESMTP) was defined in RFC 2821. EHLO is the new command for identifying the client. Only ESMTP servers accept extended hellos. An SMTP server rejects this command, thus the client will know what type of server it communicates with. Other set of commands and parameters are defined, too.

Post-Office Protocol version 3 (POP3), standardized in RFC 1939, allows messages to be accessed by the client software (UA) on the e-mail server (MTA).

POP3 works on top of TCP and in general uses port 110. The protocol message sequence includes the following stages. After the client connects to the server, it waits for the server to state it is ready. Once the server confirms its availability, the client starts sending commands, which determine the server to perform actions and respond with status messages.

POP3 requires sequential passing through three states: authorization, transaction, and update.

Table 3.1 IMAP vs. POP3

Protocol	RFC	TCP Port	Email store	Email read	Mailboxes	Partial message
POP3	1939	110	Client	Offline	Simple	No
IMAP	2060	143	Server	Online	Multiple	Yes

During the *authorization* phase the client sends username and password details to the server. The following commands are involved:

- USER username—identifies the username;
- PASS password—indicates the password.

During the *transaction* phase the client retrieves the list of messages or a particular one. The client may mark for deletion some of the messages. The following commands are involved:

- LIST—lists e-mails received in order;
- RETR no—retrieves message number no;
- DELE no—marks for deletion message number no.

During the *update* phase, the QUIT command is sent (QUIT starts the update), and the server finishes deleting all the messages marked for deletion, then it sends a disconnect message and disconnects the client.

POP3 allows the client to download the messages locally (on the client machine) and manipulate them offline.

Internet Message Access Protocol (IMAP), standardized in RFC 2060, is also used to access the e-mail messages on the server.

IMAP works on top of TCP and in general listens at port 143. The protocol message sequence includes the following stages. After the client connects to the server, it waits for the server to state it is ready. After the server confirms its status, the client sends commands and the server responds with status messages, after performing the required actions.

IMAP assumes that the server keeps all messages and the client accesses them online. IMAP enables the user to use multiple mailboxes and permits e-mail access from multiple locations.

Specific commands are defined by IMAP for searching messages, reading messages or part of them, creating, manipulating multiple mailboxes, addressing an e-mail by attributes (e.g., from source), etc.

Table 3.1 summarizes the main differences between IMAP and POP3.

3.3.2 The World Wide Web

The World Wide Web or the Web, as it is widely known, represents a framework allowing client machines to access linked documents spread over millions of servers all over the Internet.

Figure 3.14 show the principle of accessing web documents over the Internet.

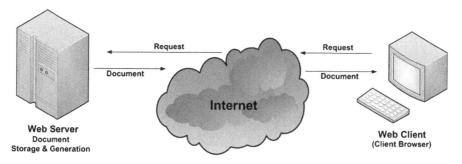

Fig. 3.14 World Wide Web document delivery process

The web documents or web pages, or just pages, consist of a collection of text, images, and lately video content. A web page may also contain links to other web pages. These links are called hyperlinks and can be attached to most of the elements of a web page but mostly to text and images.

The web pages are displayed on the client machine by an application called a browser. Internet Explorer, Firefox, and Chrome are among the most popular.

Web content transfer accounts for most data transfers over the Internet. It involves communications between Web clients (browsers) and Web servers where clients request a piece of Web content from servers and the servers respond delivering it (Fig. 3.14). In general, a series of response requests are part of a web communication session.

The web pages are stored or generated by a web server and are delivered to the client on request. The protocol used by the web client (browser) to interact with a web-server is Hypertext Transfer Protocol (HTTP). HTTP is standardized in RFC 1945 and RFC 2616, and works in general on top of TCP. HTTP uses in general port 80, but other ports can be used as well. There may be one (HTTP v.1.0) or multiple simultaneous connections (HTTP v. 1.1) initiated by the client to the server. Client sends commands and server responds with command status messages. In general, each session involves at least one request response.

Web pages or documents can be classified into three categories: Static, Active, and Dynamic.

Static documents are identically delivered at every request and to any user. These documents are modified by replacing the original file on the server. These documents are created using languages such as HTML, XML, XHTML, CSS, XSL, and are easy to create. Fast to retrieve, these documents do not require much processing on the server or client. Being static, these types of documents can be cached on the client's machine or in nearby servers for faster delivery.

Despite the performance advantages, static documents are difficult to maintain consistent and up to date, offer little user personalization and are not suitable to create large sites.

Active documents are static documents containing executable code which is executed at the client, basically by the browser. Most common executable code executed at the client side is Javascript and Java Applets.

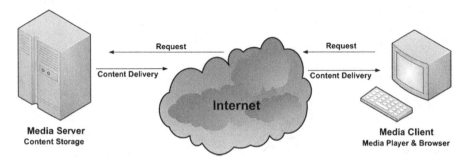

Fig. 3.15 Multimedia content delivery process

Among the advantages are user interactivity, limited user personalization, data display customization, cache friendly, and distributed resource requirements (the code runs on the client machine hence no server resource is required).

Among the disadvantages is the fact that the user runs unknown code which may pose security issues. Also, running code on the client machine may lead to increased delays depending on the performance of the machine used.

Dynamic documents are generated on the fly by the server, at client request. This type of document enables user personalization, supports database access, data display customization and can use time and date sensitive code.

Among the disadvantages of using dynamic documents are their complexity, high resource requirements on the server side and the fact that they are not cache friendly.

Among the most popular technologies for dynamic documents processing are Hypertext Processor (PHP), Java Servlets, and Java Server Pages (JSP).

3.3.3 Multimedia-Based Services

Multimedia represents content of different forms including text, images, audio, video, and animations. Multimedia content is increasingly popular nowadays and accounts for a high share of the data traffic transported over the Internet.

Even the web documents discussed in the previous section contain at least some images and text, which turns them into multimedia content.

However, multimedia applications include a wide range of scenarios from IP Television-to-media streaming to hand-held devices to delivering web documents including images and embedded video or animations.

At its basics, a multimedia application involves various types of content transferred over the network between a media server (can be a web server) and a media client, as presented in Fig. 3.15.

As mentioned before, multimedia includes various forms of content, each type have different requirements in terms of network bandwidth and timely delivery.

Text, usually requires low bandwidth and no real-time constraints. Text is usually required for subtitles, annotations, and meta-data as well as standard content

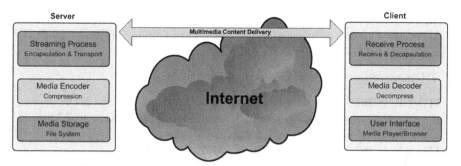

Fig. 3.16 Steps involved by multimedia content delivery process

in web document. Audio requires relatively low bandwidth and has real-time constraints. Still images require higher bandwidths (depending on the size and encoding of the image) and no real-time constraints. Animation consists of a set of still images displayed successively and require higher bandwidth (depending on the size and encoding of the image) and no real-time constraints.

One of the most prevailing form of content involved by multimedia applications is video content. Video content consists of a sequence of still images named frames displayed in a predefined order and at precise timing to create the illusion of motion. It requires high bandwidth and has real-time constraints. The raw frames of a video clip would require a huge amount of data storage, even for today standards, and would be impractical to transfer over the network. To exemplify, a 120 minute video in standard VGA (640×480) resolution at 25 frames per second requires about 154 gigabytes of storage.

In order to reduce the amount of data and make video storage and streaming effective, compression techniques have to be used. Consequently, during video encoding, compression algorithms are employed to reduce the amount of data required to store and transport the video data.

As a consequence, streaming video content from a server to a client involves three main steps: compression, encapsulation, and transport. The process is illustrated in Fig. 3.16.

Video compression relies on a good understanding of the human psycho-visual perception system which allows for the exploitation of redundancies in the video signals. Compression can be lossless or lossy, depending of the possibility to recover the original image identically or not.

Video compression standards have been developed by the Moving Picture Experts Group (MPEG) and International Telecommunication Union (ITU).

MPEG compression standards include:

- MPEG-1—Combined audio–video signal, average bit-rate of 1 Mbps in Standard input format (SIF), 352×288 pixels at 25 frames/s or 352×240 pixels at 29.97 frames/s;
- MPEG-2—Compression of standard definition (SD) and high definition (HD) interlaced video signals. Very high bitrates (up to 20 Mbps) and high picture quality;

- MPEG-3—Addressed HDTV compression, was discontinued;
- MPEG-4—Consists of two distinct compression algorithms: MPEG-4 Part 2 (Visual) and MPEG-4 Part 10 (AVC).

ITU compression standards include the H.26x family:

- ITU-T R. H.261—Teleconferencing and videophone applications, ISDN lines as the transport network infrastructure. Bitrates range from 40 Kbps to 2 Mbps in multiplies of 64 Kbps;
- ITU-T R. H.262—It is identical with the MPEG-2 standard;
- ITU-T R. H.263—Similar to H.261, provides better performance and flexibility. Low bit-rate (below 64 Kbps), however, this target has been relaxed;
- ITU-T R. H.264—Identical with MPEG-4 (AVC). Has become a key technology for multimedia applications. H.264 provides good video quality while substantially reducing the bit rates and latency.

Proprietary compression solutions include:

- VC-1 SMPTE 421M—Standardized by the Society of Motion Picture and Television Engineers (SMPTE). Video codec specification in the next generation optical media formats, such as HD-DVD and Blu-ray. It is developed by Microsoft and was originally known as the Microsoft Windows Media 9;
- Audio Video Coding Standard (AVS)—Audio Video coding Standard Workgroup of China. AVS Part 2 designed for HDTV. AVS Part7 (AVS-P7) for low complexity, low picture resolution applications for the mobile environment;
- Apple QuickTime—Developed by Apple;
- Real Media—Developed by Progressive Networks.

Compression converts data to be stored efficiently. Encapsulation wraps the compressed data in a container which specifies how the data should be stored, transported, and displayed. Encapsulated multimedia content includes video and audio streams, meta-data, subtitles, and synchronization information. Multimedia container formats include audio container formats and flexible container formats.

Audio container formats include:

- Audio Interchange File Format (AIFF) (Mac OS);
- Waveform Audio File Format (WAV) (Windows);
- MPEG-1 or MPEG-2 Audio Layer III (MP3).

Flexible containers include audio, video and other types of data:

- 3GP—3G Mobile phones (Third Generation Partnership Project);
- AVI—Audio Video Interleave (Microsoft Windows container);
- FLV—Internet video delivery with Flash Player (Adobe Systems);
- MOV—QuickTime File Format (Apple Inc.);
- MPEG-TS—MPEG-2 transport stream for digital broadcasting and for transportation over unreliable media;
- MP4—MPEG-4 Part 14, audio and video container for MPEG-4.

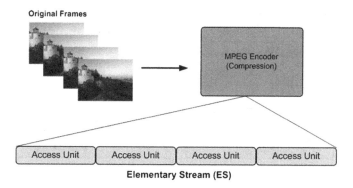

Fig. 3.17 MPEG-2 elementary stream

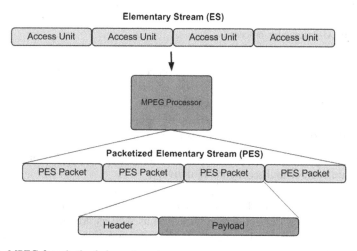

Fig. 3.18 MPEG-2 packetized elementary stream

To exemplify we present the MPEG-2 encapsulation process.

The original video frames are first compressed by the MPEG-2 video compressor. The result is split in access units. An access unit represents the fundamental unit of encoding; for video this is usually an encoded frame. The process is shown in Fig. 3.17.

The compressed content stored in access units is further split into a Packetized Elementary Stream.

The format of the packets is presented in Fig. 3.18.

The payload contains an integral number of access units. The header consists of a packet start code prefix (3 bytes), stream ID (1 byte), PES packet length (2 bytes), optional PES header (variable length), and stuffing bytes.

The optional PES header includes:

- Data Alignment Indicator—The payload starts with video or audio;
- Copyright Information—Copyright protected;

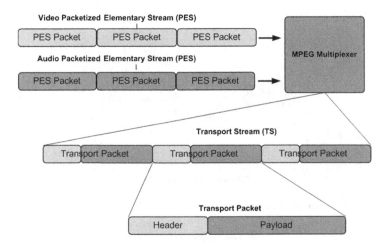

Fig. 3.19 MPEG-2 streaming process

- Presentation Time Stamp (PTS)—synchronizes a set of elementary streams and controls the playback rate;
- Elementary Stream Clock Reference (ESCR);
- Elementary Stream Rate—the ES encoding rate;
- CRC—Monitors errors in the previous PES packet.

Multimedia content delivery or transport may use one of three major techniques: broadcast, unicast, or multicast content delivery.

Broadcasting is cost-effective in terms of bandwidth and resource utilization. However, video-on-demand-like services decrease broadcasting popularity.

Unicast supports video-on-demand services as well as broadcast services. Network resources are used only when necessary and support content adaptation for each user separately.

Multicast is beneficial for group content delivery in applications such as video conferencing. However, the management of multicast groups is difficult and complex.

The process of streaming the packetized elementary streams is presented in Fig. 3.19. The packetized elementary stream is further split into transport packets, each consisting of a header and a payload.

The transport packets have fixed sizes of 188 bytes and a payload of 184 bytes. The header of 4 bytes consists of:

- Synchronization byte—0x47 (0100 0111);
- Three flag bits—Transport error, Payload Start Indicator, Priority;
- Packet Identifier (PID)—13 bits;
- Scrambling control—2 bits, used for payload encryption.
- Adaption Control (2 bits):

    - 01—No adaptation field, payload only;
    - 10—Adaptation field only, no payload;

- 11—Adaptation field followed by payload;
- 00—RESERVED.

• Continuity Counter (4 bits).

Multimedia content can be distributed over any transport protocol such as TCP and UDP. For real-time multimedia streaming, where a certain level of packet loss is acceptable, UDP is preferred over TCP. TCP's congestion control and reliability may affect the real-time delivery of transport stream packets. In the context of real-time streaming of video or audio data, a packet arriving late is as good as a lost packet.

Congestion represents a major issue especially in the context of bandwidth-hungry multimedia applications. Adaptive multimedia streaming applications alter both the encoding and transmission process parameters in order to reduce the amount of data required to describe the content and consequently to be delivered in order to match the available network capacity.

Protocols specific to real-time data delivery were also developed.

Real-time Transport Protocol (RTP) is used for delivering multimedia data over the IP networks. RTP uses transport layer protocols such as UDP and is considered an application layer protocol which delivers multimedia data itself.

Real-time Transport Control Protocol (RTCP) controls data delivery over RTP. RTP and RTCP use different port numbers (even and odd). RTCP delivers control packets carrying information such as throughput, loss, and jitter, information which is not used by RTP, but it is usable by the application directly (bit-rate adaptation). In this context, RTP cannot guarantee the Quality of Service (QoS) at all.

Real Time Streaming Protocol (RTSP) enables a client to have the features of a VCR, such as play, stop, and pause. It is used in conjunction with RTP for delivering multimedia data.

3.4 Conclusions

This chapter has presented the network protocol stacks for the theoretical ISO OSI reference model and the practical TCP/IP model, and has described the layer-based hierarchical data delivery paradigm. As network programming mostly concerns application and transport layers, most relevant protocols at these layers were presented.

The chapter has also described in details services as highly important components of the network framework and has discussed the e-mail, World Wide Web, and multimedia-based services as the most relevant.

The next chapter introduces basic network programming aspects in the context of supporting these services.

References

1. Postel J (1981) Transmission control protocol. Edited by Jon Postel. Available at http://rfc.sunsite.dk/rfc/rfc793.html

2. Postel J (August 1980) User datagram protocol. RFC 768, Internet engineering task force
3. Ramakrishnan K, Floyd S, Black D (2001) The addition of explicit congestion notification (ECN) to IP
4. Allman M, Paxson V, Stevens W (1999) TCP congestion control
5. Krasic C, Li K, Walpole J (2001) The case for streaming multimedia with TCP. In: 8th international workshop on interactive distributed multimedia systems (iDMS 2001), pp 213–218
6. Pantos R (October 2012) E.W.M.: Apple's http live streaming. Technical report, International internet draft
7. Stockhammer T (2011) Dynamic adaptive streaming over http –: standards and design principles. In: Proceedings of the second annual ACM conference on multimedia systems. MMSys '11. ACM, New York, NY, pp 133–144
8. Sandeep (2001) An experimental study of TCP's energy consumption over a wireless link. In: European personal mobile communications conference, IEEE
9. Zorzi M, Rao RR (2001) Energy efficiency of TCP in a local wireless environment. Mob Netw Appl 6:265–278
10. Giannoulis S, Antonopoulos C, Topalis E, Athanasopoulos A, Prayati A, Koubias S TCP vs. UDP performance evaluation for CBR traffic on wireless multihop networks
11. Jacobson V (1995) Congestion avoidance and control. SIGCOMM Comput Commun Rev 25:157–187
12. Jacobson V (April 1990) Modified TCP congestion avoidance algorithm. end2end-interest mailing list
13. Hoe JC (June 1995) Start-up dynamics of TCP's congestion control and avoidance schemes. Master's thesis, Massachusetts Institute of Technology
14. Mathis M, Mahdavi J, Floyd S, Romanow A (October 1996) TCP selective acknowledgment options. RFC 2018 (proposed standard)
15. Fall K, Floyd S (1996) Simulation-based comparisons of Tahoe, Reno and SACK TCP. SIGCOMM Comput Commun Rev 26:5–21
16. Seddik-Ghaleb A, Ghamri-Doudane Y, Senouci SM (2006) A performance study of tcp variants in terms of energy consumption and average goodput within a static ad hoc environment. In: Proceedings of the 2006 international conference on wireless communications and mobile computing. IWCMC '06. ACM, New York, NY, pp 503–508
17. Brakmo LS, O'Malley SW, Peterson LL (1994) In: TCP Vegas: new techniques for congestion detection and avoidance, pp 24–35
18. Mascolo S, Casetti C, Gerla M, Sanadidi MY, Wang R (2001) TCP westwood: bandwidth estimation for enhanced transport over wireless links. In: Proceedings of the 7th annual international conference on mobile computing and networking. MobiCom '01. ACM, New York, NY, pp 287–297
19. Postel J, Reynolds J (October 1985) File transfer protocol. RFC 959 (standard) Updated by RFCs 2228, 2640, 2773, 3659, 5797
20. Bellovin S (1994) Firewall-friendly FTP
21. Horowitz M, Lunt S (October 1997) FTP security extensions. RFC 2228 (proposed standard)

Chapter 4
Basic Network Programming

Abstract This chapter introduces some of the basic principles used for developing network-based applications. Multi-programming and multi-tasking paradigms are introduced as two of the basic concepts of programming. Threads and processes are discussed, emphasizing multi-threaded application development in Java. Inter-thread and inter-process communication techniques and paradigms are also presented, as some of the basic mechanisms for network applications communication.

4.1 Introduction

Network application programming uses high level programming languages and involves a set of principles and techniques. Implementation requires access to various APIs and support from different application development environments. This chapter introduces some of the basic principles used for developing network-based applications using Java programming language. However, the basic concepts and techniques remain the same regardless of the programming language employed and represent the basis for building data communication-based applications.

This chapter discusses the concept of multi-programming, which involves multi-tasking, and presents how it is implemented in standard operating systems. Multi-programming is a very important technique to both achieve computation parallelism and exploit the multi-core architectures of most of the current processors. The chapter also describes some basic aspects of the multi-programming paradigm including processes, threads, inter-thread communication and synchronization, and inter-process communications.

4.2 Multi-programming and Multi-tasking

Originally, uni-programming was the solution of choice for technical reasons. It involves only one user program running on any computer at a time. This was a feasible solution for the early computers which were, in fact, processing machines dedicated to performing a single critical task such as bulk data processing, statistical data analysis, or enterprise resource planning.

B. Ciubotaru, G.-M. Muntean, *Advanced Network Programming – Principles and Techniques*, Computer Communications and Networks, DOI 10.1007/978-1-4471-5292-7_4, © Springer-Verlag London 2013

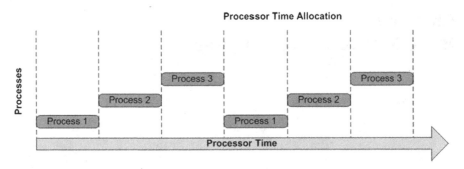

Fig. 4.1 Multi-tasking paradigm

The development of personal computers, and the related diversification in application types determined a definite trend towards widening of user processing requirements. This has lead to uni-programming becoming deprecated. Multi-programming has emerged as a processor allocation paradigm where multiple user programs run on the same computer at the same time.

The main problem with multi-programming is the limited number of CPUs (often a single one) the host machine has. Current CPU architectures involve multiple processing units (cores), which increase the parallel processing capacity of the machine. However, the number of independent processing cores still does not match the number of user programs running at the same time. This is an obvious situation which requires an allocation solution such as all the programs to be able to access the CPU. However, the more user programs run simultaneously on the same machine, the higher the pressure put on the allocation of CPU time.

In this context, the solution to the multi-programming problem is represented by the multi-tasking paradigm. Multi-tasking creates the illusion of concurrency (parallel execution of user programs) by allocating chunks of processor time to each of the running applications sequentially. Originally, each application has been associated with sequential tasks and a single process to run them. However, application development and deployment has moved forward and further benefits from the already described processing parallelism by assigning the same application's tasks to multiple processes which can individually request CPU time.

This software approach to achieve parallel processing requires that the operating systems perform fast switching of CPU between different processes. As a consequence, at any given time a single process only runs on any one processing unit (core). Consequently, the number of processes which run in parallel on a machine is equal to the existing number of processing units on that machine. However, the fast switching between processes creates the illusion (from user perspective) of all processes running in parallel.

Figure 4.1 graphically presents an illustration of the multi-tasking concept. In this figure, three distinct processes are allocated processor time by a single core CPU in a round-robin manner.

Fig. 4.2 Process state transition

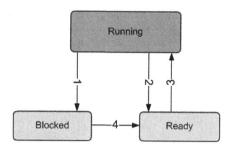

4.3 Processes

A process is a running program sequence along with all the resources that its code can affect (also known as process context). The process context includes the process state, an image of the executable machine code corresponding to the program, allocated memory, descriptors of resources used by the process such as file descriptors or handlers, security attributes such as process owner and process permissions, and last, but not least, processor state like content of registers and physical memory addressing.

The process state represents the status of the process with respect to processor time usage. A process may be in one of three states:

- Running—The process is using the CPU (it has been allocated processor time and the processes machine code is physically executed by the processor).
- Blocked—The process is unable to run until some external event occurs (e.g., data is received from the network). CPU could be free during this period if none of the existing processes is in position to run.
- Ready (Runnable)—The process is ready to run (does not have to wait for any event to occur), but it is temporarily stopped by the operating system to let other processes run on the same CPU.

Figure 4.2 graphically presents the state transitions occurring during the lifetime of a process. Depending on the operating system's scheduling algorithm and the particularities of the process (user application), the status of the process will periodically oscillate between the three states described in the figure.

Figure 4.2 illustrates all possible state transitions which may occur in the following situations:

- Transition 1—Occurs when a process cannot continue, as it is waiting for some external event. For example, when a process initiates a connection to the server, the process will be blocked until the server replies.
- Transition 2—Caused by the process scheduler when it decides to temporarily stop the execution of the current process and give another process the chance to run. The process is interrupted and its state is saved in order to resume operation from the same point it was interrupted without any disruption.
- Transition 3—Caused by the process scheduler when it decides to give a ready process the chance to run. Transitions 2 and 3 are basically creating the illusion of processing parallelism.

Fig. 4.3 Process scheduling

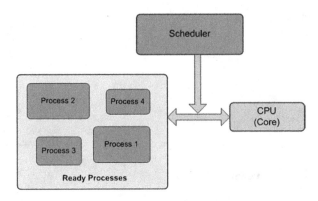

- Transition 4—Occurs when the external event that the blocked process was wait-ing for (such as the arrival of some input messages) occurs. This transition is usually triggered by a processor interruption signal generated by the correspond-ing I/O peripheral or a network interface.

When multiple processes are in the READY state, the operating system must de-cide which one of them to run first. It employs a scheduling algorithm to determine the processes which will be allocated processor time and in what order. Schedul-ing algorithms, as graphically depicted in Fig. 4.3, also determine when to stop one process and give CPU time to another process. Scheduling algorithms may do this voluntary ("non-preemptive scheduling") or forced ("preemptive scheduling").

Non-preemptive scheduling involves the processes giving up processor time will-ingly to allow other processes to run. This usually happens when the currently run-ning process has to switch to the BLOCKED state, while waiting for external event. When preemptive scheduling is used, the currently running process is forced into the READY state to allow other processes to run. Preemptive scheduling can be performed according to a scheduling policy.

There are various scheduling policies including:

- Priority scheduling—processes with higher priority will be allocated processor time more often. Process priority is an important feature when critical applica-tions are running on the host machine. Moreover, when less important tasks or less time-critical applications run (e.g., operating system updates), they may be allocated lower priority in order to minimize the impact on other running appli-cations.
- First come–first served—the first process in the queue of READY process will be allocated processor time. This treats all the process equally, and there is no method to prioritize critical processes.
- Shortest job first—the process requiring less processor time will be given prior-ity. This leaves longer processes with lower priority and may jeopardize to some extent their operation if many light processes are running at the same time.
- Shortest remaining job first—the processes requiring the shortest time to com-plete will be given the highest priority. This approach involves giving priority

Fig. 4.4 Thread scheduling

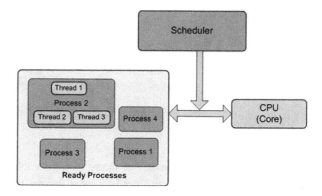

to processes which are about to finish their operation, leading to a faster de-congestion of the process queue.

- Round-robin—equal processor time slices are assigned to all processes.

4.4 Threads

A thread is a sequence of a program that performs certain tasks and executes within a process. Often threads are seen as lightweight processes, as they have their own stack, but share memory and data as well as descriptors of resources with other threads within the same process.

Similar to processes, threads may be allocated different priorities depending on their role within the application process. Thread priority can be associated to the thread during its creation and can be changed during the operation of the thread.

Threads can run in preemptive mode (operating system interrupts thread execution at regular intervals to give processing time to other threads) or in cooperative mode (a thread can access the CPU for as long as it needs).

Threads and their scheduling to access the processor time is illustrated in Fig. 4.4.

4.5 Multi-threading

Multi-threading provides another level of parallelism for task execution, with less overhead. When multiple threads exist, different tasks can be performed in parallel using common data and resources. Thread context switching is less complex and faster than process context switching, making multi-treading an efficient way to emulate parallelism. Thread switching efficiency is mainly determined by the fact that threads own less resources than processes which need to be saved prior to switching the context (they share resources such as memory and descriptors with other threads).

Fig. 4.5 Multi-threading

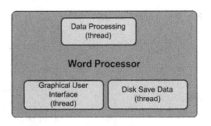

In general, a process consists of many threads, each running at the same time within the process context and performing a unique task. An example of multi-threading is graphically presented in Fig. 4.5. In this example, a word processor application (process) may use multiple threads, each performing a particular task. The graphical user interface (GUI) is running a separate thread, the data processing module has its own thread as well as the module dealing with saving data on the disk.

Despite the evident benefits multi-threading brings, in terms of application design, the number of threads should be kept to the minimum, in order not to overload the system with non-necessary context switches. Additionally, threads should be employed when there are clear benefits from using parallel processing only, as involving multi-threading in a highly sequential series of tasks only adds complexity to otherwise a simple solution.

Thread priorities have to be managed according to the application purpose and requirements. A thread which manages time-critical tasks should be given higher priority than the other threads. Such an example is the graphical user interface (GUI) which should be allocated a dedicated thread with a higher priority than other threads in order to keep the interaction with the user within the corresponding real-time requirements.

4.6 Multi-threading in Java

Java provides built-in support for multi-threaded programming. It offers two methods for using threads within an application. A thread can be created by extending the *Thread* class, or by implementing the *Runnable* interface. Both are equally efficient in terms of using the threads, but the latter is sometimes preferred as it both provides a clearer separation between the behavior of the thread and the thread itself and enables better reuse.

Next these two approaches are shown in a hands-on manner by providing the step-by-step solution design and implementation when trying to perform parallel activities within the same application.

4.6.1 *Extending* **Thread** *Class*

This example will both count and repeatedly display Hello! *messages, while availing from processing parallelism.*

- Step 1—Divide application work in tasks and allocate each of them to a thread:

```
/*CountThread does the counting*/
/*HelloThread does the printing*/
```

- Step 2—CountThread extends the Thread class:

```
/*CountThread increments a value and prints it.*/
class CountThread extends Thread
{
  /*time the thread is paused for ( in ms).*/
  int   pause;
  /*number of times the message is printed.*/
  private static final int TIMES = 10;

  /*run() is the method doing the actual thread task.*/
  public void run()
  {
    /*i is incremented and printed within
    the for loop.*/
    for (int i=0; i<TIMES; i++)
    {
      try
      {
        /*print the value of i.*/
        System.out.println(i);

        /*generate a random sleep interval.*/
        pause = (int)(Math.random() * 3000);

        /*put the thread to sleep.*/
        sleep(pause);
      }
      catch (InterruptedException e)
      {
        /*print the exception message when necessary.*/
        System.out.println(e.toString());
      }
    }
  }
}
```

● Step 3—HelloThread extends the Thread class:

```
/*HelloThread prints "Hello!" at random intervals.*/
class HelloThread extends Thread
{
  /*time the thread is paused for (expressed in ms).*/
  int  pause;
  /*number of times the message is printed.*/
  private static final int TIMES = 10;

  /*run() is the method doing the actual thread task.*/
  public void run()
  {

    /*"Hello" is printed TIMES times.*/
    for (int i=0; i<TIMES; i++)
    {
      try
      {
        /*print the message.*/
        System.out.println("Hello!");

        /*generate a random sleep interval.*/
        pause = (int)(Math.random() * 3000);

        /*put the thread to sleep.*/
        sleep(pause);
      }
      catch (InterruptedException e)
      {
        /*print the exception message.*/
        System.out.println(e.toString());
      }
    }
  }
}
```

● Step 4—Instantiate the two thread classes and start their execution:

```
/*main thread application.*/
public class ThreadHelloCount
{
  public static void main(String[] args)
  {
    /*create the CountThread thread.*/
    CountThread count = new CountThread();
```

```
    /*create the HelloThread thread.*/
    HelloThread hello = new HelloThread();

    /*start the CountThread instance.*/
    count.start();

    /*start the HelloThread instance.*/
    hello.start();
    }
}
```

Note that when dividing application work in tasks with the aim to have them associated with threads for parallel execution, each task has to be able to execute independently from the other tasks because otherwise the execution concurrency provides no benefit to the overall application. The run() method of the Thread class is overridden here to perform the core activity of the tasks. The run() method is invoked by the start() method, when the thread is started. The two threads execute loops in which counting and/or printing occurs. After each iteration, a call to the sleep() method determines the threads to suspend their execution. As a result the threads will be in the BLOCKED state until the sleep duration of time indicated when sleep() was called elapses and the threads return to the READY state. This allows the scheduler to perform its scheduling activity and have the threads interleave their execution. However, no activity is performed before the two thread classes are instantiated and their start() methods are called. This is done in the main() method of the main thread application class ThreadHelloCount.

4.6.2 *Implementing* **Runnable** *Interface*

Next is an example of multi-threading using implementations of the *Runnable* interface to create threads. The example will perform in parallel repeat printing of the current date and repeat display of a user message.

• Step 1—Divide application work in tasks and allocate each of them to a class:

```
/*DateRunnable does the current date and time printing*/
/*MsgRunnable does the user message printing*/
```

• Step 2—DateRunnable implements the Runnable interface:

```
import java.util.Date;

/*Prints date and time at random intervals.*/
class DateRunnable implements Runnable
{
```

```
/*current date.*/
private Date date;
/*number of times the message is printed.*/
private static final int TIMES = 10;

/*constructor for the DateRunnable class.*/
public DateRunnable(Date aDate)
{
  date = aDate;
}

/*run() is the method that does the thread task.*/
public void run()
{
  /*the for loop prints the message TIMES times.*/
  for (int i=0; i<TIMES; i++)
  {
    try
    {
      /*create a new Date object */
      /*containing the current date.*/
      Date nowDate = new Date();

      /*prints the date provided (date)*/
      /*and the current date.*/
      System.out.println("started:"
              + date + " now:" + nowDate);

      /*generate a random wait interval.*/
      int pause = (int)(Math.random() * 3000);

      /*the thread will sleep.*/
      Thread.sleep(pause);
    }
    catch (InterruptedException e)
    {
      /*print the exception message.*/
      System.out.println(e.toString());
    }
  }
}
}
```

• Step 3—MsgRunnable implements the Runnable interface:

```
/*MsgRunnable prints a user message at random
```

```
 *intervals.*/
class MsgRunnable implements Runnable
{
  /*message to be printed.*/
  private String message;
  /*number of times the message is printed.*/
  private static final int TIMES = 10;
  /*constructor for the MsgRunnable class.*/
  public MsgRunnable(String aMessage)
  {
    message = aMessage;
  }

  /*run() is the method that does the thread task.*/
  public void run()
  {
    /*the for loop will iterate TIMES times to print
     *the message.*/
    for (int i=0; i<TIMES; i++)
    {
      try
      {
        /*print the message.*/
        System.out.println(message);

        /*generate a random wait interval.*/
        int pause = (int)(Math.random() * 3000);

        /*the thread will sleep.*/
        Thread.sleep(pause);
      }
      catch (InterruptedException e)
      {
        /*print the exception message.*/
        System.out.println(e.toString());
      }
    }
  }
}
```

- Step 4—Instantiate the two runnable classes, create threads, and start their execution:

```
import java.util.Date;

/*main thread application.*/
```

```
public class RunnableMsgDate
{
  public static void main(String[] args)
  {
    /*create runnable objects*/
    MsgRunnable mr = new MsgRunnable("Hello!");
    DateRunnable dr = new DateRunnable (new Date());

    /*create thread objects*/
    Thread mt = new Thread(mr);
    Thread dt = new Thread(dr);

    /*start threads*/
    mt.start();
    dt.start();
  }
}
```

The same comments stand regarding the division of application work in independent tasks for thread-based parallel execution in order to avail from any performance benefits. In this example, the *run()* method of the *Runnable* interface is implemented in a runnable class in order to execute the tasks when invoked. The runnable class needs to be instantiated, then associated with a thread before the thread execution start will determine the *run()* method to be invoked (by the Thread's *start()* method). The two runnable classes execute loops in which the current date or a user message is printed. After each iteration, a call to the Thread's *sleep()* method determines execution suspension for the period of time indicated as a parameter in the *sleep()* method call. When this period elapses, the associated threads return to the READY state and are eligible for execution scheduling by the scheduler. However, thread executions start only after the two runnable classes get instantiated, two thread classes are created and associated with the corresponding runnable instances and the two thread *start()* methods are called. This is done in the *main()* method of the main thread application class *RunnableMsgDate*.

There are several important methods of the Thread class which are used for dealing with threads:

- *void start()*—Causes the thread to start its execution (JVM calls thread's run() method);
- *void run()*—Executes thread's task. If the thread was constructed from another Runnable object, it calls automatically that object's run() method;
- *void setName(String name)* and *String getName()*—Change and retrieve the name of the Thread when called;
- *int getPriority()* and *void setPriority(int)*—Get and set thread's priority. The possible values are between 1 and 10;

Fig. 4.6 Inter-thread
communication

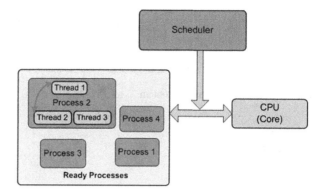

- *static void sleep(long)* and *static void sleep(long, long)*—Cause the thread to cease execution for the specified number of milliseconds and milliseconds + nanoseconds, respectively.
- *static void yield()*—Causes the thread to temporarily pause and allows other threads to execute;
- *void join(long millisec)*—It is usually invoked by the parent thread causing it to block until the child thread terminates or the specified number of milliseconds pass.
- *boolean isAlive()*—Return true if the thread is alive.

The only method of the Runnable interface is *void run()* and it requires implementation as can be seen in the example already presented.

4.7   Inter-thread and Inter-process Communication

4.7.1   Inter-thread Communication

The inter-thread communication focuses on exchanging data between different threads. As threads execute on the same machine and they share the process data space, inter-thread communication is mostly performed using common data variables. The principle of inter-thread communication is graphically presented in Fig. 4.6.

As multiple threads executing in parallel may access and modify the same data variables, the results may not be predictable. In order to solve this issue, only one thread is allowed to modify the data at a time (inter-thread synchronization is required). There are various mechanisms available to enable inter-thread communication and they are presented in details in [1], including:

- Shared memory;
- Semaphores;
- Message passing;

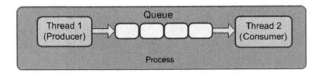

Fig. 4.7 Consumer–producer problem

- Signals;
- Named pipes.

4.7.2 Producer–Consumer Problem

A basic thread synchronization scenario is the producer–consumer problem, as presented in Fig. 4.7. Some threads store items in a queue (producers), while other threads collect items from the queue (consumers) and use them. The queue is a shared memory space and needs to be protected from access by the multiple producer and consumer threads. Next this mechanism will be described in the context of the solution.

An example of inter-thread communication synchronization based on the producer–consumer problem.

- Step 1—Divide the problem and solution in producer, consumer, and shared queue classes:

```
/*class implementing the shared queue*/
class SynchQueue;
/*class extending Thread dealing with the producer*/
class Producer extends Thread;
/*class extending Thread dealing with the consumer*/
class Consumer extends Thread;
```

- Step 2—Design the shared queue class:

```
/*class implementing the shared queue*/
class SynchQueue {
   /*indicate the location of queue's front and back.*/
   /*the consumer reads from the front*/
   /*the producer writes to the back.*/
   private int front = 0, back = 0;
   /*indicates the number of items in the queue.*/
   private int noItems = 0;
   /*queue buffer*/
   private int[] tabItems;
   /*maximum number of items in the queue.*/
   private int maxnoItems;
```

```
/*SynchQueue constructor.*/
public SynchQueue (int maxsize)
{
  maxnoItems = maxsize;
  tabItems = new int[maxnoItems];
}

/*returns the number of items in the queue.*/
public int queueSize() { return noItems; }

/*method used to insert elements in the queue.*/
public synchronized void insert (int item)
{
  /*check for space availability.*/
  while (noItems == maxnoItems)
  {
    try
    {
      /*waits for consumers to free space.*/
      wait();
    }
    catch(InterruptedException ex) {};
  }
  /*insert the item at the back.*/
  tabItems[back] = item;
  /*move the back index one step.*/
  back = (back + 1) \% maxnoItems;
  /*increment the number of items.*/
  noItems += 1;
  /*notify all threads waiting*/
  /*for the object that it is free.*/
  notifyAll();
}

/*method used to remove objects from the queue.*/
public synchronized int remove()
{
  int item;
  /*wait if the queue is empty.*/
  while (noItems == 0)
  {
    try
    {
      wait();
```

```
        }
        catch(InterruptedException ex)
        {
        };
    }
    /*retrieve the item at the front.*/
    item = tabItems[front];
    /*move the from index one step.*/
    front = (front + 1) \% maxnoItems;
    /*decrease the number of items.*/
    noItems -= 1;
    /*notify all threads waiting*/
    /*as space has been freed.*/
    notifyAll();

    return item;
  }
}
```

- Step 3—Design the consumer class extending Thread:

```
/*the consumer thread class.*/
class Consumer extends Thread
{
  /*the queue member.*/
  private SynchQueue synQue;

  /*constructor takes the queue as a parameter.*/
  public Consumer(SynchQueue que)
  {
     synQue = que;
  }
  /*run() method performs the consumer task.*/
  public void run()
  {
    int item = 0;
    do
    {
      /*retrieve an item from the queue.*/
      item = synQue.remove();
      /*print the thread name and the item.*/
      System.out.println
         ("Consumer:" + this + " value:" + item);
    }
    while (item != -1);
    /*iterate until the value of*/
```

```
    /*the item retrieved is -1.*/
  }
}
```

- Step 4—Design the producer class extending Thread:

```
/*the producer thread class.*/
class Producer extends Thread
{
  /*the queue member.*/
  private SynchQueue synQue;
  /*min and max values for the items.*/
  private int minItem, maxItem;

  /*constructor taking the queue and */
  /*min and max no item values as parameters.*/
  public Producer(SynchQueue que, int min, int no)
  {
    synQue = que;
    minItem = min; maxItem = min + no;
  }

  /*run() method performs the producer task.*/
  public void run()
  {
    /*loop used to generate items.*/
    for (int item = minItem; item <= maxItem; item ++)
    {
      /*print the item and thread name.*/
      System.out.println
        ("Producer:" + this + " value:" + item);
      /*insert the item in the queue.*/
      synQue.insert(item);
    }
  }
}
```

- Step 5—Design the producer-consumer class:

```
/*Creates a number of producers (noProd)*/
/*and consumers (noCons) and one synchronized queue.*/
/*Starts them and eventually terminates the process*/
/*by inserting  1 items in the queue noCons times.*/
class MultiProdCons
{
  public static void main(String[] args)
  {
```

```
/*number of consumers and producers.*/
int noCons = 3, noProds = 4;

/*create the 5 element queue.*/
SynchQueue sque = new SynchQueue(5);

/*create the consumers and producers.*/
Consumer[] cons  = new Consumer[noCons];
Producer[] prods = new Producer[noProds];

/*start the consumers.*/
for (int i = 0; i < noCons; i += 1 )
{    cons[i] = new Consumer(sque);
  cons[i].start();
}

/*start the producers.*/
for (int i = 0; i < noProds; i += 1 )
{    prods[i] = new Producer(sque, i*100, 50);
  prods[i].start();
}

/*wait for the producers to finish.*/
for (int i = 0; i < noProds; i += 1 )
{    try { prods[i].join(); }
  catch(InterruptedException ex) {};
}

/*insert -1 in the queue for*/
/*each consumer to terminate.*/
for (int i = 0; i < noCons; i += 1 )
{
  sque.insert( -1 );
}

/*wait for the consumers to terminate.*/
for (int i = 0; i < noCons; i += 1 )
{    try { cons[i].join(); }
  catch(InterruptedException ex) {};
}
System.out.println( "successful completion" );
  }
}
```

The key aspect in the solution to the producer–consumer problem is the synchronized use of the queue. Java has a very strong mechanism which labels a code sequence with the keyword *synchronized* and prevents multiple threads from executing the code in parallel, protecting the integrity of the shared variables and memory space. When any thread is executing the synchronized method, all other threads that invoke any of the synchronized methods for the same object suspend their execution (enter the BLOCKED state) until the first thread finishes the execution of the synchronized method. Once this happens, another thread is allowed to execute the synchronized code in an exclusive manner, and so on.

The second aspect worth mentioning is the mechanism introduced to prevent consumer threads from using processing resources while there are no items to be retrieved from the queue (the queue is empty) and producers from executing when there is no space in the queue to place their products (the queue is full). When the queue is empty, calls to the *wait()* method send the consumer threads attempting to fetch items to the BLOCKED state. Similarly, calls to the *wait()* method send the producers attempting to generate items to the BLOCKED state when the queue is full. However, an item produced and placed in the queue or an item retrieved from the queue by a consumer determines calls to *notifyall()* enabling threads to exit from their BLOCKED state and enter READY state, waiting for the scheduler to give them processor time and resume execution. In this way, both processing concurrency and efficiency is achieved.

4.7.3 Inter-process Communication

Inter-process communication focuses on exchanging data between different processes. Communicating processes can run on the same machine or on different machines. Communication between processes that run on the same machine is similar to inter-thread communication. However, as the processes do not share the same data space, there is a need for the processes to share some memory with each other first. Communication between processes that run on different machines involves communication via networks (networking).

These inter-communicating processes must run on machines that are interconnected via a network (wired or wireless), and the data is exchanged using protocols, organized hierarchically in a protocol stack.

The principle of inter-process communication when the processes are running on the same machine or on separate machines is presented in Fig. 4.8.

4.8 Conclusions

This chapter has discussed multi-programming and multi-tasking as very important aspects of the current computational complexity and diversity of applications by making use of computation parallelism and exploiting the multi-core architectures of

Fig. 4.8 Inter-process communication: (**a**) via shared memory, (**b**) involving networking

many existing processors. The chapter has also discussed processes, threads, inter-thread communication and synchronization, and inter-process communication, and has provided examples described step-by-step which help the readers understand the major issues encountered.

References

1. Tanenbaum AS (2007) Modern operating systems, 3rd edn. Prentice Hall, Upper Saddle River, NJ

Chapter 5
Sockets

Abstract In order to support the inter-process communication, specific support has to be provided by both the operating system and the programming language used. This chapter presents and discusses sockets, as one of the major solutions employed by network programming for the inter-process communications. Sockets provide the application developer with direct basic access to transport protocols, offering data packet transport services between a sender and a receiver host over the network, while hiding the complexity and implementation details of the protocol stack below. Sockets' examples are presented in details when two of the most popular transport protocols are employed in turn: the Transmission Control Protocol (TCP) and User Datagram Protocol (UDP).

5.1 Introduction

This chapter presents and discusses sockets, as one of the major solutions employed by network programming for inter-process communications. Sockets provide the application developer the direct basic access to transport protocols, offering data packet transport services between a sender and a receiver host over the network, while hiding the complexity and implementation details of the protocol stack below. Sockets examples are presented in details when the two most popular transport protocols used in the Internet are employed in turn: the Transmission Control Protocol (TCP) and User Datagram Protocol (UDP).

5.2 Socket Definition and Types

Sockets are network communication link end-points between two applications (i.e., server and client). They offer basic transport data communication support and hide lower layer implementation details. They provide a higher level of abstraction for the communication infrastructure beneath and enable support for fast and easy network-based applications development.

The basic principle of socket-based data communication is graphically presented in Fig. 5.1.

B. Ciubotaru, G.-M. Muntean, *Advanced Network Programming – Principles and*   73
Techniques, Computer Communications and Networks,
DOI 10.1007/978-1-4471-5292-7_5, © Springer-Verlag London 2013

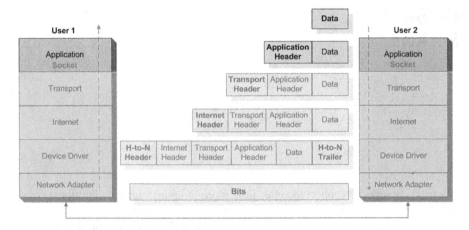

Fig. 5.1 Socket-based network data communication

There are two type of sockets that can be used for application development: transport layer sockets and application layer sockets.

Transport layer sockets make use of transport-layer protocols such as the Transmission Control Protocol (TCP) [2] and User Datagram Protocol (UDP) [1]. UDP is a connectionless non-reliable transmission of datagrams protocol, similar to the postal service. TCP is a connection-based reliable, orderly transmission of data packets, similar to the telephone service.

Application layer sockets make use of application-layer protocols such as the Hypertext Transfer Protocol (HTTP) [3] and Simple Mail Transfer Protocol (SMTP) [4]. HTTP is a TCP-based web page delivery service, while SMTP is a TCP-based e-mail delivery service.

5.3 Socket-Based Network Communications

The network communication using sockets involves several basic steps which have to be followed by the application developer in order to have a functional transport mechanism between the two communicating parties.

The first step involves creating and opening sockets. Each communicating party requires a separate socket. When creating/opening a socket, the important parameters to be provided include the IP address, port number, and communication protocol (TCP or UDP).

The second step involves establishing contact or associating the socket with another socket. In order to be able to communicate, the sockets have to use the same protocol. In general, the client knows the server's IP address, port number, and the protocol used and contacts it using these details. Depending on the protocol, it can either request a service or establish a connection.

The third step consists of exchanging data between the two parties and represents the main stage of network application's communication tasks. This step usually happens recursively. Information is sent and received by the two communicating sockets.

The last step involves closing and destroying the sockets which closes the communication end-point. After this step the socket cannot be used for communication any more.

5.3.1 UDP Sockets

When using UDP sockets the connection between the client and the server is not maintained throughout the communication session. Each datagram packet is sent as an isolated transmission when necessary. There are no guarantees that the packets arrive in order at the destination or that the packets arrive at the destination at all.

5.3.1.1 UDP Sockets—Server Side

Java UDP server communication steps include the following:

• Step 1—Create a datagram socket object.

```
DatagramSocket dgramSocket =
          new DatagramSocket(portno);
 /*1024 <= portno <= 65535*/
```

• Step 2—Create a buffer to store the incoming datagrams:

```
byte[] buffer = new byte[256];
/*-128 <= byte value <= 127*/
```

• Step 3—Create a datagram packet object for incoming datagrams:

```
DatagramPacket inPkt =
          new DatagramPacket(buffer, buffer.length);
```

• Step 4—Accept an incoming datagram:

```
dgramSocket.receive(inPkt);
```

• Step 5—Get sender's address and port number from the datagram:

```
InetAddress cliAddress = inPkt.getAddress();
int cliPort = inPkt.getPort();
```

• Step 6—Retrieve the data from the buffer:

```
String msgIn =
  new String(inPkt.getData(), 0, inPkt.getLength());
```

- Step 7—Create the response datagram:

```
msgOut = ("Message " + numMessages + ":" + messageIn);
DatagramPacket outPkt =
      new DatagramPacket(msgOut.getBytes(),
                    msgOut.length(),
                    cliAddress,
                    cliPort);
```

- Step 8—Send the response datagram:

```
dgramSocket.send(outPkt);
```

- Step 9—Repeat communication if necessary:

```
while(condition);
```

- Step 10—Close the datagram socket:

```
dgramSocket.close();
```

Java UDP socket communication may throw exceptions that need to be caught and treated. The following example shows how to catch exceptions thrown by the UDP sockets.

```
try{
      /*attempt to create the socket*/
      dgramSocket = new DatagramSocket(PORT);
   }

   catch (SocketException e) {
      /*this exception may be triggered when*/
      /*the port is already in use.*/
      System.out.println("Unable to attach to port!");
      System.exit(1);
   }
```

The following example illustrates the use of sockets to create a server application using the UDP protocols for data transport.

Server UDP Socket Communication Example:

```
import java.io.*;
import java.net.*;

/*UDP server class.*/
public class UDPEchoServer
```

Code Listing 5.1 UDPEchoServer.java

```
{
   /*port used by the server.*/
   private static final int PORT = 1234;

   /*the datagram socket specific to UDP.*/
   private static DatagramSocket dgramSocket;
   /*incoming and outgoing packets objects.*/
   private static DatagramPacket inPkt, outPkt;
   /*packet data buffer.*/
   private static byte[] buffer;

   public static void main(String[] args)
   {
      System.out.println("Opening port...\n");
      try
      {
      /*create the datagram socket*/
      dgramSocket = new DatagramSocket(PORT);
      }
      catch(SocketException e)
      {
      /*handle potential exceptions.*/
      System.out.println("Error attach port!");
      System.exit(1);
      }
      run();
   }

/*run() performs the main task of the server.*/
private static void run() {
try   {
   /*buffers for the messages to be sent and received.*/
   String msgIn,msgOut;
   /*number of messages.*/
   int numMsgs = 0;
   do {
      /*create the packet buffer.*/
      buffer = new byte[256];

      /*create the incoming packet.*/
      inPkt = new DatagramPacket(buffer,buffer.length);

      /*receive the packet from the client.*/
      dgramSocket.receive(inPkt);
```

Code Listing 5.1 (Continued)

```
/*retrieve the sender's IP address.*/
InetAddress cliAddress = inPkt.getAddress();

/*retrieve the sender's port number.*/
int cliPort = inPkt.getPort();

/*store the content of the message.*/
msgIn =
  new String(inPkt.getData(),0,inPkt.getLength());
System.out.println("Message received.");
/*increment the message number.*/
numMsgs++;

/*generate the outgoing message.*/
msgOut = ("Msg "+numMsgs+ ": "+msgIn);
/*create the outgoing packet.*/
outPkt = new DatagramPacket(msgOut.getBytes(),
        msgOut.length(),cliAddress,cliPort);

/*send the outgoing packet to the client.*/
dgramSocket.send(outPkt);
} while(true);
}
catch(IOException e) {
  e.printStackTrace();
}
finally{
  /*close the socket and release its resources.*/
  dgramSocket.close();
}
}
}
```

Code Listing 5.1   (Continued)

5.3.1.2 UDP Sockets—Client Side

Java UDP client communication steps include:

- Step 1—Create a datagram socket object:

```
DatagramSocket dgramSocket = new DatagramSocket;
/*a default port no will be selected*/
```

- Step 2—Create the outgoing datagram:

```
BufferedReader userEntry =
new BufferedReader(new InputStreamReader(System.in));

System.out.print("Enter message: ");

String msg = userEntry.readLine();

DatagramPacket outPkt =
new DatagramPacket(msg.getBytes(),
                   msg.length(), host, portno);
```

- Step 3—Send the response datagram:

```
dgramSocket.send(outPkt);
```

- Step 4: Create a buffer to store the incoming datagrams:

```
byte[] buffer = new byte[256];
```

- Step 5—Create a datagram packet object for incoming datagrams:

```
DatagramPacket inPkt =
          new DatagramPacket(buffer, buffer.length);
```

- Step 6—Accept an incoming datagram:

```
dgramSocket.receive(inPkt);
```

- Step 7—Retrieve the data from the buffer:

```
String msgIn =
new String(inPkt.getData(), 0, inPkt.getLength());
```

- Step 8—Close the datagram socket:

```
dgramSocket.close();
```

Next a client UDP socket communication example is presented.

```
import java.io.*;
import java.net.*;

/*UDP client class*/
public class UDPEchoClient

{
  /*server IP*/
  private static InetAddress host;
```

Code Listing 5.2   UDPEchoClient.java

```
/*server port*/
private static final int PORT = 1234;



/*datagram socket*/
private static DatagramSocket dgramSocket;

/*incoming and outgoing packets.*/
private static DatagramPacket inPkt, outPkt;

/*packet buffer*/
private static byte[] buff;

/*messages content storage*/
private static String msg = "", msgIn = "";


public static void main(String[] args)
{
  try
  {
  host = InetAddress.getLocalHost();
  /*or get InetAddress of server*/
  }
  catch(UnknownHostException e)
  {
  /*handle exception*/
  System.out.println("Host not found!");
  System.exit(1);
  }
  run();
}

private static void run() {
try  {
  /*create datagram socket*/
  dgramSocket = new DatagramSocket();
  /*create the buffer reader to read from the
  console*/
  BufferedReader userEntry = new BufferedReader(
      new InputStreamReader(System.in));
  do {
    System.out.print("Enter message: ");
```

Code Listing 5.2   (Continued)

```
        /*read user entry*/
        msg = userEntry.readLine();
        /*send messages until BYE is sent*/
        if (!msg.equals("BYE")) {
          /*create the packet*/
          outPkt = new DatagramPacket(msg.getBytes(),
            msg.length(), host, PORT);
          /*send the packet*/
          dgramSocket.send(outPkt);

          /*allocate packet buffer*/
          buff = new byte[256];
          /*create incoming packet*/
          inPkt = new DatagramPacket(buff, buff.length);
          /*receive incoming packet*/
          dgramSocket.receive(inPkt);
          /*store packet content*/
          msgIn = new String(inPkt.getData(),
            0, inPkt.getLength());
          System.out.println("SERVER: " + msgIn);
        }
      } while (!msg.equals("BYE"));
    }

    catch(IOException e){
      e.printStackTrace();
    }
    finally{
      /*close the socket and release its resources*/
      dgramSocket.close();
      }
    }
}
```

Code Listing 5.2 (Continued)

5.3.2 TCP Sockets

As TCP is a connection-oriented protocol, when TCP sockets are used, connections are established between client and server hosts. Client and server TCP sockets are created first and are bound for the duration of the data communication session. Following connection establishment, TCP packets are sent to the partner's socket.

These packets are guaranteed to arrive (if lost, retransmission occurs) and are received in order at the destination.

Exchanging messages using TCP sockets involves a set of steps that must be followed by the application developer. Next these steps are presented, with the focus on server and client side, respectively.

5.3.2.1 TCP Sockets—Server Side

Java TCP server communication steps:

• Step 1—Create a TCP server socket object.

```
ServerSocket servSock = new ServerSocket(portno);
/*1024 <= portno <= 65535*/
```

• Step 2—Set the server to wait (block) for clients to connect.

```
Socket sock = servSock.accept();
/*sock is a socket object.*/
```

• Step 3—Set input and output streams.

```
BufferedReader in =
new BufferedReader(
  new InputStreamReader(sock.getInputStream()));

PrintWriter out =
new PrintWriter(sock.getOutputStream(), true);
```

• Step 4—Send and receive data.

```
out.println("Waiting...");
String msg = in.readLine();
```

• Step 5—Close the connection.

```
sock.close();
```

Server TCP Socket Communication Example:

```
import java.io.*;
import java.net.*;

/*TCP-based echo server*/
public class TCPEchoServer
{
```

Code Listing 5.3 TCPEchoServer.java

```
/*server socket*/
private static ServerSocket servSock;
/*server port*/
private static final int PORT = 1234;

public static void main(String[] args)
{
  System.out.println("Opening port\n");
  try
  {
    /*Create the server socket*/
    servSock = new ServerSocket(PORT);
  }
  catch(SocketException e)
  {

    /*handle potential exceptions*/
    System.out.println("Error attach port!");
    System.exit(1);
  }
  catch (IOException e)
  {
    /*handle potential exceptions*/
    System.out.println("Error create socket!");
    System.exit(1);
  }

  /*perform the echo service indefinitely*/
  do {
    run();
  }
  while (true);
}

private static void run() {
  /*data socket*/
  Socket sock = null;
  try  {
    /*listen for incoming connections*/
    link = servSock.accept();
    /*create a socket buffer reader*/
    BufferedReader in = new BufferedReader(
      new InputStreamReader(sock.getInputStream()));
    /*create the socket writer*/
```

Code Listing 5.3 (Continued)

```
PrintWriter out = new PrintWriter(
  sock.getOutputStream(),true);

int numMsgs = 0;
/*read from the data socket*/
String msg = in.readLine();
while (!msg.equals("BYE"))
{
  System.out.println("Message received.");
  numMsgs++;
  out.println("Message " + numMsgs + ": " + msg);

  msg = in.readLine();
}
out.println(numMsgs + " messages received.");
}
catch(IOException e) {
  e.printStackTrace();    }
finally{
  /*close the socket*/
  try {
    sock.close();
  } catch (IOException e) {
    e.printStackTrace();
  }
}
}
}
```

Code Listing 5.3 (Continued)

5.3.2.2 TCP Sockets—Client Side

Java TCP client communication steps:

- Step 1—Create a TCP client socket and establish a connection to the server.

```
InetAddress srvIPAddr;
int srvPortNo = 1234;
Socket sock = new Socket(srvIPAddr.getLocalHost(),
                         srvPortNo);
/*sock is a socket object*/
```

- Step 2—Set input and output streams.

```
BufferedReader in =
new BufferedReader(
  new InputStreamReader(sock.getInputStream()));

PrintWriter out =
new PrintWriter(sock.getOutputStream(), bAutoFlush);
```

- Step 3—Send and receive data.

```
out.println("Waiting for data");
String msgIn = in.readLine();
```

- Step 4—Close the connection.

```
sock.close();
```

Client TCP socket communication example:

```
import java.io.*;
import java.net.*;

/*TCP client class*/
public class TCPEchoClient
{
  /*server IP*/
  private static InetAddress host;
  /*server port*/
  private static final int PORT = 1234;

  public static void main(String[] args)
  {
    System.out.println("Opening port\n");
    try
    {
      /*create server IP address  object*/
      host = InetAddress.getLocalHost();
    }
    catch(UnknownHostException e)
    {
      System.out.println("Host not found!");
      System.exit(1);
    }
    run();
  }
```

Code Listing 5.4   TCPEchoClient.java

```java
private static void run()
{
  Socket link = null;
  try
  {
    /*create data socket*/
    sock = new Socket(host, PORT);
    /*create socket reader and writer*/
    BufferedReader in = new BufferedReader(new
       InputStreamReader (sock.getInputStream()));
    PrintWriter out = new PrintWriter(
       sock.getOutputStream(), true);

    /*Set up stream for user entry*/
    BufferedReader reader =
       new BufferedReader(new
          InputStreamReader(System.in));

    /*storage for message and response message*/
    String msgOut, msgIn;
    do
    {
      System.out.print("Enter message: ");
      /*read user message*/
      msgOut =  reader.readLine();

      /*send the message*/
      out.println(msgOut);

      /*read the response*/
      msgIn = in.readLine();
      System.out.println("SERVER> " + msgIn);
    } while (!message.equals("BYE"));
  }

  catch(IOException e)
  {
    e.printStackTrace();
  }

  finally
  {
    /*close the data socket*/
```

Code Listing 5.4 (Continued)

```
        try {
          sock.close();
        } catch (IOException e) {
          e.printStackTrace();
        }
      }
    }
}
```

Code Listing 5.4 (Continued)

5.4 Conclusions

This chapter has introduced sockets as the most popular solution for inter-process communications. Sockets have been introduced at the application and transport layer, respectively, allowing for network programming to focus on higher layer aspects, while the implementation details of the lower layer protocol stack are hidden. The chapter has described the socket-based network programming stages step-by-step with the help of examples. The sockets examples presented in details employ in turn TCP and UDP, respectively.

References

1. Postel J (August 1980) User datagram protocol. RFC 768, Internet engineering task force
2. Postel J (1981) RFC 793—Transmission control protocol (TCP). RFC 793
3. Fielding R, Gettys J, Mogul J, Frystyk H, Masinter L, Leach P, Berners-Lee T (1999) RFC 2616—Hypertext transfer protocol (HTTP/1.1). RFC 2616
4. Klensin J (2008) RFC 5321—Simple mail transfer protocol (SMTP). RFC 5321

Chapter 6
Socket-Based Client–Server Communication

Abstract Sockets offer the basic mechanisms for data communication between two processes, each running on a distinct machine. This chapter describes the socket-based client–server communication mechanism and details the basics of client–server applications programming, including multi-threaded servers. Unicast, multicast, and broadcast communication paradigms are also introduced in this chapter.

6.1 Introduction

Client–server is a request–response remote communication model that involves processes requesting services from other processes which offer these services via the network.

The processes offering services by executing certain tasks following remote process requests are known as servers. In general, the servers receive requests from remote processes, execute the tasks associated with these services, and dispatch responses back to the requesting entities. Examples of services include database information retrieval and updates, file system access services, and dedicated user-application tasks.

The processes that contact the servers and request them to perform services are known as clients. In general, client processes manage user-interfaces, validate data entered by users, dispatch requests to servers, collect servers' responses, and process and/or display the information received.

The client and server definitions were introduced in relation to service requesting and service providing processes, but they can equally be used for applications and machines. Server applications run in general on powerful computers which are often located in dedicated places such as data centers. Client applications usually run on user devices which may be desktop-PCs, laptop-PCs, netbooks, gaming consoles, or mobile hand-held devices. The machines which host client applications are often referred to as clients, and the computers which run server applications are known as servers. Although theoretically both the server and the client applications may run on the same physical machine, this is almost never the case, mostly due to the different requirements in terms of processing power of these machines.

Both client-side and server-side machines may run in parallel several client and server applications, respectively.

B. Ciubotaru, G.-M. Muntean, *Advanced Network Programming – Principles and Techniques*, Computer Communications and Networks, DOI 10.1007/978-1-4471-5292-7_6, © Springer-Verlag London 2013

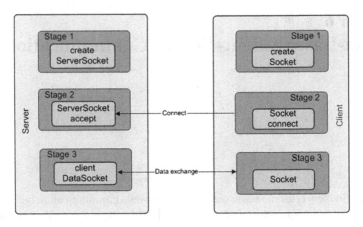

Fig. 6.1 Client–server communication steps

For example, a standard client machine would normally run several applications such as a web browser, an e-mail client, and maybe a media player receiving a video stream over the Internet. All these applications act as clients accessing services and content (e.g., web documents, e-mail messages, and multimedia content) from remote server applications.

Similarly, server machines may run several applications in parallel. A good example would be a data center server machine running a wéb server (e.g., Apache) and a database server (e.g. MySQL) in parallel. Although the scope is common for the two services (web content delivery and database services), they represent distinct applications running on the same physical hardware platform. However, most of the time there is a dedicated server machine (or servers) which runs a server application, offering a single service of which multiple client applications can avail. The next sections will present step-by-step socket-based network programming solutions to implement such a client–server paradigm. The chapter discusses unicast, multicast, and broadcast communications and presents in this context relevant data transfer application examples.

6.2 Basic Client–Server Application Programming

Server and client applications often use sockets to initiate communication sessions and perform data and/or message exchange in a request–response manner. Basic socket-based solutions enable one connection to be established between a client and a server at a time only. The idea behind this simple solution is graphically illustrated in Fig. 6.1 and is described step-by-step in the context of both UDP and TCP socket-based connectivity.

However, in most cases servers need to deal with multiple clients at a time, and consequently more advanced solutions are required. A very good option which provides good scalability is to make use of a thread-based approach for building the server application.

6.3 Multi-threaded Server Applications

A server application capable of handling multiple simultaneous clients can be built by making use of both multi-threading support and socket-based communications. Although theoretically infinite, the number of clients that a server can handle simultaneously is, in fact, limited. Indeed, the processing resources of the operating system and the physical machine on which the server application runs, as well as transport capacity of the network over which data is exchanged, limit the number of independent communication sessions established and managed simultaneously. We will present this approach in the context of a multi-threaded TCP server application example, which simply echoes the message received from the client application.

This multi-threaded TCP server application makes use of a specially built socket communicating thread class which, given the communication socket-based link has been established, exchanges messages with the client application. The major steps for building this server application component are as follows:

- Step 1—Create a server class which extends Thread.

  ```
  public class SingleTCPEchoServer extends Thread
  ```

- Step 2—Get a handle to an already established communicating socket.

  ```
  /*private socket variable*/
  private static Socket sock;

  /*set the data socket*/
  sock = s;
  ```

- Step 3—Create reader and writer objects for socket communication.

  ```
  /*BufferReader used to read data from data socket*/
  private BufferedReader in;
  /*PrinterWriter used to write to the data socket*/
  private PrintWriter out;

  /*create the BufferReader for reading from socket*/
  in = new BufferedReader(new InputStreamReader(
      sock.getInputStream()));
  /*create the PrintWriter for socket writing*/
  out = new PrintWriter(sock.getOutputStream(),true);
  ```

- Step 4—Override run() to receive and send data.

  ```
  /*read message from the data socket (client)*/
  ```

```
String msg = in.readLine();

/*send the reply message to the client*/
out.println("Message " + numMessages + ": " + msg);
```

- Step 5—Start the thread.

```
/*call the run() method*/
start();
```

- Step 6—Deal with potential exceptions.

```
try{ [...] }
catch (IOException e) { [...] }
```

The full thread-based TCP socket server application example is presented next.

```
import java.io.*;
import java.net.Socket;

/*single-threaded server class*/
/*handles client communication*/
public class SingleTCPEchoServer extends Thread {

  /*client data socket*/
  private static Socket sock;

  /*server port*/
  private static final int PORT = 1234;

  /*BufferReader used to read data from data socket*/
  private BufferedReader in;

  /*PrinterWriter used to write to the data socket*/
  private PrintWriter out;

  /*Constructor for the single threaded server*/
  public SingleTCPEchoServer(Socket s)
    throws IOException {

    /*set the data socket*/
    sock = s;

    /*create the BufferReader from data socket*/
```

Code Listing 6.1 SingleTCPEchoServer.java

```
    in = new BufferedReader(new InputStreamReader(
      sock.getInputStream()));

    /*create the PrintWriter for data socket*/
    out = new PrintWriter(
        sock.getOutputStream(),true);

    /*If any of the above calls throws an exception,
    the caller will close the socket.
    Otherwise the thread will close it.*/

    /*call the run() method*/
    start();
  }

/*run() method performs the actual task*/
public void run()
{
  try {
    int numMessages = 0;

    /*read message from the data socket (client)*/
    String msg = in.readLine();
    /*verify if the message is BYE*/
    while (!msg.equals("BYE"))
    {
      System.out.println("Message received.");

      /*count the number of messages received*/
      numMessages++;

      /*send the reply message to the client*/
      out.println("Message " + numMessages +
                  ": " + msg);

      /*read the next message*/
      msg = in.readLine();
    }

    /*at this point BYE has been received*/
    /*the server reports the number of received
    messages*/
    out.println(numMessages + " messages received.");
    }
```

Code Listing 6.1 (Continued)

```
catch (IOException e)
{
  e.printStackTrace();
}
finally
{
  try

  {
    System.out.println("\n Closing connection");
    /*close the data socket*/
    sock.close();
  }
  catch(IOException e)
  {
    System.out.println("Unable to disconnect!");

    System.exit(1);
  }
}
} /*run()*/
} /*SingleTCPEchoServer*/
```

Code Listing 6.1 (Continued)

The multi-threaded TCP server application is, in fact, a dispatcher which creates a ServerSocket at the server which waits for incoming connection requests from client applications. This wait is performed through a blocking call to accept(). As soon as a client request is received, the call to accept() completes, and a new single TCP server application thread, built as already described, will be created. If successful in establishing the connection with the client, accept() returns a communicating Socket which is passed as a parameter to the newly created single TCP thread, enabling direct communication between this newly created server thread and the client. After the new thread is started, the multi-threaded server application call again accept() waiting for another client connection request. This sequence of operations continues over and over again and is limited just by hardware and software resources of the server machine. This process is illustrated in Fig. 6.2 and described step-by-step next.

- Step 1—Create a server socket at a given port number.

```
/*The server socket is defined as a class member.*/
private static ServerSocket servSock;
/*Create the server socket to listen on PORT*/
servSock = new ServerSocket(PORT);
```

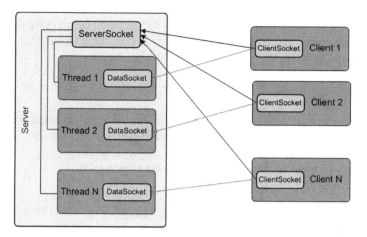

Figure 6.2 Multi-threaded server paradigm

- Step 2—In a loop wait for client connection requests.

```
do
{
   /*Blocks until a connection occurs.*/
   Socket socket = servSock.accept();
   [...]
} while (true);
```

- Step 3—For each client create a thread server to communicate via socket.

```
do {
   [...]
   /*Create a thread server to handle the client.*/
   new SingleTCPEchoServer(socket);

} while (true);
```

- Step 4—Deal with potential exceptions.

```
try{ [...] }
catch (IOException e) { [...] }
```

The complete multi-threaded TCP socket-based server application example is provided below.

```
import java.io.*;
import java.net.*;
```

Code Listing 6.2 MultiTCPEchoServer.java

```
/*Class implementing the multi-threaded echo server.*/
/*This server receives a message from the clients
 *and replies with the same message back.
 */
public class MultiTCPEchoServer {

   /*The server socket is defined as a class member.*/
   private static ServerSocket servSock;
   /*The port number is defined as a member.*/
   /*The server will listen on this port.*/
   private static final int PORT = 1234;

   /*Data socket is defined as a member.*/
   /*Socket to be used for */
   /*communication with the client.*/
   Socket sock = null;

   /*Constructor.*/
   public MultiTCPEchoServer() { }

   /*The main function to be run
    *when the server application stars.*/
   public static void main (String[] args)
       throws IOException
   {
   System.out.println("Opening port\n");

   try
   {
      /*Create the server socket to listen on PORT*/
      servSock = new ServerSocket(PORT);

   }
   catch (IOException e)
   {
      /*Handles potential exceptions
       *thrown while the server socket is created.*/
      /*Most common exception is triggered
       *when the chosen port is already used*/
      System.out.println("Port error!");
      System.exit(1);
   }
```

Code Listing 6.2 (Continued)

```
   /*At this point the server socket
    *was successfully created.*/
   try
   {
     /*main server loop.*/
     do
     {
       /*Server accepts connections from client.*/
       /*The Accept method blocks
        *until a connection occurs.*/
       Socket socket = servSock.accept();
       try
       {
         /*Create a single-threaded server.*/
         /*This will handle the client.*/
         new SingleTCPEchoServer(socket);
       }

       catch(IOException e)
       {
         /*Handle potential exceptions.*/
         /*As the creation of the
          *single-threaded server failed,
          *communication with the client can not start,
          *so the data socket is closed.
          */
         socket.close();
       }
     } while (true);
   }
   finally
   {
     /*When the server end its operation,
      *the server socket is closed.
      */
     servSock.close();
   }
 }
}
```

Code Listing 6.2 (Continued)

This multi-threaded TCP socket-based server application example works with a TCP socket-based client application similar to the one presented in the chapter on Sockets when discussing TCP connectivity.

6.4 Unicast, Multicast, and Broadcast Communications

Unicast refers to one-to-one communication and in general is performed by the sender following a receiver request.

Broadcast communication is when a single sender transmits data to all the devices connected to the network having an IP address in a certain range. This transmission can target all local subnet devices, all nodes in the local network, etc.

Multi-casting involves one-to-many communications between a sender and a set of receivers. These receivers must belong to a multicast group, which has to be established prior to any data communication. This multicast group (defined using a class D IP address) has to be established with network support. Unfortunately, not all networks enable multicast transmissions. All class D IP addresses are multicast addresses and range from 224.0.0.0 to 235.255.255.255. Any such IP address can be allocated to the newly formed multicast group, provided that it has not been already used in the same network domain.

The sender has to send data to the multicast group IP address. The receivers need to join the multicast group in order to receive data from the transmitting sender. However, the sender is not required to join the multicast group in order to transmit data.

All members of the multicast group will receive a copy of the data transmitted by the server. This is enabled by the multicast-enabled routers which support multicast tree-like routing of packets by multiplicating data packets and sending them towards the receivers which belong to the multicast group. In order to stop receiving data, the clients have to leave the multicast group.

As TCP is a point-to-point protocol and is most suitable for unicast transmissions, it cannot be used for multi-cast data delivery. Instead, UDP is the transport protocol used for multicast datagram packet distribution.

In terms of implementation, broadcast data transmission can be seen as an extension of multi-cast. In order to achieve broadcasting, all connected devices need to join the same multicast group, and consequently they will all receive a copy of the packets sent by the sender. In this context, broadcast data communications represent a special case of multicast and will not be dealt with separately.

In order to receive data from the server in a multicast manner, several steps have to be performed by the application. In the following paragraphs, these steps are detailed in the context of multicast receiver and sender applications, respectively.

Java multicast receiving data application:

- Step 1—Define port and address of multicast group to join:

```
/*multicast group port number*/
/*the server will send data to this port*/
int PORT = 5000;
/*multicast group IP address*/
String GROUP = "225.4.5.6";
```

- Step 2—Create MulticastSocket object and bind it to port PORT

```
/*MulticastSocket is a specific class
 *implementing multicast communication endpoints*/
MulticastSocket ms = new MulticastSocket(PORT);
```

- Step 3—Join the multicast group with address GROUP

```
/*MulticastGroup class provides joinGroup method
 *used to join the group using its IP*/
ms.joinGroup(InetAddress.getByName(GROUP));
```

- Step 4—Create a DatagramPacket and receive a packet.

```
/*allocate the packet buffer*/
byte buf[] = byte[1024];
/*create the packet*/
DatagramPacket pack =
  new DatagramPacket(buf, buf.length);
/*receive a packet from the multicast socket*/
ms.receive(pack);
```

- Step 5—Use the data received (print it on screen).

```
/*print the details of the sender (server)*/
System.out.println("Received data from: "
        + pack.getAddress().toString() + ":"
        + pack.getPort() + " with length: "
        +  pack.getLength());
/*print the message*/
System.out.write(pack.getData(), 0,
                 pack.getLength());
/*print a new line to separate the messages.*/
System.out.println();
```

- Step 6—Leave the multicast group and close the socket.

```
/*use leaveGroup to leave the multicast group*/
ms.leaveGroup(InetAddress.getByName(group));
/*close the multicast socket*/
ms.close();
```

On the sender side, the application has to follow another set of steps in order to be able to send data to a multicast group. In the following paragraphs, these steps are detailed.

Java multicast sending data application:

- Step 1—Define port, address of multicast group to send to and time-to-live.

```
/*port number to which the packets will be send*/
int PORT = 5000;
```

```
/*the multicast group IP address*/
String GROUP = "225.4.5.6";
/*time-to-live for packets sent
to the multicast group*/
byte TTL = 3;

/*Note: The TTL sets the IP time-to-live
specifying over how many "hops"
the packets will be forwarded in the
MulticastGroup before they expire.*/
```

- Step 2—Create MulticastSocket object.

```
/*create the multicast socket*/
MulticastSocket ms = new MulticastSocket();
```

- Step 3—Create a DatagramPacket and copy some data in it.

```
/*create the packet buffer*/
byte buf[] = byte[1024];
/*generate a message into the buffer*/
for (int i = 0; i < buf.length; i++)
  buf[i] = (byte)i;
/*create the datagram packet*/
/*the multicast IP address is used
 *for the creation of this packet*/
DatagramPacket pack =
  new DatagramPacket(buf, buf.length,
    InetAddress.getByName(GROUP), PORT);
```

- Step 4—Send the DatagramPacket to the multicast group.

```
/*send the packet specifying
the TTL as a parameter*/
ms.send(pack, TTL);
```

- Step 5—Close the socket.

```
/*close the multicast socket*/
ms.close();
```

6.5 Conclusion

This chapter has introduced the client–server communication paradigm and in its
context has presented a step-by-step socket-based network programming example
to implement a relevant application. The chapter then discussed unicast, multicast,
and broadcast communications and presented a multi-cast data transfer application
example which can also be used for data broadcast.

Chapter 7
Support for Communication-Based Services

Abstract In most cases, network communication is all about providing and accessing services. This chapter introduces the support offered by the Java programming language for various communication-based services. Control and diagnostic services including Packet InterNet Groper and Internet Control Message Protocol are presented. Electronic mail services making use of the SMTP and POP3 protocols, file transfer services using FTP, and web content transfer via HTTP are described. Java database connectivity services and programming support for database management systems communication are also discussed. The chapter ends with a presentation of the increasingly popular multimedia content delivery services.

7.1 Introduction

All network applications and services require some form of communication support and often they employ the client–server paradigm. Such applications and services include control and diagnostic services, e-mail, file transfer, web content exchange, and database access services.

Control and diagnostic services require communication mechanisms to support status information exchange in request–response manner and transmission of messages (often regular) to communication partners for information purposes via networks.

The e-mail service involves e-mail clients running on user terminals exchanging electronic messages with e-mail servers. These servers provide support for message storage and forwarding to destination e-mail servers via the network. Remote clients communicate with the e-mail servers for access to the received electronic messages and/or for sending other information. The e-mail service is based on both client–server and server–server network communications.

File transfer applications also use a client–server model. File transfer client applications running on user devices allow for local file access and, most importantly, remote file access in terms of upload and download to and from file servers. Additionally, these file applications have limited file management functions such as folder creation, deletion, etc., both locally and remotely.

Web applications use network communications support to enable the delivery of web documents to web clients (i.e., web browsers such as Firefox, Internet Explorer,

B. Ciubotaru, G.-M. Muntean, *Advanced Network Programming – Principles and Techniques*, Computer Communications and Networks, DOI 10.1007/978-1-4471-5292-7_7, © Springer-Verlag London 2013

Chrome, or Safari). The web clients send requests for the documents (web-pages) to web servers which either retrieve or generate them dynamically and deliver them to the client via networks.

Remote database access services can be seen as a particular case of web applications which involve clients establishing network connectivity with servers which have access to databases. Once security aspects have been cleared, the clients are able to run remote queries on the database, retrieve, and process the data.

This chapter presents the protocols these communication-based applications and services rely on and describes step-by-step, with the help of examples, how applications built on top of these protocols can be developed using Java.

7.2 Control and Diagnostic Services

7.2.1 Packet InterNet Groper

Packet InterNet Groper (PING) is a network utility available in most of the operating systems used today. PING is used in diagnosing network problems as well as requesting and receiving performance-related information in terms of delay and packet loss.

The name (PING) comes from an active sonar terminology which sends a sound pulse and then listens for the echo in order to detect objects underwater. Similar to the sonar, PING sends one or several data packets to a host and waits for an identical reply from the destination machine.

PING assumes that if the host machine replies to the received packet, it exists and is connected to the network. Moreover, PING measures the time elapsed between sending the data packet and receiving the echo packet from the target host (round-trip-time). Lost packets are also recorded so packer loss can also be estimated. These two aspects provide a significant metric for learning about the status of a host and for estimating the performance of the network connecting the host to the client machine.

PING uses the Internet Control Message Protocol (ICMP) protocol to send the data packet and receive the expected echo packet as response [12].

7.2.2 Internet Control Message Protocol

ICMP [12] is an unreliable transport layer protocol that uses network layer services offered by the IP protocol [13]. ICMP was standardized as RFC 792 in 1981, making it not only one the oldest protocols in operation today, but also one still widely used by network administrators.

ICMP verifies the correct operation of an IP host and checks that routers are correctly routing packets to the specified destination address.

Fig. 7.1 Internet Control Message Protocol (ICMP)

Fig. 7.2 ICMP packet format

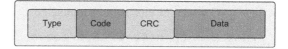

The basic principle of ICMP is presented in Fig. 7.1. It can be seen how a simple ICMP request packet is sent from the client host machine to the remote host via the network and the target machine replies with an identical copy of the message received addressed this time to the sender.

The ICMP packet fields include Type, Code, ICMP Header Checksum (CRC), and Data.

Type is an 8 bit field and indicates the type of the ICMP message. Mostly used types are Echo reply (0), Destination unreachable (3), Echo request (8), Time exceeded (11). Based on the Type field, the format of the ICMP packet may change.

Code is an 8 bit field which further qualifies the ICMP message type by offering extra information. For instance, for a Type=3 message (destination unreachable), most often used codes are Net Unreachable (0), Host Unreachable (1), Protocol Unreachable (2), and Port Unreachable (3).

ICMP Header Checksum is a 16 bit field and represents the checksum for the whole ICMP message. This field is used to determine if the packet has been received correctly and no information has been altered in transit. The data in this field is the 16-bit one's complement of the one's complement sum of the ICMP message starting with the Type field.

Data is a variable-length field which contains the data specific to the message type indicated by Type and Code fields.

The detailed format of data packets used by ICMP is illustrated in Fig. 7.2.

7.2.3 PING Java Example

Java does not offer direct support to implement applications that use PING to diagnose hosts within the network and check network basic functionality. There is a complete Oracle PING implementation example [14], but it is very complex and often difficult to understand in terms of network connectivity support. Instead, a simpler PING solution which uses the java.nio.DatagramChannel class and extends an existing solution [15] is presented. This solution involves several implementation steps, which are described next.

- Step 1—Import a network datagram I/O class

```
import java.nio.DatagramChannel;
```

- Step 2—Create and open a DatagramChannel.

```
/*Create and open a DatagramChannel object*/
DatagramChannel ch = DatagramChannel.open();
```

- Step 3—Connect the channel to a remote host.

```
/*Set remote host IP Address and port no*/
InetSocketAddress addr =
  new InetSocketAddress("136.206.35.201", 7);
/*Connect the channel*/
ch.connect(addr);
```

- Step 4—Prepare send and receive buffers.

```
/*Create the buffer for the outgoing packet*/
ByteBuffer sbuff =
  ByteBuffer.wrap("PING".getBytes());

/*Create the buffer for the incoming packet*/
ByteBuffer rbuff =
  ByteBuffer.allocate("PING".getBytes().length);
```

- Step 5—Send and receive packets.

```
/*Send an outgoing packet*/
ch.send(sbuff, addr);
/*Wait for the response*/
Thread.sleep(200);
/*Receive the echo packet if any*/
ch.receive(rbuff);
String rtxt = new String(rbuff.array());
```

- Step 6—Check the content of receiving packet.

```
if (rtxt.equals("PING"))
  System.out.println("PING: Remote host is OK.");
else
  System.out.println("PING: Communication issue.");
```

In order for this basic PING example to work, remote host's echo services need to be enabled and also permissive rules have to be set in the network's firewalls. Unfortunately, many operating systems have the echo service disabled by default.

The basic PING Java example is presented next.

```java
import java.net.*;
import java.nio.*;
import java.nio.channels.*;

/*method to send ping messages and receive responses*/
public void basicPing()
{
  try {
    /*Count number of tries*/
    int count = 0;

    /*Create the buffer for the outgoing packet*/
    ByteBuffer sbuff =
      ByteBuffer.wrap("PING".getBytes());

    /*Create the buffer for the incoming packet.
     *As the incoming packet is expected to be
     *an identical copy of the outgoing packet
     *the same buffer size has been used.
     */
    ByteBuffer rbuff =
      ByteBuffer.allocate("PING".getBytes().length);

    /*Connect the channel to the remote host
     *using an InetSocketAddress
     *using the default echo port 7
     */
    InetSocketAddress addr =
      new InetSocketAddress("136.206.35.201", 7);

    /*Create and open a DatagramChannel*/
    DatagramChannel ch = DatagramChannel.open();

    /*Set the channel as non-blocking*/
    ch.configureBlocking(false);

    /*Connect the channel*/
    ch.connect(addr);
    String rtxt = "";
    do
    {
    /*Send the outgoing packet*/
    ch.send(sbuff, addr);
```

Code Listing 7.1 PingClient.java—basicPing()

```
    /*Wait for the response*/
    Thread.sleep(200);

    /*Receive the echo packet if any*/
    ch.receive(rbuff);
    rtxt = new String(rbuff.array());


    /*increment count*/
    count++;
    }
    while (!rtxt.equals("PING") && count < 3);
    if (rtxt.equals("PING"))
       System.out.println("PING: Remote host is OK");
    else
       System.out.println("PING: Communication issue");
  }
  catch(Exception e)
  {
    /*Print the exception message.*/
    System.out.println(e.getMessage());
  }
}
```

Code Listing 7.1 (Continued)

7.3 Electronic Mail Services

Lately, electronic mail services (e-mail) are one of the most widely used means of communications. Exchanging e-mails involves clients sending electronic messages to other clients. In practice, sending client applications enable messages to be written and sent to local e-mail hosts (e-mail servers) which in turn forward them to the receiving clients' remote e-mail servers via the network. The remote clients contact their e-mail servers and if there are received messages, they are retrieved and offered for reading to the users.

In this context, the e-mail service system is composed of User Agents (UA) and Message Transfer Agents (MTA). The UAs allow the users to send and retrieve messages and may also provide graphical user interfaces. The MTAs enable transfers of messages from the source host to the destination. In general, UAs are deployed at the clients and MTAs operate at the e-mail servers.

This e-mail message exchange system involves several services provided by UA and MTA modules.

Composition is provided by UAs and refers to the creation of both original and reply messages at the level of clients.

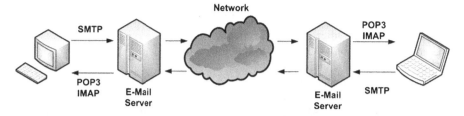

Figure 7.3 E-mail message exchange system—components, protocols, and principle

Figure 7.4 E-mail message
format

Message *transfer* is supported by MTAs and refers to the delivery of messages from source to destination, including local client–server data exchange in which UAs are also involved.

Reporting is also provided by MTAs and involves informing the sender about the status of the messages sent.

Displaying is provided by UAs through the user interface and involves presenting the messages so that they can be accessed by the users. Depending on the type of content, sometimes the messages need to be converted before displaying. Often other programs are invoked, such as plug-ins (embedded in the e-mail client applications) or stand-alone applications (independent from the e-mail client applications).

Disposition, managed by the UAs, refers to what the remote user does with the messages (e.g., save, delete, etc.).

Figure 7.3 shows the basic principle of the e-mail service, including the message exchange system major components and communication protocols. These protocols are the Simple Mail Transfer Protocol (SMTP), Post-Office Protocol version 3 (POP3), and Internet Message Access Protocol (IMAP).

The **e-mail message structure** involves an envelope, a header, and a body, as outlined in Fig. 7.4. This has been formalized in RFC 822 [16] and RFC 2822 [17]. The envelope encapsulates the message and contains all the information required to transport the message such as destination address, priority, and security level. The header contains the control information required to display the message (e.g., date, subject). The body represents the message content, which is most useful to the human user. The message body was originally text only, but lately there was a clear need to allow for addition of other media formats.

The **Multipurpose Internet Mail Extensions (MIME)** is a standard (RFC 1341, RFC 2045-2049) [18], [19] that extends the original format of the e-mail messages to support extra features and encoding rules for non-ASCII messages. These features include characters with accents (e.g., in French, German, etc.), text in non-Latin alphabets (e.g., Cyrillic, Hebrew, etc.), text in non-alphabetic languages (e.g., Chinese, Japanese), non-text data (e.g., multimedia, images, audio), etc.

MIME defines five new message headers. The new headers include:

- MIME-Version—Indicates MIME version;
- Content-Description—String describing the content;
- Content-Id—Unique identifier;
- Content-Transfer-Encoding—How body is wrapped for transmission (e.g., 7-bit ASCII, 8-bit codes, base64 binary, etc.);
- Content-Type—Type and format of content. The standard defines 7 types of content as follows: Text (Plain, Enriched), Image (Gif, Jpeg), Audio (Basic), Video (Mpeg), Application, Message (RFC 822, Partial, External-body), and Multipart.

Messages not including the MIME-Version header are assumed to be in English plain text.

Simple Mail Transfer Protocol (SMTP), standardized as RFC 821 [20], allows messages to be sent from UA located at the client to MTA situated at server side. SMTP works on top of TCP and in general uses port 25.

The client initiates the TCP connection with the server and waits for the server to state it is ready for data reception. After the server confirms it is ready, the communication sequence commences in a command–response manner. The client sends commands, and the server responds with command status messages. Status messages include ASCII encoded numeric codes and details in text. The order of the commands is very important for the success of the message sending operation.

SMTP commands include:

- HELO—identifies the client;
- MAIL FROM:—starts a mail transfer session and identifies the mail sender;
- RCPT TO:—identifies the mail recipient; There may be multiple RCPT TO: commands;
- DATA:—sender ready to transmit a series of lines of text, each ending with CR&LF. A line containing a period only indicates the end of the data;
- QUIT:—request to finish the session and close the connection.

The extended SMTP (ESMTP) was defined in RFC 2821 [21]. EHLO is the new command for identifying the client as RFC 2821 compatible. If the SMTP server recognizes this command, often it sends a list of the available ESMTP commands back to the client. They include AUTH used for authentication purposes, START-TLS employed for secure data transfer, and SIZE used to allow the client to indicate the message size or the server to specify the available buffer space. Other set of commands and parameters are also defined.

The **Post-Office Protocol version 3 (POP3)**, standardized in RFC 1939 [22], allows messages stored on the e-mail server to be accessed by the client. POP3 involves collaboration between the client-located UA and server's MTA. POP3 works on top of TCP and in general uses port 110.

POP3 requires a client–server connection to be established before client–server message exchange is permitted. The protocol message sequence includes the following stages. After the client connects to the server, it waits for the server to state it is ready. Once the server confirms its availability, the client starts sending commands which determine the server to perform actions and respond with status messages.

Table 7.1 IMAP vs. POP3

Protocol	RFC	TCP port	Email store	Email read	Mailboxes	Partial message
POP3	1939	110	Client	Offline	Simple	No
IMAP	2060	143	Server	Online	Multiple	Yes

POP3 requires sequential passing through three states: Authorization, Transaction, Update.

During the *Authorization* phase the client sends username and password details to the server. The following commands are involved:

- USER username—specifies the username;
- PASS password—indicates the password.

Only the authorized clients are allowed to proceed to the next stage.

During the *Transactions* phase, the client is allowed to retrieve the list of messages or a particular one, in a similar command–response fashion. The client may mark for deletion some (or all) of the messages. The following commands are involved:

- LIST—lists the e-mails received in order;
- RETR no—retrieves message number no;
- DELE no—marks for deletion message number no.

During the *Update* phase, the QUIT command is sent by the client and when receiving it, the server actually deletes all messages marked for deletion then sends a disconnect message, and disconnects the client.

POP3 allows the client to download the messages to the client's machine and manipulate them offline.

The **Internet Message Access Protocol (IMAP)**, standardized in RFC 2060 [23], is also used to enable client access to the e-mail messages on the server. IMAP works on top of TCP and in general listens at port 143.

The fundamental difference between POP3 and IMAP is that the latter assumes that the server keeps all the messages and the client accesses them online only. There is no message copy retrieved and stored by the client locally.

Additionally, IMAP enables the user to have and manipulate multiple mailboxes and permits e-mail access from multiple locations.

IMAP requires client–server connectivity as well. The command–response IMAP message sequence includes the following stages. The client connects to the server and waits for the server to state it is ready. After the server send its ready status confirmation, the client sends commands and the server performs the command-related actions and sends responses with action status messages to the client.

Specific commands are defined by IMAP for searching for messages, reading messages or part of them, addressing an e-mail by attributes (e.g., from source), creating and managing multiple mailboxes, etc.

A summary of IMAP and POP3 features are described in a comparative Table 7.1.

7.3.1 SMTP Java Example

This section illustrates via Java examples how e-mail messages can be sent to the e-mail server via SMTP. There are two distinct methods. The first approach uses basic socket communication, but it is more complex and requires extensive knowledge of the SMTP protocol. The second method uses the JavaMail API, and it is less complex, as the API hides the protocol-related implementation complexity.

7.3.1.1 Socket-based SMTP Example

In order to build the socket-based SMTP Java example, several major steps need to be followed. The steps are listed below.

- Step 1—Import the required packages:

```java
import java.io.*;
import java.net.*;
import java.util.*;
import java.text.*;
```

- Step 2—Prepare server details and SMTP fields:

```java
/*set the server details*/
private String host = new String("136.206.35.46");
private int port = 25;

/*set email message parameters*/
String from = new String("jack@eeng.dcu.ie");
String to = new String("jane@eeng.dcu.ie");
String cc = new String("john@eeng.dcu.ie");
String bcc = new String("jill@eeng.dcu.ie");
String subj = new String("SMTP email");
String body = new String("Message body!");
```

- Step 3—Establish socket connection with the server:

```java
/*create and open the socket*/
sock = new Socket(host, port);

/*create the I/O data streams*/
os = new DataOutputStream(sock.getOutputStream());
is = new DataInputStream(sock.getInputStream());
if(sock != null && os != null && is != null)
{
    /*Connection successful.*/
    System.out.println("Connected OK!");
    /*Send email.*/
```

```
    [...]
}
else
{
  /*Unsuccessful connection.*/
  System.out.println("Connection error!");
}
```

- Step 4—Communicate with the server using SMTP commands:

```
/*communicate with the server using SMTP commands*/
os.writeBytes("HELO\r\n");
/*set email message details*/
/*sender address*/
os.writeBytes("MAIL From: <" + from + ">\r\n");

/*destination email address*/
os.writeBytes("RCPT To: <" + to + ">\r\n");

/*CC email address*/
os.writeBytes("RCPT Cc: <" + cc + ">\r\n");

/*BCC email address*/
os.writeBytes("RCPT Bcc: <" + bcc + ">\r\n");

/*email message and header*/
os.writeBytes("DATA\r\n");

os.writeBytes("X-Mailer: Via Java\r\n");
os.writeBytes("DATE:"+dFormat.format(dDate)+"\r\n");
os.writeBytes("From: source <" + from + ">\r\n");
os.writeBytes("To: destination <" + to + ">\r\n");
os.writeBytes("Cc: CC dest. <" + cc + ">\r\n");

/*message content*/
os.writeBytes("Subject: "+ subj +"\r\n");
os.writeBytes(body + " \r\n");

/*indicates the end of message data*/
os.writeBytes("\r\n.\r\n");
```

- Step 5—Send the message:

```
/*start the SMTP update phase*/
os.writeBytes("QUIT\r\n");
```

- Step 6—Check for server's answer:

```
String rcv;
while((rcv = is.readLine()) != null) {
  if(rcv.indexOf("Ok") != -1)
  {
    /*Server success confirmation*/
    [...]
  }
}
```

- Step 7—Deal with all exceptions:

```
try
{
  [...]
}
catch()
{
  [...]
}
```

Next the complete SMTP example using sockets is presented.

```
import java.io.*;
import java.net.*;
import java.util.*;
import java.text.*;   // Used for date formatting.

/*class implementing the email service*/
public class SockSMTPeMail
{
  /*socket used for communication with the server*/
  private Socket sock = null;

  /*data streams for reading/writing to/from the
   socket*/
  private DataOutputStream os = null;
  private DataInputStream is = null;

  /*server details*/
  private String host = null;
  private int port = 25;

  /*email message parameters*/
  String from = null;
```

Code Listing 7.2 SockSMTPeMail.java

```
String to = null;
String cc = null;
String bcc = null;
String subj = null;
String body = null;

/*args are the command line arguments*/
public static void main(String[] args)
{
  SockSMTPeMail mail = new SockSMTPeMail();
  mail.SendMail();
}

public void SendMail()
{
  /*set the server details*/
  String host = new String("136.206.35.46");
  int port = 25;

  /*set email message parameters*/
  from = new String("jack@eeng.dcu.ie");
  to = new String("jane@eeng.dcu.ie");
  cc = new String("john@eeng.dcu.ie");
  bcc = new String("jill@eeng.dcu.ie");
  subj = new String("SMTP email");
  body = new String("Message body!");

  /*get and format the current date and time*/
  Date dDate = new Date();
  DateFormat dFormat;
  dFormat = DateFormat.getDateInstance(
    DateFormat.FULL, Locale.US);

  try
  {
    /*create and open the socket*/
    sock = new Socket(host, port);

    /*create the I/O data streams*/
    os = new DataOutputStream(sock.getOutputStream());
    is = new DataInputStream(sock.getInputStream());

    if(sock != null && os != null && is != null)
```

Code Listing 7.2 (Continued)

```
{
    /*Connection successful.*/
    System.out.println("Connected OK!");
    try
    {
      os.writeBytes("HELO\r\n");
      /*set email message details*/
      /*sender address*/
      os.writeBytes("MAIL From: <"
                    + from + ">\r\n");

      /*destination email address*/
      os.writeBytes("RCPT To: <" + to + ">\r\n");

      /*CC email address*/
      os.writeBytes("RCPT Cc: <" + cc + ">\r\n");

      /*BCC email address*/
      os.writeBytes("RCPT Bcc: <" + bcc + ">\r\n");

      /*email message and header*/
      os.writeBytes("DATA\r\n");

      os.writeBytes("X-Mailer: Via Java\r\n");
      os.writeBytes("DATE: " +
        dFormat.format(dDate) + "\r\n");
      os.writeBytes("From: source <"
                    + from + ">\r\n");
      os.writeBytes("To: destination <"
                    + to + ">\r\n");
      os.writeBytes("Cc: CC dest. <"
                    + cc + ">\r\n");

      /*message content*/
      os.writeBytes("Subject: "+ subj +"\r\n");
      os.writeBytes(body + " \r\n");

      /*specify the end of message data*/
      os.writeBytes("\r\n.\r\n");

      /*sends the message by issuing the QUIT
      command*/
      os.writeBytes("QUIT\r\n");
```

Code Listing 7.2 (Continued)

```
            /*check the server reply against OK*/
            String rcv;
            while((rcv = is.readLine()) != null)
            {
              System.out.println(rcv);
              if(rcv.indexOf("Ok") != -1)
              /*Server success confirmation*/
                break;
            }
          }
          catch(Exception e)
          {
            System.out.println("Communication error.");
          }
        }
        else
        {
          /*Unsuccessful connection.*/
          System.out.println("Connection error!");
        }
      }
    catch(Exception e)
    {
      System.out.println("Host " + host + "unknown");
    }
  }
}
```

Code Listing 7.2 (Continued)

7.3.1.2 JavaMail API-Based SMTP example

The second approach to building SMTP Java applications is to use the JavaMail API. The following major steps need to be considered.

- Step 1—Download JavaMail package and unzip it.

  ```
  http://www.oracle.com/technetwork/java/javamail/
    index.html
  ```

- Step 2—Update your CLASSPATH to include:

  ```
  mail.jar; mailapi.jar;
  pop3.jar; smtp.jar; activation.jar
  ```

- Step 3—Import the required packages:

  ```
  import javax.mail.*;
  ```

```
import javax.mail.internet.*;
import java.util.*;
```

- Step 4—Prepare server details and SMTP fields:

```
/*set the server details*/
srv = new String("136.206.35.46");

/*set email message parameters*/
String from = new String("jack@eeng.dcu.ie");
String to = new String("jane@eeng.dcu.ie");
String cc = new String("john@eeng.dcu.ie");
String bcc = new String("jill@eeng.dcu.ie");
String subj = new String("SMTP email");
String body = new String("Message body!");
```

- Step 5—Get the communication with the server session:

```
/*get the default comms. session,
 *or start a new one*/
Properties props = System.getProperties();
props.put("JavaMailSMTPeMail", srv);
Session session =
    Session.getDefaultInstance(props, null);
```

- Step 6—Prepare the message:

```
/*create a new message*/
Message msg = new MimeMessage(session);
/*set the message fields*/
msg.setFrom(new InternetAddress(from));
msg.setRecipients(Message.RecipientType.TO,
        InternetAddress.parse(to, false));
msg.setRecipients(Message.RecipientType.CC
        InternetAddress.parse(cc, false));
msg.setRecipients(Message.RecipientType.BCC
        InternetAddress.parse(bcc, false));
/*Set the message subject and body*/
msg.setSubject(subj);
msg.setText(body);
```

- Step 7—Send message to the server:

```
/*send the message*/
Transport.send(msg);

System.out.println("Message sent OK.");
```

- Step 8—Deal with all exceptions:

```
try
{
    [...]
}
catch()
{
    [...]
}
```

A complete simple SMTP example using JavaMail API built based on the examples provided in the JavaMail documentation [24] is presented next. The JavaMail API documentation also includes examples which make use of the extended SMTP features such as authentication.

```
import javax.mail.*;
import javax.mail.internet.*;
import java.util.*;

public class JavaMailSMTPeMail
{
    /*server details*/
    private String srv = null;

    /*email message parameters*/
    String from = null;
    String to = null;
    String cc = null;
    String bcc = null;
    String subj = null;
    String body = null;

    /*Main method to send a message to the SMTP server*/
    public static void main(String[] args)
    {
        JavaMailSMTPeMail mail = new JavaMailSMTPeMail();
        mail.SendMail();
    }

    public void SendMail()
    {
        /*set the server details*/
        srv = new String("136.206.35.46");
```

Code Listing 7.3 JavaMailSMTPeMail.java

```
/*set email message parameters*/

from = new String("jack@eeng.dcu.ie");
to = new String("jane@eeng.dcu.ie");
cc = new String("john@eeng.dcu.ie");
bcc = new String("jill@eeng.dcu.ie");
subj = new String("SMTP email");
body = new String("Message body!");

try
{
  /*get the default comms.
   *session, or start a new one*/
  Properties props = System.getProperties();
  props.put("JavaMailSMTPeMail", srv);
  Session session =
      Session.getDefaultInstance(props, null);

  /*create a new message*/
  Message msg = new MimeMessage(session);
  /*set the message fields*/
  msg.setFrom(new InternetAddress(from));
  msg.setRecipients(Message.RecipientType.TO,
    InternetAddress.parse(to, false));
  msg.setRecipients(Message.RecipientType.CC,
    InternetAddress.parse(cc, false));
  msg.setRecipients(Message.RecipientType.BCC,
    InternetAddress.parse(bcc, false));
  /*Set the message subject and body*/
  msg.setSubject(subj);
  msg.setText(body);

  /*set other header information*/
  msg.setSentDate(new Date());

  /*send the message*/
  Transport.send(msg);

  System.out.println("Message sent OK.");
}
catch (Exception ex)
```

Code Listing 7.3 (Continued)

```
    {
       ex.printStackTrace();
    }
    System.exit(0);
  }
}
```

Code Listing 7.3 (Continued)

7.3.2 POP3 Java Example

This section provides a Java example to illustrate how e-mail messages can be retrieved from the e-mail server via POP3. This example makes use of the JavaMail API which hides the POP3-related implementation aspects.

- Step 1—Download JavaMail package and unzip it.

```
http://www.oracle.com/technetwork/java/javamail/
   index.html
```

- Step 2—Update your CLASSPATH to include:

```
mail.jar; mailapi.jar; pop3.jar;
smtp.jar; activation.jar
```

- Step 3—Import the required packages:

```
import javax.mail.*;
import javax.mail.internet.*;
import java.util.*;
import java.io.*;
```

- Step 4—Prepare parameters for server authentication:

```
/*set server details*/
String srv = new String("136.206.35.46");
String user = new String("john");
String pass = new String("Secret@19_02_13");
```

- Step 5—Get the session and connect to the server:

```
/*get the default session*/
Properties props = System.getProperties();
Session session = null;
session = Session.getDefaultInstance(props, null);

/*get a POP3 message store, and connect to it*/
store = session.getStore("pop3");
store.connect(srv, user, pass);
```

- Step 6—Open Inbox folder and access all e-mails:

```
/*get the INBOX*/
folder = folder.getFolder("INBOX");
if (folder == null)
  throw new Exception("No POP3 INBOX");

/*open the folder (read only)*/
folder.open(Folder.READ_ONLY);

/*get the messages and print them*/
Message[] msgs = folder.getMessages();
for (int i = 0; i < msgs.length; i++)
  printEmail(msgs[i]);
```

- Step 7—Print an e-mail message:

```
/*get header information*/
String from = null;
from = ((InternetAddress)msg.getFrom()[0])
       .getPersonal();
if (from == null)
  from=((InternetAddress)msg.getFrom()[0])
       .getAddress();
/*print sender details*/
 System.out.println("FROM: "+from);

/*get and print the subject*/
String subj = msg.getSubject();
System.out.println("SUBJECT: "+subject);

/*get the message itself*/
Part msgPart = msg;
Object content = msgPart.getContent();

/*or its first body part
 *if it is a multipart message*/
if (content instanceof Multipart)
{
  msgPart = ((Multipart)content).getBodyPart(0);
  System.out.println("[ Multipart Message ]");
}

/*get the content type*/
String ct = msgPart.getContentType();

/*if the content is plain text, print it*/
```

```
System.out.println("CONTENT:" + ct);
if (ct.startsWith("text/plain") ||
  ct.startsWith("text/html"))
{
  InputStream is = msgPart.getInputStream();
  BufferedReader br = null;
  br = new BufferedReader(new InputStreamReader(is));

  String line = br.readLine();

  while (line != null)
  {
    System.out.println(line);
    line = br.readLine();
  }
}
System.out.println("");
```

- Step 8—Deal with all exceptions:

```
try
{
  [...]
}
catch()
{
  [...]
}
```

A complete POP3 example using JavaMail API built based on the examples provided in the JavaMail documentation [24] is presented next.

```
import javax.mail.*;
import javax.mail.internet.*;
import java.util.*;
import java.io.*;

public class JavaMailPOP3eMail
{
  /*store server details*/
  String srv = null;
  String user = null;
  String pass = null;
```

Code Listing 7.4 JavaMailPOP3eMail.java

```
public static void main(String[] args)
{
  JavaMailPOP3eMail mail = new JavaMailPOP3eMail();
  mail.SendMail();
}

public void SendMail()
{
  /*set server details*/
  srv = new String("136.206.35.46");
  user = new String("john");
  pass = new String("Secret@19_02_13");

  /*save store and folder details*/
  Store store = null;
  Folder folder = null;

  try
  {
    /*get the default session*/
    Properties props = System.getProperties();
    Session session = null;
    session = Session.getDefaultInstance(props, null);

    /*get a POP3 message store, and connect to it*/
    store = session.getStore("pop3");
    store.connect(srv, user, pass);

    /*get the default folder*/
    folder = store.getDefaultFolder();
    if (folder == null)
      throw new Exception("No default folder");

    /*get the INBOX*/
    folder = folder.getFolder("INBOX");
    if (folder == null)
      throw new Exception("No POP3 INBOX");

    /*open the folder (read only)*/
    folder.open(Folder.READ_ONLY);

    /*get the messages and print them*/
    Message[] msgs = folder.getMessages();
```

Code Listing 7.4 (Continued)

```
      for (int i = 0; i < msgs.length; i++)
      {
        printEmail(msgs[i]);
      }
    }
    catch (Exception ex)
    {
      ex.printStackTrace();
    }
    finally
    {
      /*close session*/
      try
      {
        if (folder != null)
          folder.close(false);
        if (store != null)
          store.close();
      }
      catch (Exception ex2)
      {
        ex2.printStackTrace();
      }
    }
  }

  /*print email*/
  public static void printEmail(Message msg)
  {
    try
    {
      /*get header information*/
      String from = null;
      from = ((InternetAddress)msg.getFrom()[0])
                .getPersonal();
      if (from == null)
        from=((InternetAddress)msg.getFrom()[0])
                .getAddress();
      /*print sender details*/
      System.out.println("FROM: "+from);

      /*get and print the subject*/
      String subj = msg.getSubject();
```

Code Listing 7.4 (Continued)

```
      System.out.println("SUBJECT: "+subj);

      /*get the message itself*/
      Part msgPart = msg;
      Object content = msgPart.getContent();

      /*or its first body part
       *if it is a multipart message*/
      if (content instanceof Multipart)
      {
        msgPart = ((Multipart)content).getBodyPart(0);
        System.out.println("[ Multipart Message ]");
      }

      /*get the content type*/
      String ct = msgPart.getContentType();

      /*if the content is plain text, print it*/
      System.out.println("CONTENT:" + ct);
      if (ct.startsWith("text/plain")
          || ct.startsWith("text/html"))
      {
        InputStream is = msgPart.getInputStream();
        BufferedReader br = null;
        br = new BufferedReader(new
            InputStreamReader(is));
        String line = br.readLine();
        while (line != null)
        {
          System.out.println(line);
          line = br.readLine();
        }
      }
      System.out.println("");
    }
    catch (Exception ex)
    {
      ex.printStackTrace();
    }
  }
}
```

Code Listing 7.4 (Continued)

Figure 7.5 FTP session

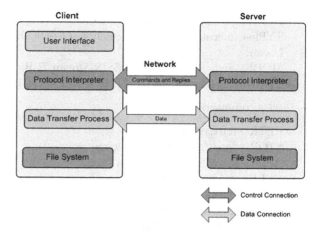

7.4   File Transfer Protocol Service

File transfers account for both a high number of flows and huge amount of data transferred over the current networks. They involve clients transferring file content in reliable and efficient manner to and from a remote server.

These file transfers make use of the File Transfer Protocol (FTP) which was developed in 1985 and is still used today. The protocol has been first standardized in RFC 959 [8], and then various extensions have been proposed to enhance flexibility and security (RFC 1579, RFC 2228) [9, 10].

FTP works on top of TCP and in general uses port 21; however, in some situations the server administrator may choose to use different ports. FTP involves a client connecting to the server and sending commands during a communication session. The server responds with actions and command status messages. In general, each such session involves at least one file transfer.

The basic principle of file transfers using FTP is outlined in Fig. 7.5.

Theoretically, FTP involves two connections: for control and data. FTP commands and replies are exchanged via the control connection, while data is exchanged over the data connection. There is a requirement for the control connection to be working when data is transferred over its dedicated connection. In practice, a single connection is used for both data and control information exchange.

The FTP commands belong to one of the following three categories.

- *Access control* commands include:

  - USER—indicates the user;
  - PASS—indicates the password;
  - CWD—changes directory;
  - CDUP—changes directory to parent;
  - QUIT—logouts.

- *Transfer parameter* commands include:

  - PORT—publishes local data port;

- PASV—makes server passive (listen);
- TYPE—indicates data representation (A-ASCII, E-EBCDIC, I-Image, L-Local);
- MODE—indicates transfer mode (S-Stream, B-Block, C-Compressed);
- STRU—sets file structure (F-FILE, R-RECORD, P-PAGE).

- *Service* commands include:

  - RETR—retrieves file;
  - STOR—sends and stores the file remotely;
  - APPE—sends file and appends;
  - DELE—deletes the file;
  - MKD—makes a new directory;
  - RMD—removes a directory;
  - PWD—prints working directory;
  - LIST—lists files.

Every command must generate some action and at least one reply from the server. This enables the synchronization of requests sent by clients and actions performed by the server and also allows the clients to know the server status. In general, the reply is a single line; however, multiple lines are also accepted. The reply must contain a three digit status code which enables machines to assess the server status and a text message which describes the server status in human language.

There are several issues involved when using FTP for file transfers. Security is an important issue for many companies that have installed firewalls. Firewalls prevent unauthorized users from getting access to the networks. However, firewalls may also inadvertently prevent valid users from accessing some resources, including files. When FTP is involved, the network administrators must design rules for classes of FTP connections which may be a costly and error prone process.

Another issue is standardization. There are many FTP client applications with different interpretations of the FTP protocol. Consequently, FTP server administrators must know how to support all of these different client application types.

An alternative to classic FTP is a Web-based file transfer. A Web-based file transfer client runs within the Web browser. There is no need for any software to install, license to purchase or software to maintain. Additionally, there is no need to set-up firewall rules for each user class.

7.4.1 Simple FTP Java Client Example

A Java FTP client can be implemented in three ways.

The first approach requires the implementation of an own FTPClient class. This solution can use standard sockets and FTP commands to interact and exchange data files with the file server. The second approach is to find an existing implementation of an FTPClient class and make use of it in order to perform the file transfer. The third possibility is to employ a Web-based FTP client.

The simple FTP Java client file transfer example presented next uses the second approach and makes use of the FTPClient implementation available as part of the Apache Commons Net API [25]. The Apache Commons Net API-based FTP client file transfer application implementation involves the following steps.

- Step 1—Download Apache Commons Net API version 3.2.

```
http://commons.apache.org/net/download_net.cgi
```

- Step 2—Update your CLASSPATH to include:

```
commons-net-3.2.jar
```

- Step 3—Import the required packages:

```
import java.io.*;
import org.apache.commons.net.ftp.FTP;
import org.apache.commons.net.ftp.FTPClient;
```

- Step 4—Prepare parameters for server authentication:

```
/*sets server parameters*/
String srv = new String("136.206.35.46");
int port = 21;
String user = new String("john");
String pass = new String("Secret@19_02_13");
```

- Step 5—Create the FTPClient object:

```
FtpClient client = new FtpClient(host);
```

- Step 6—Connect, login to the FTP server, and set transfer mode:

```
/*connects to FTP server*/
ftpClient.connect(srv, port);
/*authenticates on the server*/
ftpClient.login(user, pass);

/*sets connection to client-server mode*/
ftpClient.enterLocalPassiveMode();
/*sets transferred file type*/
ftpClient.setFileType(FTP.BINARY_FILE_TYPE);
```

- Step 7—Set local and remote files and perform transfer:

```
/*remote file*/
String rf = "/remotefolder/remotefile.txt";
/*local file*/
File lf = new File("C:/localfolder/localfile.txt");

/*enables data writing*/
OutputStream os =
```

```
   new BufferedOutputStream(new FileOutputStream(lf));

   /*gets remote file content*/
   if(ftpClient.retrieveFile(rf, os))
      System.out.println("File transfer success.");
```

- Step 8—Close output stream, perform server logout and disconnect:

```
   /*closes output stream*/
   os.close();
   /*logouts and disconnects*/
   if (ftpClient.isConnected())
   {
      ftpClient.logout();
         ftpClient.disconnect();
   }
```

- Step 9—Deal with all exceptions:

```
   try
   {
      [...]
   }
   catch()
   {
      [...]
   }
```

The complete Apache Commons Net API-based FTP download client Java example application is included next. An alternative FTP download solution which makes use of the Apache Commons Net API FTPClient's InputStream retrieveFileStream(String remote) method is presented in [26].

```
import java.io.*;

import org.apache.commons.net.ftp.FTP;
import org.apache.commons.net.ftp.FTPClient;

public class ApacheJavaFTP
{
   public static void main(String[] args)
   {
      /*sets server parameters*/
      String srv = new String("136.206.35.46");
      int port = 21;
```

Code Listing 7.5 ApacheJavaFTP.java

```
String user = new String("john");
String pass = new String("Secret@19_02_13");

/*creates FTPClient object*/
FTPClient ftpClient = new FTPClient();
try
{
  /*connects to FTP server*/
  ftpClient.connect(srv, port);
  /*authenticates on the server*/
  ftpClient.login(user, pass);

  /*sets connection to client-server mode*/
  ftpClient.enterLocalPassiveMode();
  /*sets transferred file type*/
  ftpClient.setFileType(FTP.BINARY_FILE_TYPE);

  /*remote file*/
  String rf = "/remotefolder/remotefile.txt";
  /*local file*/
  File lf =
  new File("C:/localfolder/localfile.txt");

  /*enables data writing*/
  OutputStream os =
  new BufferedOutputStream(new
        FileOutputStream(lf));

  /*gets remote file content*/
  if(ftpClient.retrieveFile(rf, os))
    System.out.println("File transfer success.");

  /*closes output stream*/
  os.close();
}
catch (IOException ex)
{
  System.out.println("Error: " + ex.getMessage());
  ex.printStackTrace();
}
finally
{
  try
```

Code Listing 7.5 (Continued)

```
    {
      /*logouts and disconnects*/
      if (ftpClient.isConnected())
      {
        ftpClient.logout();
        ftpClient.disconnect();
      }
    }
    catch (IOException ex)
    {
      ex.printStackTrace();
    }
  }
 }
}
```

Code Listing 7.5 (Continued)

7.5 Web Content Transfer Service

Web content transfers account for most data exchange over the Internet. They involve communications between Web clients (browsers) and Web servers as illustrated in Fig. 7.6.

These communications are performed based on the Hypertext Transfer Protocol (HTTP), whose version 1.0 was standardized as RFC 1945 [27] and version 1.1 was standardized as RFC 2616 [11]. HTTP works in general on top of TCP. The default port number is 80, but other ports can also be used. Communications are performed in sessions. During these sessions, clients make requests to severs for Web content and the servers respond performing Web content transfers to the requesting clients. The servers also respond with status messages for client information purpose. In general, each session involves at least one client–server request–response and at least one Web content transfer.

In terms of HTTP connections, there may be one (HTTP v.1.0) or multiple simultaneous connections (HTTP v.1.1) between each client–server pair, approaches which mostly differ in terms of efficiency. When HTTP v.1.0 is employed, the HTTP requests and responses are exchanged sequentially. For each Web item to be transferred, a single TCP connection is established, an HTTP request is sent, an HTTP response is received, and then TCP connection is released. In HTTP v.1.1, persistent connections are used, and one or more TCP connections are established between client and server. HTTP requests are sent and HTTP responses are received over all connections. Pipelining is sometimes used (sending multiple requests before responses are received). Figure 7.7 illustrates the HTTP-based Web document delivery process.

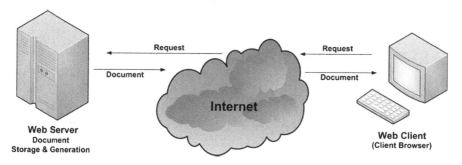

Figure 7.6 World Wide Web document delivery process

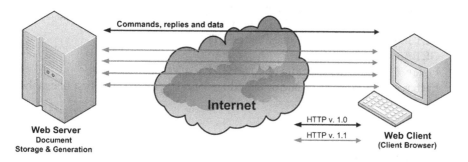

Figure 7.7 Web document delivery process using HTTP

As already mentioned, the HTTP-based client–server interaction is performed using a series of requests–responses. Each request consists of one or more lines of text (ASCII). The first line is the *Request-line* and includes:

- Name of the HTTP method;
- Universal Resource Identifier (URI) of the Web resource;
- HTTP version.

The HTTP method names are case sensitive. Method-related *Headers* follow the Request-line. Depending on the method, *Content* will follow after a blank line or not.

Next the HTTP methods are presented, indicating their names and a brief description.

- GET—request to retrieve a Web page;
- HEAD—request to read a Web page's header;
- PUT—request to store a Web page;
- POST—append to a Web page;
- DELETE—remove the Web page;
- TRACE—echo incoming request;
- CONNECT—reserved for future use;
- OPTIONS—query certain options.

Figure 7.8 HTTP request
and response structure

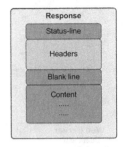

The location of Web resources are indicated using URIs. URIs were defined in RFC 2396 [28] and are either *relative*, listing the resource relative path, or *absolute*, indicating the protocol, host, port, and path.

Next are two examples of valid HTTP requests.

GET http://www.dcu.ie:80/index.html HTTP/1.1

GET /index.html HTTP/1.1

Figure 7.8 shows the structure of both HTTP request and response.

Each response consists of one or more lines of text (ASCII). The first line is the *Status-line* and includes:

- HTTP version;
- A three digit status code;
- A human readable status message.

Response-related *Headers* follow the Status-line and, depending on the response type, *Content* will be present after a blank line or not.

The status codes are determined by the server response following client request. The first status code digit divides responses in five categories:

- 1—Information;
- 2—Success;
- 3—Redirection;
- 4—Client error (e.g., invalid request);
- 5—Server error.

The second digit indicates the type of error that has occurred, if any (e.g., file system, command syntax error). The third digit further qualifies the error.

There may be zero or more HTTP headers after each request or response. Each header consists of a single line of the following format:

- Attribute name
- ":"
- Space
- Attribute value

Both attribute name and value are text-based.

Request headers give information to the server about the client in terms of client type, what content is accepted, who makes the request, etc. Each header line ends with a CRLF (\r \n).

Table 7.2 HTTP header structure

Message header	Type	Content
User-agent	Request	Info about browser and platform
Accept	Request	Type of pages the client can handle
Host	Request	Server's DNS name
Authorization	Request	List of client's credentials
Cookie	Request	Send a previously set cookie
Date	Request–response	Date and time message was sent
Server	Response	Information about server
Content-length	Response	Page length in bytes
Content-type	Response	Page's MIMO type
Set-Cookie	Response	Sets a new cookie

Response headers provide information to the client about the returned data in terms of document type, size, encoding, last modified time, etc. Response header lines also end with a CRLF (\r \n).

Table 7.2 presents the most important HTTP message headers, their meaning, and whether or not they are used as part of the request and/or response.

7.5.1 HTTP Java Client Example

Next the major steps to follow when designing a HTTP-based Web content transfer Java application are presented.

- Step 1—Import required packages:

```
import java.io.*;
import java.net.*;
```

- Step 2—Set path of file to transfer:

```
String path =
new String("http://www.eeng.dcu.ie/index.html");
```

- Step 3—From path create the URL object:

```
URL url = new URL(path);
```

- Step 4—Open an input stream from the url:

```
is = new DataInputStream(new
  BufferedInputStream(url.openStream()));
```

- Step 5—Read data from the stream line by line and print it:

```
String s;
while ((s = is.readLine()) != null)
  System.out.println(s);
```

- Step 6—Close the connection:

```
is.close();
```

- Step 7—Deal with exceptions:

```
try
{
  [...]
}
catch()
{
  [...]
}
```

The complete HTTP client Java example to retrieve Web content given its location at the server is presented.

```
import java.io.*;
import java.net.*;

/*HTTP client implementation*/
public class JavaHTTPClient
{
  /*main method invoked when the application starts*/
  public static void main (String[] args)
  {
    /*Process input parameters*/
    String path =
    new String("http://www.eeng.dcu.ie/index.html");
    DataInputStream is = null;

    try
    {
      /*Create URL object*/
      URL url = new URL(path);

      /*Open an input stream from the url*/
```

Code Listing 7.6　JavaHTTPClient.java

```
      is = new DataInputStream(new
        BufferedInputStream(url.openStream()));

      /*Reads line by line and prints them on the
      screen*/
      String s;
      while ((s = is.readLine()) != null)
      {
        System.out.println(s);
      }
    }
    catch (Exception e)
    {
      System.out.println("An exception occurred");
      e.printStackTrace();
      System.exit(1);
    }
    finally
    {
      /*Close the input stream*/
      try
      {
        is.close();
      }
      catch (IOException ioe)
      {
        System.out.println("IOException occured");
        ioe.printStackTrace();
        System.exit(1);
      }
    }
  }
}
```

Code Listing 7.6   (Continued)

7.6 Java Database Connectivity Services

Database management systems are a very important part of any information system. Databases are the most popular approach to storing data in an efficient and easy to access way. As a consequence, many network applications developed lately involve a database for data storage. In this context, Java software development enables support for database communication.

Figure 7.9 JDBC
architecture

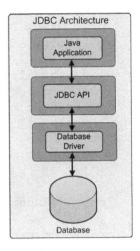

The communication between an application and a database management system occurs in a client–server manner. The user application implements the client-side modules and the database management system is in charge with the server-side modules.

Java Database Connectivity or JDBC, is a Java-based data access technology which enables database-independent connectivity between Java applications and a wide range of databases.

JDBC leverages existing database technologies and allows SQL-based database access. The process of accessing a database via this method involves establishing a connection to a database or tabular data source, sending SQL statements and retrieving and processing the results.

7.6.1 JDBC Architecture

JDBC architecture involves the following four blocks as presented in Fig. 7.9: Java Application, JDBC API, Database Driver, and Database System. These architectural blocks are be described in the context of JDBC database interaction process which involves the following steps.

Java Application calls JDBC library methods to connect and interact with the database. JDBC communicates with the Database System via the correct Database Driver (according to the database technology employed). The driver used has to match the database management system used. For example, if the data is stored in a MySQL database server, the MySQL specific driver has to be loaded. There are many drivers and database communication solutions including MySQL, Postgres, and Oracle.

The results are transferred from the Database System to the Java Application in the inverse way, via the driver and JDBC API.

Several types of database drivers can be used by applications developers.

Direct-to-Database Pure Java Driver allows JDBC calls to be converted directly into the protocol used by the database. The advantages of such a driver include good performance and no need to install special software on the client side or server. Disadvantages involve reduced optimization for server operating system and the need for a different driver for each different database.

Database Middleware Pure Java Driver allows JDBC calls to be converted into a middleware-specific protocol which is then converted into database specific protocol by a middleware server. Middleware server manages multiple database connectivity. This type of driver can be used when multiple databases need to be connected to via the same JDBC driver. It is server-based, so there is no need for a JDBC driver on the client machine. For performance reasons, the server-side component is optimized for the operating system of the server machine. The main disadvantage occurs when the middleware must run on different platforms as database-specific code must run on the middleware server.

Native API Partly Java Driver allows JDBC calls to be converted into calls on the client API for specific database systems (e.g., Oracle, Informix). Specific drivers must be loaded on each client machine. Advantages for using this type of driver include flexibility (allows access to almost any database as long as ODBC drivers are available), significantly better performance and limited Java feature set. As a disadvantage, this solution requires specific client library to be installed.

JDBC-ODBS Bridge allows JDBC to accesses the database via Microsoft's ODBC drivers. ODBC drivers must be loaded on each client machine in order for the database interaction to be performed. Advantages include flexibility, almost any database for which ODBC driver is installed can be accessed via this method. Disadvantages are represented by performance overhead and the need to install an ODBC driver on the client machine which makes it unsuitable for applets.

7.6.2 JDBC Database Access

JDBC database access can be performed by following several steps. Theses steps will be detailed with code examples in the following paragraphs.

- Step 1—Load database driver, by loading the appropriate driver class. The current class instantiates the driver class and register it with the JDBC driver manager.

```
/*Use Class::forName(String classname)*/
// Class.forName("sun.jdbc.odbc.JdbcOdbcDriver");
// Class.forName("connect.microsoft.MicrosoftDriver");
Class.forName("oracle.jdbc.driver.OracleDriver");
```

- Step 2—Establish connection with the database. Create connection URL which includes "jdbc", protocol, host, port number, database name. Host and port number are required for remote access. Connect to the database which uses DriverManager::getConnection(String URL, String username, String password) or DriverManager::getConnection(String URL). Return a reference to an object of type Connection and throw SQLException if a database access error occurs.

```
jdbcodbcURL = "jdbc:odbc:BankDatabase";
Connection link = getConnection(jdbcodbcURL);
```

- Step 3—Create a statement object. Use Connection class's method createStatement() and catch SQLException id thrown.

```
Statement st = link.createStatement();
```

- Step 4—Run the query statement.

```
/*create query*/
String query = "SELECT account, balance FROM
                   Accounts";
/*execute query and retrieve the results*/
ResultSet resultSet = st.executeQuery(query);
/*throws SQLException*/
```

- Step 5—Run the update statement.

```
/*Create update statement*/
/*Uses SQL statements INSERT, UPDATE, DELETE*/
String ins =
  "INSERT INTO Accounts (1234, "John Doe",
   "02/03/2007")";
String upd =
  "UPDATE Accounts SET (account=1234,
   name="John Doe")";
String rem =
  "DELETE FROM Accounts WHERE account=1234";

/*Execute update*/
/*Returns an int representing the row count*/
/*Throws SQLException */
int result = st.executeUpdate(ins);
int result = st.executeUpdate(upd);
int result = st.executeUpdate(rem);
```

- Step 6—Process and display the database operation results.

```
/*Process returned data*/
/*Use ResultSet's methods
 *next() - moves cursor down to the next row
 *previous() - moves cursor up to the previous row
 *XXX getXXX(String colName)
 *returns the value of designated
 *column in current row;
 *XXX can be Byte, String, Int, Date, etc.
 *XXX getXXX(int colNo)
 *returns the value of designated
```

```
*column in current row;
*XXX can be Byte, String, Int, Date, etc.
*Throw SQLException
*/
resultSet.next();
resultSet.getInt("account");
```

- Step 7—Close connection.

```
/*Close Statement object*/
/*Use Statement::close()
 *Throws SQLException*/
st.close();

/*Close Connection
 *Use Connection::close()
 *Throws SQLException*/
link.close();
```

The complete example of a Java application enabling access a database via JDBC
is presented next.

```
import java.sql.*;

/*JDBC application implementation*/
public class JDBCApp {

  /*define connection, statement and result set*/
  static Connection link;
  static Statement statement;
  static ResultSet results;

  /*main method to be invoked
   *when the application starts*/
  public static void main(String[] args)
  {
    System.out.println("Welcome to JDBC program!");
    try {
      /*load the driver*/
      Class.forName("sun.jdbc.odbc.JdbcOdbcDriver");
      /*initiate the connection*/
      link = DriverManager.getConnection
        ("jdbc:odbc:BankDatabase","","");
    }
```

Code Listing 7.7 JDBCApp.java

```
    catch(ClassNotFoundException e) {
      System.out.println("Error: Unable to load
                         driver!");
      System.exit(1);
    }
    catch(SQLException e) {
      System.out.println("Error: Connect to
                         database!");
      System.exit(1);
    }

    try {
      /*create statement*/
      statement = link.createStatement();
      /*execute the statement and retrieve the result*/
      results =
      statement.executeQuery("SELECT * FROM Accounts");
    }
    catch(SQLException e) {
      System.out.println("Error: Cannot execute
                         query!");
      e.printStackTrace();
      System.exit(1);
    }

    try {
      /*process the results*/
      while (results.next()) {
        System.out.println();
        System.out.println("Account:"
        + results.getInt(1));
        System.out.println("Holder:   "
        + results.getString(2));
        System.out.println("Balance:  "
        + results.getFloat(3));
        System.out.println("Modified: "
        + results.getDate(4));
      }
    }
    catch(SQLException e) {
      System.out.println("Error: Retrieving data!");
      e.printStackTrace();
      System.exit(1);
    }
```

Code Listing 7.7 (Continued)

```
    try {
      /*close the statement and connection*/
      statement.close();
      link.close();
    }
    catch(SQLException e) {
      System.out.println("Error: Unable to
                            disconnect!");
      e.printStackTrace();
    }
  }
}
```

Code Listing 7.7   (Continued)

7.6.3 JDBC Transactions

Most databases require protection against errors that may leave the entire data storage in an inconsistent state. For example, when multiple tables are to be updated as a result of an operation, it is important to make sure that either all operations succeed or none of them. Unfortunately, data processing, network and database errors may occur, and a mechanism should be in place to protect the database consistency.

A transaction consists of a number of statements that are related logically and make sense only if all of them are successfully executed. By default, after each database statement is executed, the changes are automatically committed to the database (auto-commit is on). As a consequence, the changes are saved on the disk and are irreversible.

Before a transaction that consists of two or more statements is performed, the auto-commit feature must be turned off (Connection::setAutoCommit(false)). This will prevent the changes to be saved to disk directly. When all the statements are executed successfully, the changes should be permanently recorded to the database by using a commit operation (Connection::commit());

All changes from the last call to commit() method are recorded without being actually saved on the disk. If an error occurs, the database must be returned to the state before transaction started and this is made by using the rollback method (Connection::rollback()). When rollback is performed, all changes from the last call to commit() are dropped.

```
Connection con =
  DriverManager.getConnection(url, username, passwd);

/*turn auto-commit off*/
con.setAutoCommit(false);

try {
```

```
  statement.executeUpdate(sqlStatement_1);
  ...
  statement.executeUpdate(sqlStatement_N);
  /*at this stages all the changes done
   *by running the above statements are recoded
   *but not saved on the disk*/

  /*commit changes as no error occurred*/
  con.commit();
}
catch (Exception e) {
  try{
     /*as an exception was thrown indicating an error*/
     /*and rollback is performed*/
     con.rollback();
  }
  catch (SQLException sqle)     {
    /*report problem rolling back*/
  }
}
finally {
  try{
     /*close connection*/
     con.close();
  }
  catch (SQLException sqle)     {
     /*report problem closing connection*/
  }
}
```

7.6.4 JDBC Metadata

All the examples presented so far assumed a known database structure. This means that the name of the tables as well as the name of the fields of each table and their order are known. Hence the statements can be formed and results can be processed using table names and columns ids.

However, often the database structure is unknown, and consequently it is necessary to have this information in order to interact with the database.

Information about database can be retrieved using *DatabaseMetaData's* methods. A reference to a *DatabaseMetaData* object is returned by Connection:: getMetaData().

Among the most important *DatabaseMetaData* methods are *ResultSet getCatalogs();* which gets all the names of catalogs available in this database, *ResultSet*

*getTables(String catalog, String schemaPattern, String tableNamePattern, String[]
types);* which retrieves a description of the tables available in the given catalog, and
boolean isReadOnly(); which checks if the database is read-only.

Data structure information can be retrieved using *ResultSetMetaData's* methods.
A reference to a *ResultSetMetaData* object is returned by *ResultSet::getMetaData();*
method.

Among the most important *ResultSetMetaData* methods are *int getColumn-
Count();* which returns the number of columns in the data-set, *String getColumn-
Name(int column-no);* which returns the column name given its order number (starting from 1, not 0), *int getColumnType(int column-no)* which returns the column type
given its order number (starting from 1, not 0!), *String getColumnTypeName(int
column-no)* which returns a string containing the indicated column's type name and
boolean isReadOnly(int column-no) which checks if the column is read-only.

Most often used column type constants (defined in *java.sql.Types*) are *Types.
NUMERIC, Types.DECIMAL, Types.INTEGER, Types.VARCHAR, Types.DATE,
Types.REAL, Types.DOUBLE, Types.FLOAT.*

The following example shows how database information can be used in a Java
application.

```
/*create a statement*/
Statement statement = link.createStatement();

/*create the query*/
String select = "SELECT * FROM Table WHERE Field =
                 Value";

/*execute the statement and retrieve the results set*/
ResultSet results = statement.executeQuery(select);

/*retrieve the ResultSetMetaData object*/
ResultSetMetaData metaData = results.getMetaData();

/*retrieve the number of fields*/
int noFields = metaData.getColumnCount();

/*check if results found*/
boolean found = results.next();

if (!found)
  System.out.println("Not found!");
else
  /*for each available column*/
  for (int i = 1; i <= noFields; i++) {
    /*display column name and column type*/
    System.out.println("Field name: "
```

```
                    + metaData.getColumnName(i));
      System.out.println("Field type:   "
                    + metaData.getColumnTypeName(i));

   /*depending on the column type*/
   /*retrieve entry value by type and display it*/
   switch (metaData.getColumnType(i))
   {
      case Types.INTEGER:
        System.out.println("Val:"+results.getInt(i));
        break;
      case Types.VARCHAR:
        System.out.println("Val:"+results.getString(i));
        break;
      case Types.NUMERIC:
        System.out.println("Val:"+results.getFloat(i));
        break;
      default:
        System.out.println("Val of unknown type");
   }
}
/*close database connection*/
link.close();
```

7.7 Multimedia Content Delivery Services

Multimedia content delivery was usually associated with broadcasting in the traditional TV distribution services. Lately, due to the development and proliferation of other multimedia based services such as video-on-demand or video conferencing, unicast and multicast content delivery became closely associated with multimedia applications.

Broadcasting has the main advantage of being cost effective in terms of bandwidth. Delivering the same content to multiple users at the same time reduces resource utilization. As the users are more likely to prefer video-on-demand-like services [29], the popularity of broadcasting decreases.

Unicast has the main advantage of supporting video-on-demand services, as well as broadcast services. Another benefit of unicast is that network resources are used only when there is a user requiring a certain service [29]. In the context of multimedia delivery to mobile devices, unicast presents the benefit of supporting content adaptation for each user separately in order to meet his/her device capabilities as well as networking resources.

Multicast is beneficial especially for group content delivery in applications like video conferencing. However, the management of multicast groups is difficult and complex.

Various wireless solutions have been proposed to address multimedia content delivery to mobile users. Three typical categories can be identified: DVB-based solutions which enhance the Digital Video Broadcasting standard for mobile devices (hand-held), solution enhancing the third generation cellular networks including UMTS with Multimedia Broadcast Multicast Service (MBMS) support, and content delivery solutions exploiting the widespread popularity of WLAN (802.11—WiFi).

7.7.1 Protocols Specific to Real-Time Data Delivery

The *Real-time Transport Protocol (RTP)* [30] is used for delivering multimedia data over the IP networks. RTP uses transport layer protocols such as UDP, for example, and consequently some people consider RTP as an application layer protocol. However, as RTP is used to deliver multimedia content, often specialists state it is an upper transport layer protocol.

Real-time Transport Control Protocol (RTCP) [31] controls data delivery over RTP. RTP and RTCP use different port numbers (even and odd). As opposed to RTP which delivers the content, RTCP delivers control packets such as throughput, loss, jitter, etc. This information is not used by RTP, but it is usable by the application directly for bit-rate adaptation or delivery quality assessment. In this context, RTP cannot guarantee the Quality of Service (QoS) at all. The quality of delivery is maintained by adapting the content bit-rate to the network QoS based on delivery performance information provided by RTCP.

RTCP periodically transmits control packets to all participants in the streaming session, using the same distribution mechanism as the data packets. The underlying protocol used for transport must provide multiplexing of the data and control packets by using separate port numbers with UDP.

RTCP performs four functions: provides feedback on the quality of content delivery, carries a persistent transport-level identifier for an RTP source (i.e., canonical name), provides rate adaptation for the control packets based on the number of participants, and provides minimal session control information such as participant identification.

Real Time Streaming Protocol (RTSP) [32] enables a multimedia client to have access to the video remote control features, including play, stop, pause, etc. RTSP is often used in conjunction with RTP for delivering multimedia data and enabling its control.

RTSP controls one or many time-synchronized streams of continuous media such as audio and video. RTSP does not deliver the continuous streams itself, although it supports interleaving of the continuous media stream with the control stream. This protocols acts as a virtual "remote control" allowing the user player to provide VCR-like control options (i.e., play, pause, stop).

The set of streams is defined by a presentation description; however, a specific format is not defined. RTSP does not use connections; however, the media server keeps a session tagged by an identifier. This session is not linked in any way with

Figure 7.10 RTP packet
format

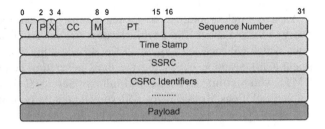

a transport level connection such as TCP connections. RTSP sessions are independent of the transport solution used. RTSP requests will be transported over TCP connections when reliability is desired or over UDP when reliability is traded for speed.

Figure 7.10 shows the fields of the RTP packet header and the payload as follows. The header has a minimum size of 12 bites.

- V—2 bits, version number;
- P—1 bit, padding flag;
- X—1 bit, packet header extension flag;
- CC—4 bits, contributing source number flag;
- M—1 bit, special event flag;
- PT—7 bits, payload type flag;
- Sequence Number—16 bits, data packet sequence number;
- Time Stamp—32 bits, time stamp;
- SSRC—32 bits, synchronization source and synchronization source flag;
- CSRC LIST—32 bits, contributing source and contributing source flag list. Can be up to 15;
- Payload—Packet payload.

The following example shows how to use the Java Media Framework (JMF) [33] to build an RTP server delivering a local video file.

```
/*Import relevant packages*/
import java.awt.*;
import java.io.IOException;
import javax.media.*;
import javax.media.protocol.*;
import javax.media.format.*;
import javax.media.control.TrackControl;

/*Define media server class*/
public class MediaServer {

    /*Define relevant member variables*/
```

Code Listing 7.8 MediaServer.java

```
private MediaLocator locator;
private String ipAddress;
private String port;
private Processor processor = null;
private DataSink  rtpTransmitter = null;
private DataSource dataOutput = null;

/*MediaServer constructor providing
source location, streaming IP and Port*/
public MediaServer(String mediaSource,
            String ipAddress, String port){
  this.locator = new MediaLocator(mediaSource);
  this.ipAddress = ipAddress;
  this.port = port;
}

/*Start the server*/
public void start() {
  /*Create processor*/
  createProcessor();
  /*Create transmitter*/
  createTransmitter();
  /*Start streaming*/
  processor.start();
}

/*Stop the server*/
public void stop() {
  /*Stop and destroy the processor*/
  processor.stop();
  processor.close();
  processor = null;

  /*Stop and destroy the transmitter*/
  rtpTransmitter.close();
  rtpTransmitter = null;
}

/*Create the processor*/
private void createProcessor() {
  try {
    /*Create data source*/
    DataSource ds =
        Manager.createDataSource(locator);
```

Code Listing 7.8 (Continued)

```
  /*Create processor*/
  processor = Manager.createProcessor(ds);
} catch (NoProcessorException e) {
  e.printStackTrace();
} catch (NoDataSourceException e) {
  e.printStackTrace();
} catch (IOException e) {
  e.printStackTrace();
}

/*Configure and realize the processor*/
processor.configure();
processor.realize();

/*wait for the processor to initialize*/
while (processor.getState() < Processor.Configured
    || processor.getState() < Processor.Realized) {
  try {
    this.wait(1000);
  } catch (InterruptedException e) {
    e.printStackTrace();
  }
}

/*Get the media file tracks*/
TrackControl [] tracks =
      processor.getTrackControls();

/*Search for a video track*/
for (int i = 0; i < tracks.length; i++) {

  Format format = tracks[i].getFormat();

  if (tracks[i].isEnabled() &&
        format instanceof VideoFormat) {

    /*Video track found*/
    Dimension size =
        ((VideoFormat)format).getSize();

    float frameRate =
        ((VideoFormat)format).getFrameRate();
    /*Make the width and height multiples of 8*/
    int w = 0;
```

Code Listing 7.8 (Continued)

```
            if(size.width % 8 == 0){
              w = size.width;
            } else{
              w = (int)(size.width / 8) * 8;
            }

            int h = 0;
            if(size.height % 8 == 0){
              h = size.height;
            }else{
              h = (int)(size.height / 8) * 8;
            }

            VideoFormat videoFormat =
                    new VideoFormat(VideoFormat.H263_RTP,
                    new Dimension(w, h),
                    Format.NOT_SPECIFIED,
                    Format.byteArray, frameRate);
            tracks[i].setFormat(videoFormat);
        } else
            tracks[i].setEnabled(false);
    }
    /*Initialize the output content descriptor
    to RAW_RTP*/
    ContentDescriptor cd =
        new ContentDescriptor(ContentDescriptor.RAW_
                              RTP);
    processor.setContentDescriptor(cd);
    /*Retrieve the output data source*/
    dataOutput = processor.getDataOutput();
}

/*Create the transmitter*/
private void createTransmitter() {
try {
  /*Define the streaming URL*/
  String rtpURL =
    "rtp://" + ipAddress + ":" + port + "/video";
  /*Create the transmitter and start streaming*/
  MediaLocator outputLocator =
      new MediaLocator(rtpURL);
  rtpTransmitter =
      Manager.createDataSink(dataOutput,
                              outputLocator);
```

Code Listing 7.8 (Continued)

```
    rtpTransmitter.open();
    rtpTransmitter.start();
    dataOutput.start();
    } catch (NoDataSinkException e) {
      e.printStackTrace();
    } catch (SecurityException e) {
      e.printStackTrace();
    } catch (IOException e) {
      e.printStackTrace();
    }
  }

  public static void main(String [] args) {
    try {
      MediaServer vt =
      new MediaServer("file:\\video.avi", "localhost",
                      "1024");
      vt.start();
      Thread.currentThread().sleep(60000);
      vt.stop();
    } catch (InterruptedException e) {
      e.printStackTrace();
    }
  }
}
```

Code Listing 7.8 (Continued)

7.7.2 Multimedia Delivery over Cellular Networks

In cellular networks, multimedia delivery was introduced starting from the 2.5G technologies and continuing with the current 3G technologies. The packet-switched streaming (PSS) standard developed by the Third Generation Partnership Project (3GPP) provides the means of content transportation for streaming and downloading applications. PSS uses various protocols for content delivery and information exchange. Content is delivered using RTP over UDP. Other types of media including text and graphics are delivered over HTTP. RTSP is used for control information exchange. PSS supports user quality of experience monitoring which permits content adaptation for improving user satisfaction.

Apart from the transport mechanisms, PSS also specifies a set of media codecs including Adaptive Multirate (AMR), H.263 [34], H.264 [35], MPEG-4 Advanced Video Codec (AVC) [36], and MPEG-4 [37].

For further improvement of user perceived quality, PSS also includes an Adaptive Streaming feature [38] which is useful for adapting the content to network condition variations as well as variations in network characteristics due to handovers between systems [29] like GPRS to WCDMA and vice-versa.

The *IP Multimedia Subsystem (IMS)* [39] was developed within 3GPP as a service platform to provide multimedia services over 3G networks. IMS uses the Session Initiation Protocol (SIP) for signaling and session control, RTP for media transport and IPv6 at the network layer. The IMS platform is not directly involved in media transport (only in session control) [39], but QoS is maintained by collaboration between the IMS platform and the transport network. The Policy Decision Function (PDF) is the IMS sub-module which is responsible for QoS negotiation according to the application requirements.

3GPP also proposed the *Multimedia Broadcast/Multicast Service (MBMS)* for UMTS [40]. MBMS delivers multimedia content to a group of users in a point-to-multipoint manner using UMTS MBMS transmission bearer. MBMS is composed of two modules, the MBMS bearer service which deals with transmission procedures below the IP layer and the MBMS user service which manages streaming and downloading methods and procedures. The streaming methods used by MBMS are similar to PSS in terms of transfer protocols (e.g., RTP) and codecs.

Broadcast and Multicast Services (BCMCS) [41] protocol is similar to MBMS but was developed by 3GPP2 for the CDMA2000 protocol family for 3G networks. Similar to MBMS, BCMCS provides point-to-multipoint content delivery and guarantees QoS for two way multimedia applications. Content adaptation may be performed using SVC which was also introduced in MPEG-4 standard as *FGS (MPEG-4 FGS)* [42].

7.7.3 DVB-based Multimedia Delivery

The Digital Video Broadcasting (DVB) [43] standards offer point-to-multipoint data services with high data rates for multimedia (especially TV) content delivery to end users. Apart from the satellite versions (DVB-S) [44], DVB also standardized a terrestrial wireless data service via DVB-T [5]. Although DVB-T broadcasts multimedia content to static and mobile users, including vehicular receivers, it is not optimized for highly mobile hand-held devices. However, the most recent DVB-T2 [45] is highly efficient and addresses many of the shortcomings of the previously-proposed DVB-T.

Consequently, the DVB community has developed DVB-H (hand-held) [6] for multimedia content delivery to mobile devices.

DVB-H specifies the protocol layers below the network layer only, and consequently there was a need for an Internet Protocol (IP) [46] interface for higher transport layers which was defined by the IP-based Data Broadcast (IP Datacast) [7] specification which was also introduced.

IP Datacast specified the protocols for higher layers in concordance with the Internet protocol stack. For the transport layer, UDP was chosen with RTP for real-time media broadcasting and File Delivery over Unidirectional Transport (FLUTE) [47] for non-real-time data transfer like download-based media delivery.

For media encoding, DVB-H aims for high compatibility between network components and terminals; therefore, MPEG-4/H.264 was chosen for video encoding as well as the Microsoft Windows Media 9 based VC-1 codec [48]. For audio MPEG 4, AAC+ [49] is recommended.

IP Datacast was developed towards a hybrid interoperability of several types of networks in order to benefit from their advantages and balance their disadvantages.

DVB-H has the advantage of being highly scalable with the number of users unlike cellular networks or WLANs which are basically point-to-point and suffer from severe QoS drops when congested. On the other hand, DVB-H interactivity is quite limited.

Considering these aspects, using a hybrid solution where the content management layer decides which network to use for delivery of a certain service depending on its popularity (the number of users requesting the same service at the same time) or its interactivity requirements may improve the overall quality of the service as perceived by the user.

7.7.4 Multimedia Delivery over WLAN

Wireless LAN is probably the most successful and cost-effective option for multimedia delivery. With encouraging link layer data rates, IEEE 802.11 based WLANs popularity is constantly increasing and many flavors have been proposed, addressing different wireless communications aspects including using different frequencies, supporting increased bitrates, focusing on mesh networks or on vehicular communications: IEEE 802.11b, IEEE 802.11a, IEEE 802.11g, IEEE 802.11s [4], IEEE 802.11p, etc.

Despite all the positive aspects WLANs suffer from the same unpredictability of the wireless links as well as from severe QoS drops when the wireless medium gets congested with the increase in the number of simultaneous hosts engaged in data sessions.

The IEEE 802.11 standards describe only the physical and MAC layer. There are several enhancements proposed for supporting multimedia applications including the IEEE 802.11e [1] and IEEE 802.11n [3] which provide QoS support features in the MAC layer. There are also various prioritization schemes [2] which allow traffic differentiation depending on the type of traffic (priority class).

WLANs use the Internet protocol stack for higher layers, consequently all the multimedia streaming solutions designed for the Internet may be used in scenarios including WLANs. Although WLANs are compatible with the IP based network paradigm, their particularities especially regarding the error prone and highly dynamic wireless links have to be considered by the higher layers in order to provide a high quality multimedia streaming service.

7.8 Adaptive Multimedia Delivery

User satisfaction is crucial for the success of any multimedia-based application. Various performance issues arise when multimedia content is delivered over best-effort networks to users with heterogeneous device capabilities and expectations. However, network conditions in terms of available bandwidth, packet loss, packet delay, and delay jitter have a major impact on the quality of delivered multimedia content and its timeliness, ultimately affecting the end-user perceived quality, or as it is most recently termed Quality of Experience (QoE).

In order to avoid the negative impact dynamic network conditions have on the multimedia content, measures have to be taken to adapt the streaming process to follow and match the current network capacity. If short term variations can be overcome by using buffering techniques [50], for long time-scale network dynamics rate adaptation techniques are among the most efficient solutions.

Several adaptive streaming solutions were proposed at the network and transport layer including TFRCP [51], LDA+ [52], and RAP [53]. These solutions present a reasonable performance in terms of QoS, but their major drawback is a poor correlation with the actual end-user perceived quality.

More advanced adaptive streaming techniques from the point of view of maintaining a high level of user perceived quality were developed at the application layer. Such a solution with good performance in terms of user perceived quality is LQA [54]. Cross-layer methods get closer to the user and try to achieve higher perceptual quality of streamed multimedia content. A good survey of these solutions can be found in [55].

The Quality Oriented Adaptation Scheme (QOAS) [56] involves a user perceived quality estimation in the feedback-based multimedia adaptation process. Consequently, QOAS shows significant improvements in end-user perceived quality when used for streaming multimedia content in both wired and wireless networking environments.

Diverse solutions were proposed for adaptive multimedia transmissions over wireless access networks [57] or wireless ad-hoc networks [58]. Among the proposed solutions are adaptation mechanisms at the level of layers [57] or objects [59], fine-granular scalability schemes [60], and perception-based approaches [61].

However, all these solutions involve content adjustments which affect equally the whole area of the video frames, regardless of different user interest in various frame regions as research on regions of interest (ROI) has demonstrated [62].

A cross-layer adaptive multimedia streaming solution was proposed in [63]. Unlike the other solutions discussed above, this one makes distinction between various elements of the video content by identifying, classifying, and assigning different priorities, and consequently different QoS levels for each element or group of elements. However, this solution does not consider the variation in user attention focus during the video sequence.

An ROI-based adaptive scheme is introduced in [64]. Unlike in the case of ROIAS, each macro-block is categorized as ROI or non-ROI based on a saliency map computed using luminance contrast, color-double-opponent, texture, skin color, and motion vector.

ROI-based adaptation of video content is also discussed in [65]. Although techniques for estimating the ROI within a video frame are presented, the adaptation consists in adjusting the frame resolution to match the maximum display resolution.

A similar approach is presented in [66]. Unlike ROIAS, the proposed solution focuses on resolution adaptation and targets specific types of content (i.e., news, interviews) where the ROI is predefined at the beginning of the material and then is tracked throughout the playback.

Although ROI is considered in the adaptation process, the above mentioned solutions do not reach the level of generality and performance in terms of smoothness and adaptability.

7.9 Conclusion

This chapter has presented the major communication-based services, has introduced the protocols these services rely on, and has described step-by-step, with the help of examples, how applications built on top of these protocols can be developed using Java.

References

1. IEEE (2005) IEEE standard for local and metropolitan area networks specific requirements—Part 11: Wireless LAN medium access control (MAC) and physical layer (PHY) specifications MAC enhancements for QoS
2. Xiao Y (2005) Performance analysis of priority schemes for IEEE 802.11 and IEEE 802.11e wireless LANs. IEEE Trans Wirel Commun 4(4):1506–1515
3. IEEE (September 2008) IEEE draft standard for local and metropolitan area network-specific requirements—Part 11: Wireless LAN medium access control (MAC) and physical layer (PHY) specifications mendment 5: enhancements for higher throughput
4. IEEE (December 2009) IEEE draft standard for information technology—telecommunications and information exchange between system—LAN/MAN specific requirements—Part 11: Wireless medium access control (MAC) and physical layer (PHY) specifications: amendment 10: mesh networking
5. Ladebusch U, Liss C (2006) Terrestrial DVB (DVB-T): a broadcast technology for stationary portable and mobile use. Proc IEEE 94(1):183–193
6. DVB (November 2004) Transmission system for handheld terminals (DVB-H), ETSI EN 302304 v1.1.1
7. Kornfeld M, May G (2007) DVB-H and IP datacast mdash; broadcast to handheld devices. IEEE Trans Broadcast 53(1):161–170
8. Postel J, Reynolds J (October 1985) File transfer protocol. RFC 959 (standard) Updated by RFCs 2228, 2640, 2773, 3659, 5797
9. Bellovin S (1994) Firewall-friendly FTP
10. Horowitz M, Lunt S (October 1997) FTP security extensions. RFC 2228 (proposed standard)
11. Fielding R, Gettys J, Mogul J, Frystyk H, Masinter L, Leach P, Berners-Lee T (1999) RFC 2616—Hypertext transfer protocol (HTTP/1.1). RFC 2616
12. Postel J (1981) RFC 792—Internet control message protocol (ICMP). RFC 792
13. Postel J (1981) RFC 791—Internet protocol (IP). RFC 791

14. Oracle: Complex ping with Java NIO
15. Odulio J (2005) Simple ping with Java NIO. Personal and Technical Journal on Software Development. ISSN: 1793-2343
16. Crocker DH (1982) RFC 822—Standard for ARPA internet text messages. RFC 822
17. Resnick P (2001) RFC 2822—Internet message format. RFC 2822
18. Borenstein N (1992) F.N.: RFC 1341—MIME: Mechanisms for specifying and describing the format of internet message bodies. RFC 1341
19. Freed N (1996) B.N.: RFC 2045—multipurpose internet mail extensions (MIME) Part one: format of internet message bodies. RFC 2045
20. Postel J (1982) Rfc 821—simple mail transfer protocol (SMTP). RFC 821
21. Klensin J (2001) RFC 2821—Simple mail transfer protocol (SMTP). RFC 2821
22. Myers J (1996) R.M.: RFC 1939—Post-office protocol version 3 (POP3). RFC 1939
23. Crispin M (1996) RFC 2060—Internet message access protocol (IMAP). RFC 2060
24. Oracle: Javamail API
25. Apache: Apache commons net API
26. http://www.codejava.net (download files from an FTP server)
27. Berners-Lee T (1996) F.R.F.H.: RFC 1945—Hypertext transfer protocol—HTTP/1.0. RFC 1945
28. Berners-Lee T, Fielding R, Masinter L (1998) RFC 2396—Uniform resource identifiers (URI): Generic syntax. RFC 2396
29. Hartung F, Horn U, Huschke J, Kampmann M, Lohmar T, Lundevall M (2007) Delivery of broadcast services in 3G networks. IEEE Trans Broadcast 53(1):188–199
30. Schulzrinne H, Casner S, Frederick R, Jacobson V (2003) RFC 3550 RTP: a transport protocol for real-time applications
31. HU1TEMA, C (2003) Rfc3605. Real time control protocol (RTCP) attribute in session description protocol (SDP)
32. Schulzrinne H, Rao A, Lanphier R (1998) RFC2326. Real time streaming protocol. Available on http://www.ietf.org/rfc/rfc2326.txt
33. Gordon R, Talley S (1999) Essential JMF: developer's Java media players. Prentice Hall, New York
34. ITU-T (February 1998) ITU-T recommendation H.263—Video coding for low bit rate communication
35. ITU-T (2003) ITU-T recommendation H.264—ISO/IEC 14496-10 AVC—Draft ITU-T recommendation and final draft international standard of joint video specification
36. ISO (2005) International standard ISO/IEC 14496-10 MPEG-4 AVC
37. ISO (2004) International standard ISO/IEC 14496-2 MPEG-4 visual
38. Frojdh P, Horn U, Kampmann M, Nohlgren A, Westerlund M (2006) Adaptive streaming within the 3GPP packet-switched streaming service. IEEE Netw 20(2):34–40
39. Cuevas A, Moreno J, Vidales P, Einsiedler H (2006) The IMS service platform: a solution for next-generation network operators to be more than bit pipes. IEEE Commun Mag 44(8):75–81
40. 3GPP (March 2006) Multimedia broadcast/multicast service (MBMS); Stage 1 (Release 7) Tech rep 3G TS 22.146 V7.1.0
41. 3GPP2 (April 2006) Broadcast multicast service for CDMA2000 1x systems C.S0077 Rev. 1.0
42. Kang K, Kim T (2009) Improved error control for real-time video broadcasting over CDMA2000 networks. IEEE Trans Veh Technol 58(1):188–197
43. Reimers U (1998) DVB
44. Morello A, Mignone V (2006) DVB-S2: the second generation standard for satellite broadband services. Proc IEEE 94(1):210–227
45. Vangelista L, Benvenuto N, Tomasin S, Nokes C, Stott J, Filippi A, Vlot M, Mignone V, Morello A (2009) Key technologies for next-generation terrestrial digital television standard DVB-T2. IEEE Commun Mag 47(10):146–153
46. Postel J (1981) Internet protocol

47. Paila T, Roca V, Walsh R, Luby M, Lehtonen R (2012) FLUTE-file delivery over unidirectional transport

48. Fan CP, Su GA (2009) Efficient fast 1-D 8×8 inverse integer transform for VC-1 application. IEEE Trans Circuits Syst Video Technol 19(4):584–590

49. Varga I (2004) Audio codec for mobile multimedia applications. In: IEEE 6th workshop on multimedia signal processing, 2004, IEEE, pp 450–453

50. Fitzek F, Reisslein M (2001) A prefetching protocol for continuous media streaming in wireless environments. IEEE J Sel Areas Commun 19(10):2015–2028

51. Padhye J, Padhye J, Towsley D, Kurose J, Towsley D, Koodli R (1999) A model based TCP-friendly rate control protocol

52. Sisalem D, Wolisz A (2000) LDA+ TCP-friendly adaptation: a measurement and comparison study. In: The 10th international workshop on network and operating systems support for digital audio and video (NOSSDAV'2000), pp 25–28

53. Rejaie R, H M, Yu H Estrin D (1999) Proxy caching mechanism for multimedia playback streams in the Internet. In: Proceedings of the 4th international web caching workshop

54. Rejaie R, Yu H, Handley M, Estrin D (2000) Multimedia proxy caching mechanism for quality adaptive streaming applications in the Internet. In: Proceedings of IEEE nineteenth annual joint conference of the IEEE computer and communications societies, INFOCOM 2000, vol 2, pp 980–989

55. van Der Schaar M, Sai Shankar N (2005) Cross-layer wireless multimedia transmission: challenges, principles, and new paradigms. IEEE Wirel Commun 12(4):50–58

56. Muntean GM, Perry P, Murphy L (2004) A new adaptive multimedia streaming system for all-IP multi-service networks. IEEE Trans Broadcast 50(1):1–10

57. Li Q, van der Schaar M (2004) Providing adaptive qos to layered video over wireless local area networks through real-time retry limit adaptation. IEEE Trans Multimed 6(2):278–290

58. Shah S, Chen K, Nahrstedt K (2003) Dynamic bandwidth management for single-hop ad hoc wireless networks. In: Proceedings of the first IEEE international conference on pervasive computing and communications, 23–26 2003 (PerCom 2003), pp 195–203

59. Cha KA (2004) Content complexity adaptation for MPEG-4 audio-visual scene. IEEE Trans Consum Electron 50(2):760–765

60. van der Schaar M, Radha H (2002) Adaptive motion-compensation fine-granular-scalability (AMC-FGS) for wireless video. IEEE Trans Circuits Syst Video Technol 12(6):360–371

61. Cranley N, Perry P, Murphy L (2005) Optimum adaptation trajectories for streamed multimedia. Multimed Syst 10(5):392–401

62. Gulliver S, Ghinea G (2004) Stars in their eyes: what eye-tracking reveals about multimedia perceptual quality. IEEE Trans Syst Man Cybern, Part A, Syst Hum 34(4):472–482

63. Ahmed T, Mehaoua A, Boutaba R, Iraqi Y (2005) Adaptive packet video streaming over IP networks: a cross-layer approach. IEEE J Sel Areas Commun 23(2):385–401

64. Chiang JC, Hsieh CS, Chang G, Jou FD, Lie WN (2010) Region-of-interest based rate control scheme with flexible quality on demand. In: IEEE international conference on multimedia and expo (ICME), 2010, pp 238–242

65. Huang T (2010) Region of interest extraction and adaptation in scalable video coding. In: Seventh international conference on fuzzy systems and knowledge discovery (FSKD), 2010, vol 5, pp 2320–2323

66. Nuriel T, Malah D (2010) Region-of-interest based adaptation of video to mobile devices. In: 4th international symposium on communications, control and signal processing (ISCCSP), 2010, pp 1–6

Chapter 8
Server-Side Network Programming

Abstract Server-side network programming involves designing and implementing programs to be run on a server. Server-side applications run as processes on a dedicated physical machine, virtual machine, or cloud infrastructure. Server-side applications receive requests from the clients and perform tasks as requested by the clients. This chapter introduces various server-side methods and techniques used to generate and deliver web documents to requesting clients, including Java specific solutions such as Java Servlets and Java Servlet Pages. Detailed examples are presented for both technologies.

8.1 Introduction

Server-side network programming involves designing and implementing programs to be run on the server.

Server-side applications run as processes on a dedicated physical machine, virtual machine or Cloud infrastructure, as schematically presented in Fig. 8.1. A server machine may run one or more applications at the same time.

Server-side applications perform tasks requested by the clients. The most popular server-side applications are Web server applications which deliver Web documents over the Internet to Web clients at their request.

A typical server-side application involves three distinct layers.

The *presentation layer* enables user access to data and translates data in user friendly content. It mainly involves graphical user interfaces and handles user inputs and data presentation to users.

The *business logic layer* deals with user-related commands, makes logic decisions, and processes data. This layer is the actual data processing layer which implements the core functionality of any application.

The *resource layer* organizes data storage and retrieval and uses a database management system or file system. This layer is mainly in charge of the persistent data storage and retrieval.

Based on the three layer model presented above, four types of server-side application architectures can be defined.

One-tier applications are usually suitable for small size applications. In this case, all layers are combined in a single entity. One single tier will deal with data storage

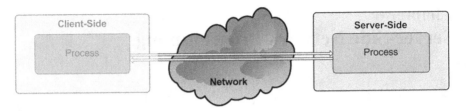

Fig. 8.1 Server-side network programming

and retrieval, data processing and decision making, as well as data presentation and user interface.

Two-tier applications are suitable for medium size applications. In this scenario, presentation has been separated from business logic. The user interface related modules are separated from the modules which deal with data processing and decision making

Three-tier applications are suitable for medium and large size applications. By separating the three layers into three tiers, the presentation layer is implemented by separate dedicated modules, the data processing tier has its own modules and the data storage tier gets its own components. Such an application is easier to develop, manage, scale, and maintain.

N-tier applications may also be implemented. This type of server-side application architectures are suitable for large size applications which add extra layers for security, efficiency, and scalability.

This chapter presents Java solutions for developing Web-based server-side applications and focuses on Servlets and Java Server Pages (JSP)-based solutions. For information purpose, brief descriptions of Common Gateway Interface (CGI) and Hypertext Pre-processor (PHP), as non-Java alternative solutions are also included.

8.2 Non-Java Server-Side Network Programming Solutions

8.2.1 Common Gateway Interface

Common Gateway Interface (CGI) is a protocol that enables remote users to access services provided at the servers. In general, a normal Web browser is located at the client-side, and at the server side there is a normal Web server. The Web server has to be able to run scripts or applications in order to provide services to the clients.

A Web server with CGI support needs to be configured such that it interprets a URL that it serves as a reference to a CGI script or application. A common convention for CGI script/application deployment is to have a cgi-bin/ directory at the base of the directory tree on the server and consider all executable files within this directory (and no other, for security reasons) to be CGI scripts/applications. Consequently, when the server receives a request, it will run the corresponding CGI script/application from the cgi-bin/ directory.

Another convention is to use .cgi file extensions for all CGI scripts. Consequently, the Web server can be configured to interpret all .cgi files as CGI scripts. Although convenient, this method opens the server to attacks if a remote user can upload its own scripts with the corresponding extension.

Any programming language such as C/C++, Visual Basic, PERL, and TCL can be used to write CGI processing code. Script-based languages are preferred due to their simple modification with no requirement in terms of code re-compile to generate the executable application and application redeployment.

Typical CGI script/application steps involve reading input data (i.e., from the standard input), processing the data provided, and generating an HTML output document to the standard output.

Among the main drawbacks of CGI are its security issues, as described above, and performance. Calling a command (CGI script) generally means the invocation of a newly created process running on the server. Starting a process consumes much more time and memory than the actual work of generating output of the task performed by the process.

This is valid especially when the program also needs to be interpreted or even compiled. Under these circumstances, if the script is called often, the resulting workload can quickly overload the server.

8.2.2 Hypertext Pre-processor

Hypertext Pre-processor (PHP) is a powerful server-side scripting language for dynamic Web-page generation. In general, a normal Web browser is located at the client-side, and a normal Web server runs at the server. For the Hypertext Pre-processor case, the Web server has to have the PHP package installed in order to be able to interpret PHP scripts.

PHP is a fully functional language which enables form processing, generation of various data types (not only text) as well as database access. PHP also provides object-oriented programming feature support.

The following code example shows how PHP scripts are specified and marked in an HTML document. In the example below, it can be seen how PHP can be used to print a message in an HTML document which is then delivered to the user. The *print* function is available within PHP.

```
<?
  print("Hello world!");
?>

<?php
  print("Hello world!");
php?>
```

```php
<script language="php">
  print("Hello world!");
</script>
```

To further exemplify the capabilities of PHP, the following code sample defines
a function which recursively deletes a folder and its content.

```php
##remDir removes all files/folders from path ($path)
function remDir($path)
{
  ##add a '/' at the end of the path if it does not
    exist
  if (substr($dir, strlen($path)-1, 1) != '/')
    $path .= '/';

  ##display the complete path
  echo $path;

  ##if the folder is opened successfully
  if ($handle = opendir($path))
  {
    ##for each sub-folder
    while ($item = readdir($handle))
    {
      ##if not current or parent folder
      if ($item != '.' && $item != '..')
      {
        ##if it is a folder
        if (is_dir($path.$item))
        {
          ##delete recursively the folder
          if (!remDir($.$item))  return false;
        }
        ##if it is file
        elseif (is_file($path.$item))
        {
          ##delete the file
          if (!unlink($path.$item))  return false;
        }
      }
    }
    ##close the parent folder
```

Code Listing 8.1 remDir.php

```
    closedir($handle);
    ##remove the parent folder
    if (!@rmdir($dir))
      return false;
    return true;
  }
  return false;
}
```

Code Listing 8.1 (Continued)

PHP presents the following main advantages. It is open source, and consequently it is developed and maintained by a large community of developers. It is relatively fast and easy to use as it is using C-like syntax. It is fairly stable and provides a powerful library support for various types of features and functionality development. PHP is also easy to port on various platforms, and the built in database support makes it a very powerful server-side application development tool.

Among the disadvantages, security is probably the main one. Since it is open source, every bug in the system can be detected within the code and weaknesses can be exploited. PHP is not suitable for large applications as it is not very modular and consequently hard to maintain. Implicit conversions may be also considered by many developers as a weak point of PHP as it can easily generate confusion and unexpected bugs in the system.

8.3 Java Servlets

8.3.1 Servlet Overview

Java Servlets are programs that run on the server side and generate content dynamically following client requests.

The Java servlet architecture and its functionality principle is graphically presented in Fig. 8.2.

The architecture involves a client–server paradigm. At the client side, a Web browser, representing the user interface or user process, sends requests to the Web server addressed to a specific servlet. Responses from the Web server originating from the servlet are expected and hopefully will be received by the Web browser, and the corresponding Web document will be displayed on the user interface.

At the server side, there is a Servlet Container which is in charge of managing the servlets. The requests originating from the client process are first received by the servlet container which then dispatches them to the corresponding servlet. Upon receiving the request, the servlet will process it, perform the business logic operations (access the required resources such as database systems or file systems, for

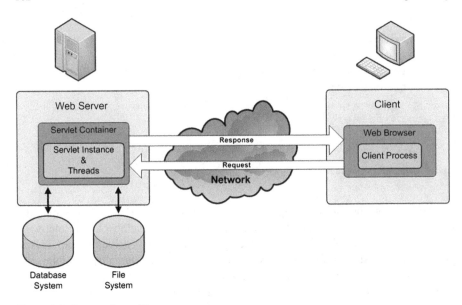

Figure 8.2 Java servlet architecture

example), and produce the results which are then sent to the client in the form of a response.

In this process, the Web browser is in charge of user inputs and data display, the servlet container is in charge of the management of servlet life cycle and with resource management, servlet deployment and security, while the servlet itself is in charge of the business logic (i.e., providing the requested service).

There are many advantages of using Java servlets for delivering dedicated services to clients over the Internet.

Efficiency. As Java Virtual Machine is always running, when starting a servlet, only a new Java thread is created, as opposed to a system process (as it happens in the case of CGI), which highly increases the efficiency and decreases the latency.

Persistency. A servlet which was already loaded by the servlet container remains in the memory and can maintain system resources such as database connectivity, offering a faster and more efficient access to resources.

Flexibility. Having access to the whole set of Java APIs, servlets represent a powerful tool for network application developers. They enable communication with Web servers, data sharing between servlets, maintaining information between requests, and managing sessions (for example, for database and file access support).

Security. Servlets are run by the Servlet Container in a restrictive sandbox, similar to that used by the Web browsers for applets (which will be discussed later in this book). This protects the whole system against malicious attacks, offering a high level of security.

Cost efficiency. There are many "free" or low-cost Web servers available for either personal use or low volume traffic. If you have a Web server, you can easily and cheaply add the servlet technology (if it is not already there!). Consequently, servlets offer a cost efficient approach to network service providing.

Convenience. Servlets take advantage of the Java platform and are supported by almost all Web servers. In general, servlet-based solutions can be deployed to any platform with no modifications, offering a highly portable solution.

8.3.2 Servlet Life-Cycle

The Servlet Container is in charge of managing servlets from various points of view. It listens and accepts requests from clients and other servlets and dispatches them to the correct servlet (indicated in the request). The container is also responsible for dispatching servlet responses to the invoking process (e.g., client).

However, the most important task performed by the servlet container is to manage servlet objects in terms of their life-cycle and access to resources.

The servlet life-cycle, as managed by the Servlet Container, consists of several stages, as illustrated in Fig. 8.3. When a request is mapped to a servlet, if an instance of the servlet does not exist, the servlet class is instantiated creating a servlet object that handles the request. Important to note is that there is a single servlet instance per servlet definition. This single servlet instance has to deal with multiple requests, often received simultaneously. Consequently, if a servlet object exists, the container creates a new thread to handle the request, which is highly time and processing efficient.

However, in this manner, different threads share the same memory space, which may cause data inconsistency. Consequently, while developing servlet applications, there is a need to include synchronization for all the methods that may be affected by the parallel processing of multiple simultaneous requests (e.g., queue management, database update, etc.).

When instantiating the servlet, the container initializes the instance by calling the *init()* method. It then invokes the *service()* method whenever a request is made, passing it request and response objects as parameters. The request parameter includes an indication of the service method invoked. For the HTTP servlets, these service methods include the HTTP methods: GET, DELETE, OPTIONS, POST, PUT, and TRACE. Most servlets follow the HTTP servlet model. However, other types of servlets with diverse different service methods can also be developed.

Depending on the service method requested to be run, the servlet thread performs different activities when executing the service() method and generates a response. This response is delivered to the calling method as part of the response object passed as a parameter.

A servlet instance runs until the container decides to destroy it. Often this happens some period of time after the last request. Typically, this period is either 15 or 30 minutes, but the system administrator can modify it.

When the container needs to remove the servlet, it finalizes the servlet by calling the *destroy()* method which destroys the servlet instance.

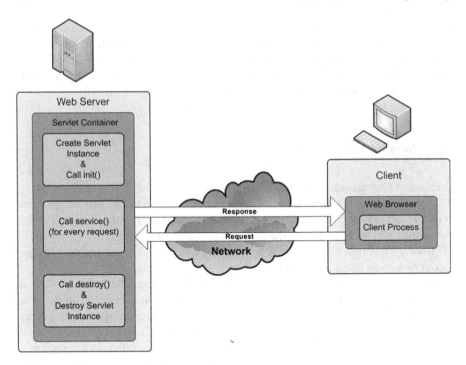

Figure 8.3 Java servlets life-cycle

Servlet Life-cycle involves the following stages:

- Creating a servlet object;
- Calling init();
- Repeatedly calling service();
- Calling destroy();
- Destroying servlet object.

Many Web servers available commercially or open source-based support Java servlets. Some of the most popular are: Apache (Tomcat) (open source, non-commercial), JBoss (open source, commercial, standards compliant), and IBM Web-Sphere (commercial).

8.3.3 Servlet Programming

Java API provides the basic functionality for implementing Java servlets. The class hierarchy is presented in Fig. 8.4 and involves an interface (*Servlet*), an abstract class (*GenericServlet*), an implementation class (*HTTPServlet*), and an application specific programmer-defined class.

Figure 8.4 Java servlets
class hierarchy

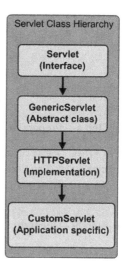

The *Servlet* interface publishes the *init()*, *destroy()*, and *service()* methods. *GenericServlet* is an abstract class implementing some of the methods involved in servlet programming. *HttpServlet* implements all the Servlet methods, including *service()*, which determines the request method type: GET, DELETE, OPTIONS, POST, PUT, or TRACE. The *service()* method then calls the corresponding default methods, for instance, *doGet()* or *doPost()*.

CustomServlet is a programmer-written class and is application specific. Depending on application requirements some methods (e.g., doGet(), doPost(), etc.) are overridden providing the application specific functionality.

8.3.3.1 Creating a Basic Servlet

Next the major steps in developing a servlet application will be presented in the context of a simple example of a HelloWorldServlet.

- Step 1—Import the required packages:

```
/*import java packages*/
import java.io.*;
import javax.servlet.*;
import javax.servlet.http.*;
```

- Step 2—Define a customer class by extending HttpServlet:

```
public class HelloWorldServlet extends HttpServlet
{
[...]
}
```

- Step 3—Override the method corresponding to the expected request:

```
public void doGet(HttpServletRequest req,
    HttpServletResponse res)
  throws ServletException, IOException
{
[...]
}
```

- Step 4—Prepare the response:

```
/*set response's content type*/
res.setContentType("text/html");
/*get the write stream for the response*/
PrintWriter out = res.getWriter();
```

- Step 5—Generate the response:

```
/*generate the response document*/
out.println("<!DOCTYPE HTML PUBLIC
    \"-//W3C//DTD HTML 4.0 " +
    "Transitional//EN\">\n" + "<HTML>\n" +
    "<HEAD><TITLE>Hello WWW</TITLE></HEAD>\n" +
    "<BODY>\n" +
    "<H1>Hello World!</H1>\n" +
    "</BODY></HTML>");
```

- Step 6—Do cleanup:

```
out.close();
```

The complete code for the HelloWorld Servlet example is presented next.

```
/*import java packages*/
import java.io.*;
import javax.servlet.*;
import javax.servlet.http.*;

/*define HelloWorldServlet
 *class extending HttpServlet*/
public class HelloWorldServlet extends HttpServlet
{
  /*override doGet() method which will be invoked
   *automatically by service()
   *when a GET request arrives*/
  public void doGet(HttpServletRequest req,
      HttpServletResponse res)
    thsrows ServletException, IOException
```

Code Listing 8.2 HelloWorldServlet.java

```
{
  /*set response's content type*/
  res.setContentType("text/html");
  /*get the write stream for the response*/
  PrintWriter out = res.getWriter();

  /*generate the header for the response*/
  String docType =
    "<!DOCTYPE HTML PUBLIC \"-//W3C//DTD HTML 4.0 " +
    "Transitional//EN\">\n";

  /*generate the response document*/
  out.println(docType + "<HTML>\n" +
    "<HEAD><TITLE>Hello WWW</TITLE></HEAD>\n" +
    "<BODY>\n" +
    "<H1>Hello World!</H1>\n" +
    "</BODY></HTML>");

  out.close();
  }
}
```

Code Listing 8.2   (Continued)

After the import of the two main Java API packages, *javax.servlet* which defines the major servlet classes and *javax.servlet.http* which provides the methods to handle service requests, the *HelloWorldServlet* class which extends *HttpServlet* is defined and the *doGet()* method is overridden.

The *doGet()* method receives references to request and response objects as parameters. The classes these two objects instantiate provide a set of methods for retrieving the information from their headers.

The following methods are used for accessing request object headers:

- getHeaders()—mostly used to retrieve headers;
- getCookies()—returns cookies;
- getAuthType()—gets authorization type;
- getRemoteUser()—gets user (e.g., obrien2);
- getRemoteAddr()—gets remote host IP Address (e.g., 136.206.35.123);
- getRemoteHost()—gets remote host name (e.g., pine.eeng.dcu.ie);
- getContentLength()—returns content length (bytes);
- getContentType()—returns content type;
- getDateHeader()—converts parameter to Date;
- getIntHeader()—converts parameter to Integer;
- getMethod()—returns the method used (e.g., GET, POST, HEAD);
- getRequestURI()—returns the URI/URL invoked;

- getProtocol()—returns the protocol used;
- getServerName()—returns the server name;
- getServerPort()—returns the server port number.

The following methods are used for assessing the response object header information:

- addCookie(Cookie c)—adds the specified cookie to the response;
- addHeader(String name, String value)—adds a response header with name and value;
- setStatus(int sc)—sets status code to the header (e.g., SC-OK, SC-BAD-REQUEST);
- setContentLength(int len)—sets content length (bytes);
- setContentType (String type)—sets content type (e.g., text/html);
- setDateHeader(String name, long date)—sets a response header with the given name and date value;
- setIntHeader(String name, int value)—sets a response header with the given name and integer value.

8.3.3.2 Initializing a Servlet

When the servlet is first instantiated, the *init()* method is called. This method allows dedicated servlet parameters to be initialized before any request is processed. The following steps need to be performed if servlet application-specific initialization is desired.

- Step 1—Set in the configuration file servlet initialization parameters in <name, value> pairs:

```
<servlet>
  <servlet-name>
    InitParamsServlet
  </servlet-name>
  <servlet-class>
    initparamsservlet.InitParamsServlet
  </servlet-class>
  <init-param>
    <param-name>msg</param-name>
    <param-value>This is the init text</param-value>
  </init-param>
  <init-param>
    <param-name>rep</param-name>
    <param-value>4</param-value>
  </init-param>
</servlet>
```

- Step 2—Map in the configuration file the servlet name on the servlet URL:

```
<servlet-mapping>
  <servlet-name>
    InitParams
  </servlet-name>
  <url-pattern>
    /servlet/InitParamsServlet
  </url-pattern>
</servlet-mapping>
```

- Step 3—Define a customer class by extending HttpServlet:

```
public class InitParamsServlet extends HttpServlet
{
[...]
}
```

- Step 4—Declare the parameters to be initialized:

```
/*private members which need to be initialized*/
private String text = null;
private int times = 1;
```

- Step 5—Override the init() method:

```
public void init(ServletConfig config)
    throws ServletException
{
[...]
}
```

- Step 6:—In init(), get the initialization parameters:

```
/*read the "msg" parameter
 *from the configuration file*/
text = config.getInitParameter("msg");

if (text == null)
  text= "No init message";

/*read the "rep" parameter
 *from the configuration file*/
String repeatString =
  config.getInitParameter("rep");

times = Integer.parseInt(repeatString);
```

- Step 7—Override the doGet() method to address GET requests:

```
public void doGet(HttpServletRequest req,
      HttpServletResponse res)
    throws ServletException, IOException
{
[...]
}
```

- Step 8—In doGet(), use the initialized parameters:

```
/*print the text message
 *a specified number of times*/
for(int i=0; i<times; i++)
{
   out.println(text + "<BR>");
}
```

- Step 9—Deal with all exceptions:

```
try
{
   [...]
}
catch()
{
   [...]
}
```

Next the complete code for the servlet initialization example is provided.

```
/*import java packages*/
import java.io.*;
import javax.servlet.*;
import javax.servlet.http.*;

/*define InitParamsServlet class extending HttpServlet*/
public class InitParamsServlet extends HttpServlet
{
   /*private members which need to be initialized*/
   private String text;
   private int times = 1;

   /*overridden init() method called when
    *the servlet is created*/
```

Code Listing 8.3 InitParamsServlet.java

```
public void init(ServletConfig config)
    throws ServletException
{
  /*Always call super.init()*/
  super.init(config);

  /*read the "msg" parameter from
   *the configuration file*/
  text = config.getInitParameter("msg");
  if (text == null)
    text= "No init message";

  try {
    /*read the "rep" parameter
     *from the configuration file*/
    String repeatString =
        config.getInitParameter("rep");
    times = Integer.parseInt(repeatString);
  }
  catch(NumberFormatException nfe)
  {
    /*handle the case where
     *repeatString is null or illegal*/
    times  = 1;
  }
}

/*override doGet() method which will be invoked
 *automatically by service()
 *when a GET request arrives*/
public void doGet(HttpServletRequest req,
        HttpServletResponse res)
      throws ServletException, IOException
{
  /*set response's content type*/
  res.setContentType("text/html");
  /*get the write stream for the response*/
  PrintWriter out = res.getWriter();

  /*generate the header for the response*/
  String docType =
    "<!DOCTYPE HTML PUBLIC
```

Code Listing 8.3   (Continued)

```
    \"-//W3C//DTD HTML 4.0 " +
    "Transitional//EN\">\n";
  /*generate the response document*/
  out.println(docType + "<HTML>\n" +
    "<HEAD><TITLE>Hello WWW</TITLE></HEAD>\n" +
    "<BODY>\n" +
    "<H1>

  /*print the text message a
   *specified number of times*/
  for(int i=0; i<times; i++)
  {
    out.println(text + "<BR>");
  }

  out.println("</H1>\n</BODY></HTML>");

  out.close();
  }
}
```

Code Listing 8.3 (Continued)

The configuration file must be stored in xml format on the server. This file is provided as a parameter to the *init()* method. The following content is a suitable configuration file for the initialization servlet example provided, which specifies a message *msg* = "This is the init text" to be printed to the client *rep* = 4 times.

```
<?xml version="1.0" encoding="UTF-8"?>

<web-app version="2.4"
    xmlns="http://java.sun.com/xml/ns/j2ee"
    xmlns:xsi=http://www.w3.org/2001/XMLSchema-instance
    xsi:schemaLocation="http://java.sun.com/xml/ns/j2ee
    http://java.sun.com/xml/ns/j2ee/web-app_2_4.xsd">

  <servlet>
    <servlet-name>
      InitParamsServlet
    </servlet-name>
```

Code Listing 8.4 config.xml

```
      <servlet-class>
         initparamsservlet.InitParamsServlet
      </servlet-class>
      <init-param>
         <param-name>msg</param-name>
         <param-value>This is the init text</param-value>
      </init-param>
      <init-param>
         <param-name>rep</param-name>
         <param-value>4</param-value>
      </init-param>
   </servlet>

   <servlet-mapping>
      <servlet-name>InitParams</servlet-name>
      <url-pattern>
         /servlet/InitParamsServlet
      </url-pattern>
   </servlet-mapping>
   <session-config>
      <session-timeout>
         30
      </session-timeout>
   </session-config>

   <welcome-file-list>
      <welcome-file>
         index.jsp
      </welcome-file>
   </welcome-file-list>
</web-app>
```

Code Listing 8.4   (Continued)

8.3.3.3 Reading Individual Client Parameters

Most of the time, in order for a servlet to provide the service it was designed for, it has to read and client's input parameters need to be interpreted. In general, these parameters are collected via forms and sent across the network via client requests.

In order to highlight the major steps in building a servlet capable of reading client parameters, an example which allows the client user to input a name and a value via a form displayed by the client Web browser is presented. When the user has already input the data and presses the submit button, the browser communicates with the server-located servlet transmitting the client data as parameters for further processing. The servlet is required to read the client parameters before processing them in an application-dependent manner. The output of the parameter processing phase is a dynamical generated Web page to be delivered to the client and be displayed by the client's browser.

The major steps in developing the client parameter-reading servlet are listed next.

- Step 1—Enable user parameters to be read by a form:

```
<form [...] >
 Propriety name:
   <input type="text" name="name"><br>
 Propriety value:
   <input type="text" name="value"><br>
 <input type="Submit">
</form>
```

- Step 2—Invoke the servlet when submitting the form:

```
<form action="/ClientParams/servlet/
               CliParamsServlet"">
  [...]
</form>
```

- Step 3—Create a customer servlet class to extend HttpServlet:

```
public class CliParamsServlet extends HttpServlet
{
[...]
}
```

- Step 4—Override the doGet() method to address GET requests:

```
public void doGet(HttpServletRequest req,
     HttpServletResponse res)
   throws ServletException, IOException
{
[...]
}
```

- Step 5—In doGet(), get and use the parameters:

```
/*get the response write stream*/
PrintWriter out = res.getWriter();
  [...]
out.println ("<HTML>" +

  [...]

  "<B>Propriety name</B>: "
  /*retrieve the user input name*/
```

```
          + req.getParameter("name") + "\n" +

          [...]

          "<B>Propriety value</B>: "
          /*retrieve the user input value*/
          + req.getParameter("value") + "\n" +

          [...]

          "</HTML>");
```

The following html code allows the client to input a name and a value via a form which when submitted will send the corresponding request to the */Client-Params/servlet/CliParamsServlet* servlet.

```
<html>
 <head>
  <meta http-equiv="Content-Type"
       content="text/html; charset=UTF-8">
  <title>Client Parameters Input Page</title>
 </head>
 <body>

 <h1>Client Parameters Input Page</h1>

 <form action=
         "/ClientParams/servlet/CliParamsServlet">
  Propriety name:
      <input type="text" name="name"><br>
  Propriety value:
      <input type="text" name="value"><br>
  <input type="Submit">
 </form>

 </body>
</html>
```

Code Listing 8.5 client.html

The complete servlet implementation is presented in the following code example.

```java
/*import java packages*/
import java.io.*;
import javax.servlet.*;
import javax.servlet.http.*;

/*define CliParamsServlet  class extending
 *HttpServlet*/
public class CliParamsServlet  extends HttpServlet
{
  /*override doGet() method which will be invoked
   *automatically by service()
   *when a GET request arrives*/
  public void doGet(HttpServletRequest req,
          HttpServletResponse res)
        throws ServletException, IOException
  {
    /*set content type*/
    res.setContentType("text/html;charset=UTF-8");
    /*get the response write stream*/
    PrintWriter out = res.getWriter();

    String title = "Client Parameters";

    /*generate the header type*/
    String docType =  "<HTML>" +
      "<!DOCTYPE HTML PUBLIC \"-//W3C//DTD HTML 4.0 " +
      "Transitional//EN\">\n";
    out.println (docType +
      "<BODY BGCOLOR=\"#FDF5E6\">\n" +
      "<H1 ALIGN=CENTER>" + title + "</H1>\n" +
      "<UL>\n" +
      "  <LI><B>Propriety name</B>: "
        /*retrieve the user input name*/
        + req.getParameter("name") + "\n" +
      "  <LI><B>Propriety value</B>: "
        /*retrieve the user input value*/
        + req.getParameter("value") + "\n" +
      "</UL>\n" +
      "</BODY></HTML>");

    out.close();
  }
}
```

Code Listing 8.6 CliParamsServlet.java

8.3.3.4 Reading All Client Parameters

To exemplify servlet–client interaction when several parameters are involved, the following html form will be used which will be displayed by the client's web browser and will allow the user to input several parameters. Next the major steps in reading all input parameters are presented. The custom servlet class extension from HttpServlet and doGet() method overriding is assumed to be also performed (but not explicitly indicated).

- Step 1—Enable user parameters to be read by the client form:

```
<form [...]>
  Name:
    <input type="text" name="name"><br>
  Surname:
    <input type="text" name="surname"><br>
  <hr>Address:
  <textarea name="address" rows=3 cols=40>
  </textarea><br>
  Credit Card:<br>
  <input type="radio" name="cardType" value="Visa">
    Visa<br>
  <input type="radio" name="cardType" value="Master">
    Master<br>
  Credit Card Number:
  <input type="password" name="cardNum"><br>
  <input type="submit" value="Send Form">
</form>
```

- Step 2—Invoke the servlet when submitting the form:

```
<form action=
  "/ClientAllParams/servlet/CliAllParamsServlet">
[...]
</form>
```

- Step 3—In the doGet() method, get and print the parameters:

```
PrintWriter out = res.getWriter();
/*generate the HTML content*/
out.println ("<HTML>\n" + "<BODY>\n");
[...]

/*retrieve the parameter list*/
Enumeration paramNames = req.getParameterNames();
/*iterate through the parameter list*/
while(paramNames.hasMoreElements())
{
```

```
/*retrieve and print parameter name*/
String paramName =
    (String)paramNames.nextElement();
out.print(paramName + "\n");

/*retrieve and print the parameter values*/
String[] paramValues =
    req.getParameterValues(paramName);

/*iterate through the parameter values*/
for(int i=0; i<paramValues.length; i++)
  out.println(paramValues[i] + "\n");
}
[...]
out.println("</BODY>\n</HTML>");
```

The full code for the HTML document which calls the all parameter printing servlet upon submission of the embedded form is presented next.

```
<!DOCTYPE HTML PUBLIC
    "-//W3C//DTD HTML 4.0 Transitional//EN">
<HTML>
<HEAD><TITLE>A Sample FORM using GET</TITLE></HEAD>
<BODY>
<H1 ALIGN="CENTER">A Sample FORM using GET</H1>
  <form action=
    "/ClientAllParams/servlet/CliAllParamsServlet">
    Name: <input type="text" name="name"><br>
    Surname: <input type="text" name="surname"><br>
    <hr>
    Address:
    <textarea name="address" rows=3 cols=40>
    </textarea><br>
    Credit Card:<br>
    <input type="radio" name="cardType" value="Visa">
      Visa<br>
    <input type="radio" name="cardType" value="Master">
      Master<br>
    Credit Card Number:
    <input type="password" name="cardNum"><br>
    <input type="submit" value="Send Form">
  </form>
</BODY>
</HTML>
```

Code Listing 8.7 all-params.html

The following full implementation of the doGet() method shows how all client parameters can be retrieved and printed in tabular fashion, by making use of the Java *Enumeration* class and its *nextElement()* and *hasmoreElements()* methods.

```
/*overrides doGet() method; to be invoked automatically
 *by service() when a GET request arrives*/
protected void doGet(HttpServletRequest req,
      HttpServletResponse res)
         throws ServletException, IOException
{
  /*set content type*/
  res.setContentType("text/html;charset=UTF-8");
  /*get the response write stream*/
  PrintWriter out = res.getWriter();

  /*generate the header type*/
  String docType =
    "<HTML>"
    + "<!DOCTYPE HTML PUBLIC \"-//W3C//DTD HTML 4.0 "
    + "Transitional//EN\">\n";

  out.println (docType +
    "<BODY>"
    + "\n<H1 ALIGN=CENTER>All Client Params</H1>\n"
    + "<TABLE BORDER=1 ALIGN=CENTER>\n"
    + "<TR>\n"
    +"<TH>Parameter Name<TH>Parameter Value(s)");

    /*retrieve the parameter list*/
    Enumeration paramNames = req.getParameterNames();

    /*iterate through the parameter list*/
    while(paramNames.hasMoreElements())
    {
      /*retrieve and print parameter name*/
      String paramName =
        (String)paramNames.nextElement();
      out.print("<TR><TD>" + paramName + "\n<TD>");
      /*retrieve and print the parameter values*/
      String[] paramValues =
        req.getParameterValues(paramName);
      if (paramValues.length == 1)
```

Code Listing 8.8 CliParamsServlet.java—doGet()

```
        {
          String paramValue = paramValues[0];
          if (paramValue.length() == 0)
            out.println("<I>No Value</I>");
          else
            out.println(paramValue);
        }
        else
        {
          out.println("<UL>");
          /*iterate through the parameter values*/
          for(int i=0; i<paramValues.length; i++)
            out.println("<LI>"
                  + paramValues[i] + "</LI>");
          out.println("</UL>");
        }
    }
  out.println("</TABLE>\n</BODY></HTML>");
}
```

Code Listing 8.8 (Continued)

8.3.3.5 Sessions

As HTTP is a stateless protocol, its request–response transactions are self-contained and independent. However, often applications require data storage from one transaction to another, as different pages are visited or information of different types is collected and/or exchanged.

In order to bridge the gap between the support HTTP provides and application needs, Java *Sessions* have been introduced. A session is a specially defined container storing data relative to a series of client transactions. In fact, such a session container stores data about client activities in form of name–value pairs, which can be accessed at request by all servlets that have access to the session object.

Using sessions requires several steps to be performed by the servlet, as described next. As this step-by-step process description focuses on sessions-oriented Java programming support, some required servlet implementation-related aspects such as HTTPServlet inheritance and doGet() override are not listed.

- Step 1—Create a session

```
/*returns the current session or
 *creates one if it does not exist.*/
HttpSession session = req.getSession(true);
```

- Step 2—Get relevant data from the input parameters

```
/*get the parameters from the servlet request.*/
```

```
String dataName = req.getParameter("name");
String dataValue = req.getParameter("value");
```

- Step 3—Store data in name–value pairs

```
/*stores (dataName, dataValue)
 *pair with the session*/
session.setAttribute(dataName, dataValue);
```

- Step 4—Retrieve the object associated with a name

```
/*retrieves the value associated with the name*/
String value =
  session.getAttribute(dataName).toString();
```

- Step 5: Remove the (name, value) association

```
/*removes the data associated with dataName*/
removeAttribute(dataName);
```

The following code example illustrates the usage of the methods for accessing session objects from a servlet. The key object *session* is an instance of the HttpSession class which stores all (name, value)-pair associations. New client parameters are read and stored in a new (name, value)-pair with the session object, then all (name, value)-pair associations are printed, including the newly added one.

```
/*override doGet() method*/
protected void doGet(HttpServletRequest req,
    HttpServletResponse res)
  throws ServletException, IOException
{
  /*set content type*/
  res.setContentType("text/html");
  /*get the response write stream*/
  PrintWriter out = res.getWriter();

  /*get the session object*/
  HttpSession session = req.getSession(true);

  /*print session-related data*/
  String id = session.getId();
  Date ctime =
    new Date(session.getCreationTime());
  Date atime =
    new Date(session.getLastAccessedTime());
  out.println("<br>Session ID: " + id);
```

Code Listing 8.9 JavaServlet.java—doGet()

```
out.println("<br>Created: " + ctime);
out.println("<br>Last accessed: " + atime);
/*get the new name
 *from servlet request*/
String dataName = req.getParameter("name");
if (dataName != null && dataName.length() > 0)
{
  /*get the new parameter
   *value from servlet request*/
  String dataValue = req.getParameter("value");
  /*set the new (name,value)
   *pair with the session*/
  session.setAttribute(dataName, dataValue);
}

/*print all session contents*/
Enumeration e = session.getAttributeNames();
/*iterate through session elements*/
while (e.hasMoreElements())
{
  /*get the name of the next element*/
  String name = (String)e.nextElement();
  /*retrieve the value*/
  String value =
    session.getAttribute(name).toString();
  out.println("<br>" + name + " = " + value);
}

out.close();
}
```

Code Listing 8.9 (Continued)

The following html code can be used to allow the user to input parameter values, call the above servlet, and pass it the parameters.

```
<html>
  <head>
    <meta http-equiv="Content-Type"
      content="text/html; charset=UTF-8">
    <title>Session Servlet Main Page</title>
  </head>
```

Code Listing 8.10 session-servlet.html

```
<body>

  <h1>Session Servlet</h1>
  <form action=
    "/SessionServlet/servlet/SessionServlet">
    Propriety name:
      <input type="text" name="name"><br>
    Propriety value:
      <input type="text" name="value"><br>
    <input type="Submit">
  </form>
</body>
</html>
```

Code Listing 8.10   (Continued)

8.3.3.6 Cookies

The previous section has presented sessions as a method to store information between user requests. When users navigate from one Web page to another, they lose
the information stored in the requests made to the server. Although a temporary data
storage solution, sessions' saved data is not persistent and expires once the client has
logged out or closed the Web browser application. As a direct consequence, the data
stored in sessions is eventually lost. However, often there is a need for accessing
information from previous sessions. This requires an additional solution to store the
data in between the sessions.

In order to solve this data persistence issue, *cookies* have been used. Cookies are
small pieces of information stored on the client machine. When the client connects
to a server, the server-specific cookies are retrieved by the browser from the client
machine. If cookies are found, information about the client previous sessions' activity can be extracted and used by the server to personalize its behavior. If no cookies
are found, new cookies can be created and stored at the client's side. The cookies
are usually stored by the Web browser, and for security reasons browsers can disable
cookies. If the client browser does not accept cookies, it will discard them.

Although the most important information cookies store is often considered the
(name, content)-pair, the cookies are stored in a container with several other fields.
There fields include:

The *name* of the cookie is typically used to identify the cookie and therefore to
retrieve and examine the cookie's content. This name cannot contain comma, space,
or other special characters (reserved). Often the *content* is a simple value, but it can
also be an array of values.

The *domain* represents the domain of the server that is to receive the cookie. The
domain of server requesting the cookie must match the domain stored in the cookie.

This mechanism prevents other servers from accessing cookies that do not belong to them.

Expiration time is a time stamp that indicates the time when the cookie expires. This time is stored in a specific format and provides a cookie with a certain lifespan.

The *path* on the server where the cookie originates from is also saved. If not specified, this path indicates the full path from where the cookie was set.

Secure field states if the cookie requires secure communication (i.e., https) or not. The default value is no.

Cookies are set using HTTP headers in the following format:

```
Set-Cookie: user=NetworkProgrammer;
   domain=.netprogramming.eu;
path=/servlet/NewCookie;
expires=Fri, 1-Mar-2013, 16:15:00 GMT;
```

In order to create, store and retrieve cookies, several steps have to be followed. These steps are indicated next and make use of the following methods:

HTTPServletResponse method *void addCookie(Cookie cookie)*. HTTPServletResponse method *Cookies[] getCookies()*. Once a cookie is retrieved, it can be manipulated using Cookie class specific methods. *String getName()* retrieves the name associated with the cookie. *String getValue()* retrieves the value associated with the cookie. *void setValue(String value)* sets the value associated with the cookie.

- Step 1—Create a cookie

```
/*returns the newly created cookie
 *object storing (cookieName, cookieValue) pair*/
Cookie cookie = new Cookie(cookieName, cookieValue);
```

- Step 2—Store the cookie at the client

```
/*stores the cookie with the
 *HTTPServletResponse void addCookie() method*/
res.addCookie(cookie);
```

- Step 3—Get all the cookies stored at the client

```
/*retrieves cookies via the HTTPServletRequest
 *Cookie[] getCookies() method*/
Cookies[] cookies = res.getCookies();
```

- Step 4—Identify a cookie given by "name" and update its value

```
/*checks all cookies names against "name"*/
/*if found, fetch its value and set a new value*/
String name = new String("name");
String newvalue = new String("newvalue");
for(int i=0; i<cookies.length; i++)
  if (name.equals(cookies[i].getName()))
  {
```

```
      String oldvalue = cookies[i].getValue();
      cookies[i].setValue(newvalue);
   }
```

Cookies can be used by servlets to store user data as the following example shows. This example retrieves the parameters from the client request: cookieName, cookieValue, searchName, and searchValue, sets a new cookie named cookieName with the value cookieValue, searches for a cookie named searchName, gets and prints its old value, and updates this cookie's content storing searchValue.

```
protected void doGet(HttpServletRequest req,
    HttpServletResponse res)
  throws ServletException, IOException
{
  res.setContentType("text/html");
  PrintWriter out = res.getWriter();

  /*read data from the Web page*/
  String cookieName =
    req.getParameter("cookiename");
  String cookieValue =
    req.getParameter("cookievalue");
  String searchName =
    req.getParameter("searchname");
    String searchValue =
    req.getParameter("searchvalue");

  /*set new cookie to the client*/
  if (cookieName != null && cookieValue != null)
  {
    Cookie cookie = null;
    try
    {

      /*create the cookie*/
      cookie = new Cookie(cookieName, cookieValue);
    }
    catch (IllegalArgumentException e)
    {
      e.printStackTrace();
    }
    /*add the cookie using the response object*/
    res.addCookie(cookie);
  }
```

Code Listing 8.11 CookieServlet.java—doGet()

```
/*get all cookies from the client*/
Cookie[] cookies = req.getCookies();

if ((cookies != null) && (cookies.length > 0))
{
  /*print all cookies' info*/
  for(int i = 0; i < cookies.length; i++)
  {
    /*print cookie's name and value*/
    out.println("<br>Cookie name:"
        + cookies[i].getName());
    out.println("<br>Cookie value:"
        + cookies[i].getValue());
    /*set cookie with the new value*/
    if (searchName.equals(cookies[i].getName()))
      cookies[i].setValue(searchValue);
  }
}
else
{
  out.println("<br> There are no cookies!");
}

out.close();
}
```

Code Listing 8.11 (Continued)

The following html code represents the cookie servlet main page. The document is visualized on the client web browser, and the form allows the user to enter several parameters: cookieName, cookieValue, searchName, and searchValue. These will be passed to the servlet *CookieSerlvet* on the client's machine for processing, as already indicated.

```
<html>
  <head>
    <meta http-equiv="Content-Type"
      content="text/html; charset=UTF-8">
    <title>Cookie Servlet Main Page</title>
  </head>
  <body>
```

Code Listing 8.12 cookie-servlet.html

```
<h1>Cookie Servlet Main Page</h1>

<a href="/CookieServlet/servlet/CookieServlet">
  Read Cookie Servlet
</a>

<br>Set Cookie Form
<form action="/CookieServlet/servlet/CookieServlet">
  Cookie attribute name:
  <input type="text" name="cookiename"><br>
  Cookie attribute value:
  <input type="text" name="cookievalue"><br>
  Cookie name to search for:
  <input type="text" name="searchname"><br>
  Cookie updated value:
  <input type="text" name="searchvalue"><br>
  <input type="Submit">
</form>
</body>
</html>
```

Code Listing 8.12 (Continued)

8.4 Java Server Pages

Java Server Pages (JSP) are web pages that have embedded Java code which runs on the server side and generates content dynamically.

Generating HTML code using servlets is inconvenient as multiple *out.println()* calls are required, even for typical HTML content generation. Writing servlets requires Java programming expertise, whereas writing HTML content can be performed by a less skilled a person. However, Java code flexibility is still provided via HTML-like tags embedded in the HTML code. As it will be seen in the following examples, JSP represents a powerful development tool for web applications.

The following example represents a html web page which contains a form allowing the user to input two values, a number and a power. When the form is submitted (by clicking the submit button), the request is sent to the server targeting the *ProcessJSP.jsp* page.

```
<html>
  <head>
    <meta http-equiv="Content-Type" content=
    "text/html">
```

Code Listing 8.13 jsp-access.html

```
  <title>JSP Page</title>
</head>
<body>
  <h1>Index JSP Page</h1>

  <form  method="POST"  action="ProcessJSP.jsp">
    Number:
      <input type="Text" name="Number" value=""
       size=5>
    Power:
      <input type="Text"  name="Power" value=""
       size=5>
    <input  type="Submit"  value = "Submit">
    <input  type="Reset"  value="Clear">
  </form>
</body>
</html>
```

Code Listing 8.13   (Continued)

The *ProcessJSP.jsp* page is presented in the following code example. The Java code is contained within specific tags:

```
<%
[...]
%>
```

The following JSP retrieves the parameters from the request, calculates the power of the number input by the user, and displays the result.

```
<html>
  <head>
    <meta http-equiv="Content-Type"
     content="text/html">
    <title>JSP Page</title>
  </head>

  <body>
  <h1>Process JSP Page</h1>
 <%
    /*retrieve the parameters*/
    String strNumber = request.getParameter("Number");
    String strPower = request.getParameter("Power");
```

Code Listing 8.14 ProcessJSP.jsp

```
      int number = Integer.parseInt(strNumber);
      int power = Integer.parseInt(strPower);
      int res = 1;
      /*calculate the power*/
      for (int i = 0; i < power; i++)
        res *= number;
    %>
    <!-- display the number and its power-->
    <b><%= number %> power <%= power %> is <%= res %></b>
    </body>
  </html>
```

Code Listing 8.14   (Continued)

JSP provides various scripting element. The following paragraphs present the major elements in order to exemplify their usage and the capabilities provided by this technology.

Java expressions are evaluated, converted into as string, and inserted in the page output at runtime. All information about the Web page request is available. The following predefined variables are available: *HTTPServletRequest request, HTTPServletResponse response, HTTPSession session,* and *JspWriter out* (a buffered version of PrintWriter).

A Java expression can be used in the following forms:

```
<%= java expression %>
```

or

```
<jsp:expression> java expression </jsp:expression>
```

For instance, the following expression displays the current date and time:

```
<%= new java.util.Date() %>
```

Properties can be set in JSP as follows:

```
<jsp:setProperty name = "author"
  property = "username" value = "John" />
```

An example which sets the name, property and value attributes is presented in the following code:

```
<jsp:setProperty>
  name = "user" property = "userID" value =
    '<%= Math.random() %>' />
```

Scriptlets represent pieces of Java code run by the server when a JSP page is invoked. The Java code will be executed at runtime and has access to the same pre-defined variables as expressions. Scriptlets can be inserted in a JSP page in the following ways:

```
<% java code %>
```

or

```
<jsp:scriptlet> java code </jsp:scriptlet>
```

The following example shows how java code can be used in a JSP page:

```
<% response.setContentType("text/plain"); %>

<% out.println("Your IP is"
     + request.getRemoteAddr()); %>

<% if (Math.random() < 0.5) { %>
  You are welcome!
  <% } else { %>
  You are NOT welcome!
  <% } %>
```

Declarations are also supported in JSP pages. Java code will be added to the JSP generated servlet and evaluated at runtime.

Declarations can be added to JSP in the following ways:

```
<%! java code %>
```

or

```
<jsp:declaration> java code </jsp:declaration>
```

The following code example indicates how two variables can be declared:

```
<%! private int balance = 0; %>
<jsp:declaration>
  private String username = "";
</jsp:declaration>
```

Often JSP requires importing new packages to have access to additional classes. In order to achieve this, the *page* directive with the *import* attribute has to be used in one of the following ways:

```
<%@ page import="packagename.classname" %>
```

or

```
<%@ page import="packagename1.classname1,
        packagename2.classname2, [...]" %>
```

The following code example shows the import of all classes from the javax.servlet.http package:

```
<%@ page import="javax.servlet.http.*" %>
```

8.5 Conclusion

This chapter has presented server-side network programming technologies, which include Common Gateway Interface (CGI) and Hypertext Pre-processor (PHP), as non-Java alternative solutions, and Java Servlets and Java Server Pages (JSP) on which the focus has been. Their key aspects are that they generate dynamic content which can consider various factors such as the values of initialization parameters, user input, environment variables, etc., and they run on the server, providing the client with the output for display.

Chapter 9
Client-Side Network Programming

Abstract Client-side network programming involves designing and writing code to be run on the client machine during client–server communication process. This chapter introduces various types of web documents used and conveyed over the Internet as well as their descriptive languages and characteristics. Java specific solutions for active and dynamic documents are introduced along with comprehensive examples to illustrate their capabilities and functionality. This includes Java Script language as well as Java Applets.

9.1 Introduction

Client-side network programming involves designing and writing code to be run on the client machine during the client–server communication process.

Although various network-based stand-alone applications can be built for the client, each serving a different purpose or invoking a specific service from the server, the most popular client-side application is a Web browser.

A Web browser runs as a client process, and its basic functionality involves communication with a Web server by making use of HTTP. Following document request, the browser also performs Web document retrieval, received document interpretation and display for the user, and responds to user actions. Most Web documents interpreted by Web browsers are HTML documents. However, the current Web browsers are more advanced and can also interpret and run specific code such as JavaScript or embed more advanced entities such as Java Applets.

Figure 9.1 illustrates the scope of the client-side network programming in terms of preparing code to run as a client process. This code may belong to stand-alone applications and be independently run, may be Java Script code to be executed by the Web browser or Java Applets code to run embedded in the Web browser.

9.2 Web Documents Classification

Based on their characteristics, three types of Web documents manipulated by networked applications can be identified.

B. Ciubotaru, G.-M. Muntean, *Advanced Network Programming – Principles and Techniques*, Computer Communications and Networks, DOI 10.1007/978-1-4471-5292-7_9, © Springer-Verlag London 2013

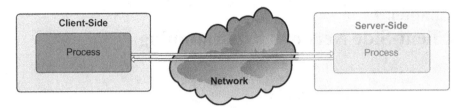

Fig. 9.1 Client-side network programming

Static documents include content which is identically delivered at every request, to any user, and to any device via any network. They do not require any additional processing at the server side following user request before content delivery. These types of documents are delivered as they are, and any modification is performed by replacing the original file with an updated file version on the server. Static documents are quick and easy to create, and are fast to retrieve as there is no request-dependent personalized processing involved which could have been time consuming. Moreover, as static documents seldom change, they are cache friendly, helping improve the delivery performance. Although using static documents has some clear advantages, there are difficulties in creating large sites, maintaining consistency and keeping up to date, and do not offer any provision for user personalization.

Active documents are basically static documents containing executable code to be run on the client side. Such a code may be a Java Script code, for example, which is interpreted and run by the client's Web browser.

Unlike the static documents, active documents offer user interactivity with limited user personalization. They support data display customization, while still being cache friendly. Cache friendliness is given by the fact that the active code (e.g., Java Script) is not changed (or it seldom changes) at the server side and can be successfully delivered from a cached location closer to the client. Although the code is static, by running it at the client side it can offer a certain level of dynamism. Moreover, the fact that active documents run code on the client-side brings further the advantage of distributed resource requirements (at client's side).

However, the fact that active documents involve code run at the client's side has two main disadvantages. The client runs unknown code which may be unsafe from a security point of view, and the active code may be slow to run if the client machine has low computational resources.

Dynamic documents are documents that are generated on the fly by the server at a client's request. The server will use, for example, Java servlets, PHP or JSP to generate the dynamic content which will be then forwarded to the client. Dynamic documents have been presented in the previous chapter on server-side network programming.

Dynamic documents enable user personalization, offer support for database access, as well as data display customization. As documents are dynamically generated for every client's request, dynamic documents can use time and date sensitive code in order to assemble the client's document.

Although dynamic documents are the solution to develop large sites and Web applications involving user interaction, they require skilled creators with strong knowledge of server-side network programming. Moreover, being dynamically generated at the server side, they have high resource requirements (computational and communication) and are not cache friendly.

9.3 Static Documents

Static documents include both content-related data and information about formatting the presentation of the content to the user. Originally data and presentation formatting-related information were combined into a single document.

The HyperText Markup Language (HTML) [1] and the Extensible HyperText Markup Language (XHTML) [2] are used to describe both data and presentation and are usually used to format the documents delivered to the client user.

Recently, content and formatting-related data are separated, and different languages are used to describe each of them.

The Extensible Markup Language (XML) [3] is used to describe data in a formalized, structured, and cross-platform way, allowing for easy data transport and manipulation. In general, no presentation-related information is included.

For formatting purposes, the Cascading Style Sheets (CSS) [4] and the Extensible Stylesheet Language (XSL) [5] can be used in conjunction with HTML and XML, respectively.

Static documents are delivered across the network using the HyperText Transfer Protocol (HTTP) [6] and the Hypertext Transfer Protocol Secure (HTTPS) [7] which enables content transfer from the server to clients over the networks in a regular or secure manner, respectively.

In order to access and retrieve any document from the server, the client request needs to provide the host details, the location of the document to be accessed, and the document name. The transfer protocol has also to be indicated. This information is specified using a Uniform Resource Locator (URL) with the structure presented in the following example.

```
<protocol>://<username>:<password>@
<host>:<port>/<path>/<name>
```

The *protocol* indicates the protocol used to deliver the document, and it is usually HTTP or HTTPS.

The *username* and *password* pair controls the access to the document. A public document is not protected by a username and a password so they will not be required.

The *host* represents the IP address of the server or the root domain name which is forwarded to the IP of the server.

The *port* specifies the port number on which the Web server is listening for connection requests from clients. The usual ports are 80 or 8080 and, if this is the case, they do not need to be specified in the URL.

The *path* and *name* uniquely indicate the location and name of the document in the server's file system.

9.3.1 HyperText Markup Language

The HyperText Markup Language (HTML) [1] is a language used to describe Web documents. A HTML file is a text file containing markup tags which are interpreted by the Web browser, informing it how to display the various components of the Web document.

HTML files are easy to create by using any plain text editor and typically have an *htm* or *html* file extension. They are composed of elements, and each element is contained inside a parent element, forming a tree-like structure in a hierarchical manner. HTML tags are used to markup HTML elements and are surrounded by angle brackets: < and >. HTML tags normally come in pairs as in the following example *<tagname>content </tagname>*. The first tag in any pair is the start tag and the second tag is the end tag, which differs from the start tag by the addition of a "/" in front of the tag name. The text between the start and end tags is the element content. The tag has effect on its content and on its children elements only. There are exceptions such as *
* which indicates a new line and which is a tab that does not have to be closed as it has no content. Generally, HTML tags are not case sensitive and most of them can have attributes. Attributes provide additional information to an HTML element such as properties.

The following example shows generally how an HTML tag is used in an HTML file, and it includes an attribute and its value:

```
<tag attribute="value"> element content </tag>
```

The following is an example of a Web document described in the HTML language:

```
<html>
  <head>
    <title>My New Page Title</title>
  </head>
  <body bgcolor="white">
    <p>A New Paragraph</p>
    <br>
    <table> [...] </table>
    [...]
  </body>
```

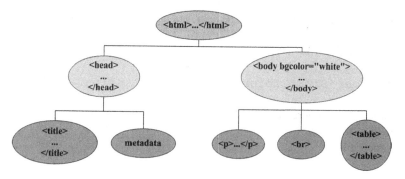

Fig. 9.2 HTML document tag hierarchy

```
</html>
```

The above HTML code example is presented in a hierarchical manner in Fig. 9.2. The *<html>* tag contains the whole document. Its direct children are *<head>* and *<body>*.

The *<head>* contains information about the document, such as the title of the document and metadata. Metadata identifies the version of the HTML used to describe the content of the document. For example, the following metadata identifies the content as HTML version 4.0 transitional.

```
<!DOCTYPE html public "-//w3c//dtd html 4.0
transitional//en">
```

The *<body>* describes the content of the document and can include many tags of diverse types. One of the important tags probably is the *<table>* tag which allows for bi-dimensional structuring of the data presentation.

Next basic tags used to construct HTML documents and format them according to application requirements are presented.

The heading tags format the text within their boundaries at different sizes. There are several heading tabs available as it can be seen in the following example:

```
<h1>Text written with heading 1</h1>
<h2>Text written with heading 2</h2>
<h3>Text written with heading 3</h3>
<h4>Text written with heading 4</h4>
<h5>Text written with heading 5</h5>
<h6>Text written with heading 6</h6>
```

Paragraphs and new lines can be specified as follows:

```
<p> Paragraph </p>
<br> Newline
```

Text presentation formatting can be achieved using the following tags:

```
<i> Italics </i>
<b> Bold </b>
<font size="SIZE" color="COLOR"> Text </font>
```

Unordered and ordered lists, including nested lists, can be included in an HTML document as follows:

Unordered list:

```
<ul>
  <li> First item
  <li> Second item
</ul>
```

Ordered list:

```
<ol>
  <li> Item one
  <li> Item two
</ol>
```

Images can be added to an HTML document using the *img* tag, which has no closing tag. Attributes such as *width* and *height* can be used to control picture dimensions.

```
<img src="http://www.netprogramming.eu/examples/
          img.jpg">
```

Anchors or links can be specified, allowing the user to navigate to other pages. In the following example, a link is attached to a text and permits the user to navigate to a different URL. The URL can be absolute or relative to the existing site.

```
<a href="page2.html">Link Text</a>
```

Forms are used to allow the user to input data, which is then sent to the Web server via requests. A form can contain several form elements such as text fields, radio buttons, check-boxes, and a submit button used to submit the form and consequently send the request to the server.

A credit card details reading form example is presented next.

```
<form name="CardForm" action="form_action.html"
  method="get">
    <input type="text" name="name"> Name
    <input type="radio" name="card" value="VISA">
```

```
<input type="radio" name="card" value="Master">
<input type="checkbox" name="choice" value="Bag">
<input type="checkbox" name="choice" value="Box">
<input type="submit" value="Submit">
</form>
```

Comments in an HTML document can be specified in the following way.

```
<!-- This is a comment -->
```

Tables are used to structure the presentation of a HTML document in a table-like format. A table has a header row with a number of items and multiple rows with several items each. The tables can be nested to create more complex layouts.

```
<table>
  <!-- Header row -->
  <th>
    <td>Item</td>
  </th>

  <!-- One row -->
  <tr>
    <td>Item</td>
  </tr>
</table>
```

9.3.2 Extensible Markup Language

Extensible Markup Language (XML) [3] is a cross-platform, extensible, and text-based standard for representing data. Unlike HTML that was designed to enable data display, XML enables data representation. XML allows for structuring, storing, and sending of information over the networks in a flexible and efficient way.

Similar to HTML, XML was also designed to describe data by using tags. However, there are no predefined XML tags, they need to be defined for each application or service specifically. XML uses a Document Type Definition (DTD) [8] or a XML Schema Definition [3] to describe data.

An example of an XML document describing a message is presented in the following code snippet.

```
<msg>
  <to>John</to>
  <from>Jack</from>
  <topic>Gentle reminder</topic>
```

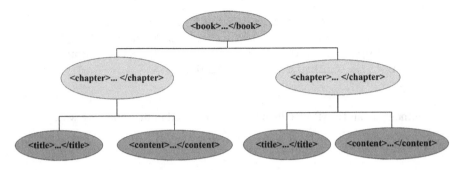

Fig. 9.3 XML document tag hierarchy example

```
<body>The deadline is Friday at 14:00!</body>
</msg>
```

Any XML document is composed of elements identified by tags, *<tagname>* *</tagname>*, which must always be closed. Each element is contained inside a parent element (tree like hierarchical structure similar to HTML). There must be a single root and each element may have attributes, if defined.

The following example shows the representation of a book in XML form. The hierarchical structure is graphically presented in Fig. 9.3.

```
<book>
  <chapter>
    <title>Title 1</title>
    <content>
      <p>Paragraph A1</p>
      [...]
    </content>
  </chapter>
  <chapter>
    <title>Title 2</title>
    <content>
      <p>Paragraph B1</p>
      [...]
    </content>
  </chapter>
  [...]
</book>
```

9.3.2.1 Document Type Definition

A Document Type Definition or DTD [8] document defines the legal building blocks of an XML document. It defines the document structure with a list of legal elements.

DTD can be declared inline in an XML document or externally. Using a DTD allows independent groups of people to use common data structures. Based on the DTD, verification of both generated and received data structure can be done.

Inline document type definition has the following format:

```
<!DOCTYPE root-element [element-declarations]>
```

An example defining a message is presented in the following code snippet:

```
<?xml version="1.0"?>
<!DOCTYPE msg [ <!ELEMENT msg (to, from, topic, body)>
<!ELEMENT to (#PCDATA)>
<!ELEMENT from (#PCDATA)>
<!ELEMENT topic (#PCDATA)>
<!ELEMENT body (#PCDATA)> ]>
```

External document type definition has the following form:

```
<!DOCTYPE root-element SYSTEM "filename">
```

The following is an example of external DTD definition usage:

```
"msg.xml" file:
<?xml version="1.0"?>
<!DOCTYPE msg SYSTEM "msg.dtd">

"msg.dtd" file:
<!ELEMENT msg (to, from, topic, body)>
<!ELEMENT to (#PCDATA)>
<!ELEMENT from (#PCDATA)>
<!ELEMENT topic (#PCDATA)>
<!ELEMENT body (#PCDATA)>
```

9.3.2.2 XML Schema Definition

XML Schema Definition or XSD [3] document describes the structure of an XML document. XSD is an XML-based alternative to DTD and can also be declared inline in an XML document or externally.

XSD defines elements and attributes that can appear in a document and their data types. It defines which elements are child elements, their order and number, whether an element is empty or can include text and default and fixed values for elements and attributes.

XSD are richer and more powerful than DTD, supporting data types and namespaces. XSD documents are written in XML and are extensible to future additions.

An example of an XSD file for representing the message introduced before is presented in the following code snippet:

```
<?xml version="1.0"?>

<xs:schema
      xmlns:xs="http://www.w3.org/2001/XMLSchema"
      targetNamespace="http://www.netprogramming.eu"
      xmlns="http://www.netprogramming.eu"
      elementFormDefault="qualified">
  <xs:element name="msg">
    <xs:complexType>
    <xs:sequence>
      <xs:element name="to" type="xs:string"/>
      <xs:element name="from" type="xs:string"/>
      <xs:element name="topic" type="xs:string"/>
      <xs:element name="body" type="xs:string"/>
    </xs:sequence>
    </xs:complexType>
  </xs:element>
</xs:schema>
```

For a better understanding of the XSD file components, their use will be further explained. From definition, *xmlns:xs="http://www.w3.org/2001/XMLSchema"* indicates that the elements and data types used in the schema come from the *"http://www.w3.org/2001/XMLSchema"* namespace and these elements and data types should be prefixed with "xs:".

The *targetNamespace="http://www.netprogramming.eu"* indicates that the elements defined by this schema *(to, from, topic, body)* come from the following namespace: *"http://www.netprogramming.eu"* .

The attribute *xmlns="http://www.netprogramming.eu"* indicates the default namespace.

The attribute *elementFormDefault="qualified"* indicates that any elements used by the XML instance document which were declared in this schema must be namespace qualified.

```
<?xml version="1.0"?>
<msg xmlns="http://www.netprogramming.eu"
     xmlns:xsi=
       "http://www.w3.org/2001/XMLSchema-instance"
     xsi:schemaLocation=
       "http://www.netprogramming.eu msg.xsd">
<msg>
  <to>John</to>
  <from>Jack</from>
  <topic>Gentle reminder</topic>
  <body>The deadline is Friday at 14:00!</body>
</msg>
```

Within the *xml* file *xmlns= "http://www.netprogramming.eu"* specifies the default namespace declaration. All the elements used in this XML document are declared in this with the following namespace *xmlns:xsi= "http://www.w3.org/2001/XMLSchema-instance"*. SchemaLocation attribute has two values, the namespace to use and the location of the XML schema, *xsi:schemaLocation= "http://www.netprogramming.eu msg.xsd"*.

XSD offer great flexibility for defining application specific data structures to be described using the XML language.

For instance, the following simple element definition includes XXX which is the name and YYY which is the data type of the element:

```
<xs:element name="XXX" type="YYY"/>
```

The most common XML schema has a lot of built-in data types including *xs:string, xs:decimal, xs:integer, xs:boolean, xs:date, xs:time,* and *xs:positiveInteger*.

Default and fixed values can be defined for the elements of the schema. For example, the following examples have ZZZ as default value and WWW as fixed value:

```
<xs:element name="XXX" type="YYY" default="ZZZ"/>

<xs:element name="XXX" type="YYY" fixed="WWW"/>
```

Optional and required elements can also be defined. In the following example, the XXX element is defined as required. Consequently, this simple element when composing a complex one will have to be present in the XML file:

```
<xs:element name="XXX" type="YYY" use="required"/>
```

Restrictions on elements values ("facets") can be defined as well. In the following example, a *gender* simple element is defined. Its value is of type string; however, it is restricted to two values, "Male" and "Female".

```
<xs:element name="gender"/>
<xs:simpleType>
<xs:restriction base="xs:string">
  <xs:enumeration value="Male"/>
  <xs:enumeration value="Female"/>
</xs:restriction>
</xs:simpleType>
```

The following example shows the definition of a custom element named "carReg" of custom type "regType". The "regType" is defined as having string type with values restricted to a specific pattern as defined in the following code snippet:

```
<xs:element name="carReg" type="regType">
<xs:simpleType name="genType">
```

```
<xs:restriction base="xs:string">
  <xs:pattern value=
    "[0-9][0-9][A-Z]([A-Z])+([0-9])*"/>
</xs:restriction>
</xs:simpleType>
</xs:element>
```

A complex element is an XML element that contains other elements and/or attributes. A complex element may be empty, may contain other elements, contain text only, or contain both other elements and text.

A complex type can be used by instantiation. In the following example, a complex type named "pers" is defined containing two element named "name" and "age". Then two elements named "employee" and "student" of type "pers" are defined, basically instantiating the type "pers":

```
<xs:element name="employee" type="pers"/>
<xs:element name="student" type="pers"/>
<xs:complexType name="pers">
  <xs:sequence>
    <xs:element name="name" type="xs:string"/>
    <xs:element name="age" type="xs:integer"/>
  </xs:sequence>
</xs:complexType>
```

Inheritance is also permitted. The following example defines a complex type named "fullpers" which extends the already defined type "pers" by adding an element called "addr" (address). Both types can be then used by instantiation:

```
<xs:element name="employee" type="fullpers"/>
<xs:element name="employee" type="pers"/>
<xs:complexType name="pers">
  <xs:sequence>
    <xs:element name="name" type="xs:string"/>
    <xs:element name="age" type="xs:integer"/>
  </xs:sequence>
</xs:complexType>
<xs:complexType name="fullpers">
  <xs:complexContent>
    <xs:extension base="pers">
      <xs:sequence>
        <xs:element name="addr" type="xs:string"/>
        <xs:element name="city" type="xs:string"/>
      </xs:sequence>
    </xs:extension>
  </xs:complexContent>
```

```
</xs:complexType>
```

Complex elements support indicators. The indicators control how elements will be used in XML documents. There are altogether seven indicators.

Order indicators may include *all, choice, and sequence.*

All requires all elements to be used as in the following example:

```
<xs:element name="employee">
  <xs:complexType>
 <xs:all>
    <xs:element name="name" type="xs:string"/>
    <xs:element name="id_number" type="xs:string"/>
 </xs:all>
  </xs:complexType>
</xs:element>
```

Choice allows one element to be chosen out of many:

```
<xs:element name="employee">
  <xs:complexType>
 <xs:choice>
    <xs:element name="manager" type="manager"/>
    <xs:element name="director" type="director"/>
 </xs:choice>
  </xs:complexType>
</xs:element>
```

Sequence specifies that the elements must appear in a specific order:

```
<xs:element name="employee">
    <xs:complexType>
 <xs:sequence>
    <xs:element name="firstname" type="xs:string"/>
    <xs:element name="lastname" type="xs:string"/>
 </xs:sequence>
  </xs:complexType>
</xs:element>
```

Occurrence indicators include *maxOccurs* and *minOccurs* and specify the minimum and maximum number of times an element can occur:

```
<xs:element name="employee" type="pers"/>
<xs:complexType name="pers">
  <xs:choice>
    <xs:element name="name" type="xs:string"/>
    <xs:element name="nick" type="xs:string"
```

```
minOccurs="0" maxOccurs="unbounded"/>
  </xs:choice>
</xs:complexType>
```

Group indicators include element groups and attribute groups and are used to define related sets of elements.

The following example defines a group called "person-details" which can be used and referenced when defining a complex element such as "person-information" which contains the elements defined by the group plus an extra element, "address":

```
<xs:group name="person-details">
  <xs:sequence>
 <xs:element name="first_name" type="xs:string"/>
 <xs:element name="last_name" type="xs:string"/>
 <xs:element name="birthday" type="xs:date"/>
  </xs:sequence>
</xs:group>

<xs:element name="person" type="person-information"/>

<xs:complexType name="person-information">
  <xs:sequence>
 <xs:group ref="person-details"/>
 <xs:element name="address" type="xs:string"/>
  </xs:sequence>
</xs:complexType>
```

When defining an XSD schema, simple elements cannot have attributes. Only complex types can have attributes. Attributes themselves are always declared as a simple type. The following is an attribute with XXX being the name and YYY the data type:

```
<xs:attribute name="XXX" type="YYY"/>
```

Similar to elements, attributes can have default and fixed values, required or not. The following example shows the usage of attributes:

```
<?xml version="1.0" encoding="ISO-8859-1" ?>
<xs:schema xmlns:xs= "http://www.w3.org/2001/
  XMLSchema">
<xs:element name="order">
<xs:complexType>
  <xs:sequence>
  [...]
  </xs:sequence>
```

```
<xs:attribute name="orderid"
   type="xs:string" use="required"/>
</xs:complexType>
</xs:schema>
```

9.4 Active Documents

Active documents are static documents which include code to be run at the client side. Active documents can generate content dynamically at the client side and provide user interactivity, limited personalization, and data display customization. The code is sent with the Web document from the server and then is run on the client machine. The advantages include less processor resources requirements at the server and the fact that the document is relatively static at the server side (it seldom changes, not being generated at the client request) which makes it cache friendly.

There are various solutions for creating active documents, including using JavaScript, Java Applets, and AJAX.

Making use of JavaScript is one of the most popular solutions. JavaScript is a script language used to improve the Web document design, validate forms, detect browsers, create cookies, create dynamic behavior, and interact with the user.

Java Applets are Java applications that are embedded in Web documents and are run by a Java-aware Web browser.

AJAX is a technique for creating better, faster, and more interactive Web applications. It uses existing technologies and languages.

9.4.1 JavaScript

JavaScript is an object-oriented scripting language that adds interactivity to Web documents. A scripting language is a lightweight programming language, but offering enough flexibility and capabilities that makes it a powerful tool for active Web documents. JavaScript code is usually embedded directly into Web (HTML) pages and is executed without preliminary compilation (JavaScript is an interpreted language). However, external files containing JavaScript code are also used in practice.

The embedded JavaScript code can be placed in the header or body of an HTML document.

The HTML head scripts usually represent code (e.g., functions) to be executed when it is called or when events are triggered. The JavaScript code, indicated in the following example as "JSCODE", is loaded in the memory before the document's body is generated:

```
<head>
<script> JSCODE </script>
```

```
[...]
</head>
```

The HTML body scripts consist of JavaScript code which is executed when the page is loaded. In the following example, "JSCODE" generates the Web page content:

```
<body>
<script> JSCODE </script>
[...]
</body>
```

In general, HTML external scripts contain code to be used by more than one Web page. Often the code is written to be reused elsewhere. The external file (e.g., "javascript-file.js") is loaded as follows:

```
<script src="javascript-file.js"> </script>
```

JavaScript offers a multitude of programming features which makes it a relatively powerful tool.

Variables can be defined, although with no explicit type associated at declaration. Declaration can be explicit (using var) or implicit at first assignment.

```
var varname = VALUE
```

or

```
varname = VALUE
```

The scope of a variable declared within a function is the body of that function (local). The scope of a variable declared outside a function is all the code after the declaration (global).

Several flow control statements can be used in JavaScript. The "if" statement can be used in a similar manner with its usage in Java or C++. The "else" branch may be present or missing. A typical "if" statement is provided as an example next:

```
if (CONDITION)
{
  BODY IF TRUE
}
else
{
  BODY IF FALSE
}
```

The "switch" statement is also similar with its corresponding statements in Java and C++. Its "default" option may be missing. An example of how "switch" can be used is shown below:

```
switch (EXPRESSION)
{
   case VALUE1: BODY IF VALUE1; break
   case VALUE2: BODY IF VALUE2; break
   ...
   default: BODY IF DEFAULT
}
```

Three types of loops can be used in JavaScript: "for", "while", and "do-while". Next is an example of a "for" loop:

```
for (INTIALIZATION;
 CONDITION; UPDATE)
{
   BODY
}
```

In "for", BODY is executed zero or more times depending on the CONDITION. UPDATE is executed after the BODY and before the CONDITION is re-evaluated. The "break" statement interrupts the execution of any loop, while the "continue" statement interrupts the execution of any iteration from within a loop.

In BODY, at least one variable affecting the CONDITION must be updated (otherwise there is a danger of creating an infinite loop).

Next is an example of a "while" loop:

```
while (CONDITION)
{
   BODY
}
```

In BODY. at least one variable affecting the CONDITION must be updated. In "while", BODY is executed one or more times depending on the CONDITION.

Next is an example of a "do-while" loop:

```
do
{
   BODY
}
while (CONDITION)
```

Arrays can also be defined within JavaScript code. Declaration and instantiation of an Array is performed using the "new" directive as follows:

```
var names = new Array()
```

Arrays can be initialized when created or after creation by initializing each element separately:

```
/*at declaration*/
var names = new Array("John", "Brian", "Sean")

/*after declaration*/
names[0] = "John";
names[1] = "Brian";
names[2] = "Sean"
```

Elements of an array can be accessed using an index or via a *for in* loop as in the following examples:

```
/*using an index*/
for (i = 0; i < names.length; i++)
{
  document.write(names[i])
}

/*using a for in loop*/
for (x in names)
{
    document.write(names[x])
}
```

For interaction with the user, a set of predefined message boxes or pop-up boxes can be used.

An *alert box* displays a text and the user has to press "OK":

```
alert("text")
```

A *confirm box* allows the user to choose either "OK" or "Cancel", and consequently the box returns "true" or "false", respectively. This type of a pop-up box can be used to get the user's confirmation to perform a certain operation:

```
confirm("text")
```

A *prompt box* allows the user to enter an input value and then click either "OK" or "Cancel". If "OK" is clicked, the box returns the input value, otherwise it returns "null". A default value can be indicated in case the user chooses not to input anything. However, she or he has to click either "OK" or "Cancel":

```
prompt("text","defaultvalue")
```

JavaScript custom functions may be defined as follows using the "function" keyword. The function may return a value using "return":

```
function NAME (VAR1, VAR2, \ldots, VARN)
{
  BODY

  return VAL
}
```

User generated events can also be handled by JavaScript code. Both mouse-related and key-related events may be captured and handled.

Mouse-related events include "onmousedown", "onmouseover", and "onclick". A mouse-related event is triggered when a mouse button is pressed, the mouse pointer is over an element, or a mouse button clicked while the pointer is on an element. Key-related events include "onkeydown" and "onkeyup". A key-related event is triggered when the key is pressed or released.

The following example shows how when the e-mail text field is modified the "verifyemail()" function is called:

```
<input type="text" size="20" id="email"
    onchange="verifyemail()">;
```

Exceptions can also be thrown, caught, and handled using the standard "try-catch" and "throw" directives.

In the following example, if an error occurs in CODE 1, CODE 2 will be executed:

```
try
{
  CODE 1
}
catch(err)
{
  CODE 2
}
```

The statement, "throw(EXCEPTION)" throws an exception that can be caught using catch.

As mentioned before, JavaScript is an object-oriented scripting language. Various objects are already defined and the application developer can further define custom objects.

Predefined objects include *Date* (with the standard methods: getTime(), get-Day(), setFullYear()), *Math* (with the following methods: random(), round(), min(), pow(), cos(), sqrt()), and *String* (with the important methods: bold(), toUpperCase(), substr(), concat(), length).

The following is a user defined object named "Car" which can be instantiated and consequently used within the Web document:

```
function Car(brand, year, color)
{
  this.brand = brand
  this.year = year
  this.color = color

  this.changeBrand=changeBrand;

  function changeBrand(brand)
  {
    this.brand=brand;
  }
}
mycar = new Car("Ferrari", 2007, "red")
```

Timer is another predefined object. Its main methods are "setTimeout()" and "clearTimeout()". In the following example, the STATEMENT is executed after MILLISECONDS time. *t* is a handler to the timer and can be used to cancel it using clearTimeout() which clears the timer:

```
var t = setTimeout("STATEMENT", MILLISECONDS)

clearTimeout(t)
```

The following is a more complex example of timer usage. In this case, a form is used to start and stop the timer. The timer will then increment a variable which will be then written to a text field of the form.

```
<html>
<head>
  <script type="text/javascript">
  // counter
  var c=0
```

Code Listing 9.1 timer.html

```
  var t
  function timedCount()
  {
    document.getElementById('txt').value=c
    c=c+1
    t=setTimeout("timedCount()", 1000)
  }
  function stopCount()
  {
    clearTimeout(t)
    alert("Timer Cancelled")
  }
  </script>
</head>
<body>
  <form>
    <input type="button" value="Start count!"
      onClick="timedCount()">
    <input type="text" id="txt">
    <input type="button" value="Stop count!"
      onClick="stopCount()">
  </form>
</body>
</html>
```

Code Listing 9.1   (Continued)

9.4.2 Java Applets

9.4.2.1 Overview

Java applets are programs written in Java that can be included in a Web page and run on client devices. When a user requests a Web document containing a Java applet, the applet's code is transferred to the user's machine and is executed by the browser's Java Virtual Machine. As they run on the client's machine, in order to protect it, important security-related limitations are imposed on applets.

As it was the case for the servlets, which were presented in the server-side network programming chapter, the applets also have a specific class hierarchy. All applets inherit the main *java.applet.Applet* base class, which has ancestors in the class hierarchy *java.lang.Object, java.awt.Container,* and *java.awt.Panel*, as presented in Fig. 9.4. More recently, the applets extended the *javax.swing.JApplet* base class (in Java 2), which also has the *java.applet.Applet* class as an ancestor.

The *Applet* base class has the following methods: *init(), start(), stop(), destroy(), paint()*. These methods need to be overridden as they do not do anything as imple-

Figure 9.4 Applet class
hierarchy

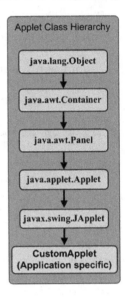

Applet Class Hierarchy

java.lang.Object

java.awt.Container

java.awt.Panel

java.applet.Applet

javax.swing.JApplet

CustomApplet
(Application specific)

mented in the *Applet* class. The *JApplet* class extends *Applet,* and some methods are
implemented in this case.

Finally, the *CustomerApplet* class is a programmer-written class implementing
the application specific functionality. Some methods (e.g., init(), paint(), etc.) are
overridden by this class.

9.4.2.2 Java Applet Life-Cycle

Java applet life-cycle begins with the creation of the applet. When the applet is
created, it is first initialized. The *init()* method is called once, only when the applet
is loaded. After the applet is created, the *start()* method is called. This method may
be called many times whenever the user revisits the page.

Running on the client machine applets usually involve a user interface. In order
to paint the user interface specific to the applet, the *paint()* method is called. This
call can occur many times, every time when the browser needs to repaint the applet
rectangular area. The *repaint()* method can be called when the applet area needs to
be voluntarily redrawn (i.e., when changes occur).

When the user leaves the page, the *stop()* method is called. This call can happen
many times, every time when the user leaves the page.

In order for the applet to be destroyed, the *destroy()* method is called. This call
occurs once only, just before the applet is unloaded.

9.4.2.3 Java Applet Examples

The following code shows an example of an applet extending the Applet class. Each method call determines to simply add the method name to a text buffer. The content of the buffer is displayed every time the applet display area is repainted.

```java
/*include the required packages*/
import java.applet.Applet;
import java.awt.Graphics;

/*define the applet class*/
public class FirstApplet extends Applet
{
  /*declare the buffer used to compose messages*/
  StringBuffer buffer;

  /*override the init() method*/
  public void init()
  {
    buffer = new StringBuffer();
    writeText("init()");
  }

  /*override the start() method*/
  public void start()
  {
    writeText("start()");
  }

  /*override the stop() method*/
  public void stop()
  {
    writeText("stop()");
  }

  /*override the destroy() method*/
  public void destroy()
  {
    writeText("destroy()");
  }
  /*implement the method which assembles text messages*/
  private void writeText(String text)
```

Code Listing 9.2 FirstApplet.java V1

```
  {
    System.out.println(text);
    buffer.append(text);
    repaint();
  }

  /*override the paint() method*/
  public void paint(Graphics g)
  {
    buffer.append("paint()");

    /*get dimensions*/
    int width = getWidth()/4;
    int height = getHeight()/4;
    /*draw a rectangle*/
    g.drawRect(width, height, getWidth()/2,
               getHeight()/2);
    /*draw the string in the middle of the rectangle*/
    g.drawString(buffer.toString(), getWidth()/2,
                 getHeight()/2);
  }
}
```

Code Listing 9.2   (Continued)

The following code shows an example of an applet extending the JApplet class:

```
/*include the required packages*/
import javax.swing.JApplet;
import java.awt.Graphics;

/*define the applet class*/
public class FirstApplet extends JApplet
{

  /*declare the buffer used to compose messages*/
  StringBuffer buffer;

  /*override the init() method*/
  public void init()
```

Code Listing 9.3 FirstApplet.java V2

```
{
  buffer = new StringBuffer();
  writeText("init()");
}

/*override the start() method*/
public void start()
{
  writeText("start()");
}

/*override the stop() method*/
public void stop()
{
  writeText("stop()");
}

/*override the destroy() method*/
public void destroy()
{
  writeText("destroy()");
}

/*implement the method which assembles text messages*/
private void writeText(String text)
{
  System.out.println(text);
  buffer.append(text);
  repaint();
}

/*override the paint() method*/
public void paint(Graphics g)
{
  buffer.append("paint()");

  /*get dimensions*/
  int width = getWidth()/4;
  int height = getHeight()/4;

  /*draw a rectangle*/
  g.drawRect(width, height,
    getWidth()/2, getHeight()/2);
```

Code Listing 9.3 (Continued)

```
    /*draw the string in the middle*/
    g.drawString(buffer.toString(),
      getWidth()/2, getHeight()/2);
  }
}
```

Code Listing 9.3 (Continued)

9.4.2.4 Java Applet Security Aspects

Applets run on the client side code originating from a remote machine (server). This poses various security risks as, first, the origin of the code has to be identified and authenticated, and second, the code must be protected against unauthorized alterations.

In general, applets loaded over the network are prevented from reading and writing files from/to the client file system, making network connections except to the originating host, starting other programs on the client machine, loading libraries, and defining native method calls (giving the applet direct access to the remote computer). Furthermore, the applet is not allowed to perform reading of some system properties or accessing any system services.

Applets loaded from the file system, and not from the network, are not imposed such strict restrictions. Applets can usually make network connections to the host they came from. Applets running within a Web browser can load HTML documents and can invoke public methods of other applets on the same page.

Each browser has a *SecurityManager* object that implements its security policies. When the *SecurityManager* detects a violation, it throws a *SecurityException*. This also applies to applets. Any applet can catch this *SecurityException* and react to it according to its application specific implementation.

9.4.2.5 Java Applet Event Handling

Both classes extended by customer applet classes (i.e., *Applet* and *JApplet*) inherit the same *java.awt.Container* base class. Consequently, all applets inherit the event-handling methods from the *Container* class. To react to an event, an applet must override the appropriate event-specific method (e.g., mouse, keyboard, etc.).

The following example shows the implementation of an applet which catches mouse events and prints a distinct message for each event type:

```
/*import the mouse
events specific packages */
import java.awt.event.MouseListener;
```

Code Listing 9.4 FirstApplet.java V3

```java
import java.awt.event.MouseEvent;

/*import the applet specific packages*/
import javax.swing.JApplet;
import java.awt.Graphics;

/*implement the applet extending JApplet
and implementing MouseListener interface*/
public class FirstApplet extends JApplet
       implements MouseListener
{
  /*define the text buffer*/
  StringBuffer buffer;

  /*override the init() method*/
  public void init()
  {
    addMouseListener(this);
    buffer = new StringBuffer();
  }

  /*overridden method, invoked when
  the mouse enters the applet rectangle*/
  public void mouseEntered(MouseEvent event)
  {
    writeText("MEnter!");
  }

  /*overridden method, invoked when
  the mouse exits the applet rectangle*/
  public void mouseExited(MouseEvent event)
  {
    writeText("MExit!");
  }

  /*overridden; invoked when mouse button is pressed*/
  public void mousePressed(MouseEvent event)
  {
    writeText("MPress!");
  }

  /*overridden; invoked when mouse button is released*/
  public void mouseReleased(MouseEvent event)
```

Code Listing 9.4 (Continued)

```
{
  writeText("MRelease!");
}

/*overridden; invoked when mouse button is clicked*/
public void mouseClicked(MouseEvent event)
{
  writeText("MClick!");
}

/*method which assembles text messages*/
private void writeText(String text)
{
  System.out.println(text);
  buffer.append(text);
  repaint();
}

/*override the paint() method*/
public void paint(Graphics g)
{
  /*draw the string in the middle*/
  g.drawString(buffer.toString(),
      getWidth()/2, getHeight()/2);
}
}
```

Code Listing 9.4 (Continued)

9.5 Conclusion

This chapter has presented the client-side network programming aspects with the focus on designing and writing the code to be run on the client machine following user request for content and its delivery from the server to the client.

The client-located Web browser communicates with the Web server requesting a document. Following the document request, the browser also performs Web document retrieval, received document interpretation and display for the user, and responds to user actions. During document interpretation, the Web browsers run JavaScript code or Java applet code.

This chapter presented details on how both JavaScript and Java applet code can be written and provided full examples to clearly illustrate the client-side network programming principles.

References

1. Connolly D, Masinter L (June 2000) The 'text/HTML' media type. Internet RFC 2854
2. Consortium, WWW, et al (2000) XHTML 1.0: The extensible hypertext markup language. A reformulation of HTML 4 in XML, vol 1
3. Whitehead E, Murata M (1998) XML media types
4. Lie H, Bos B, Lilley C (March 1998) The text/CSS media type. RFC 2318
5. Transformation X (November 1999) Version 1.0, w3c recommendation 16
6. Berners-Lee T, Fielding RT (1996) Hypertext transfer protocol–http/1.0
7. Rescorla E (2000) Rfc 2818: Http over tls. Internet engineering task force: http://www.ietf.org
8. Murata M, Laurent SS, Kohn D (January, 2001) XML media types. RFC3023

Chapter 10
Advanced Client–Server Network Programming

Abstract Client–server communication is at the basis of service provisioning over the Internet. Clients connect to servers and request specific services or tasks to be performed. Sockets have been introduced as basic communication support for client–server data exchange. This chapter introduces advanced client–server network programming techniques. These include the Remote Method Invocation paradigm which allows the clients to invoke methods on servers and retrieve the results and Java applet–servlet communication techniques alongside comprehensive examples.

10.1 Introduction

The server-side network programming is concerned with the case when following client request, the server response involves running code on the server machine. Usually a response document is generated dynamically and is delivered to the client for processing, display, and further interaction with the user. The client-side network programming involves designing and writing code to be run at the client side. Following client requests, the code gets transferred to the client side, then run on client machines. The results are displayed to the users.

The client–server network programming refers to the situation when the code runs at both the server and client side, and the corresponding server and client processes exchange data. Figure 10.1 illustrates the scope of the client–server network programming in terms of communicating client and server processes. Sockets have already been introduced as a great solution for enabling the client–server interprocess communication, while hiding lower layer implementation details from the higher layer abstract tasks.

This chapter presents two alternative solutions for the client–server communication, focusing on Remote Method Invocation (RMI) and Applet–Servlet communication. RMI offers a mechanism for the clients to remotely access services made available at the servers providing all required input data and collecting the outputs following the remote processing at server side. The Applet–Servlet communication involves applets accessing servlet services and exchanging information. Due to the security limitations, the applets have to originate from the same servers that host the

B. Ciubotaru, G.-M. Muntean, *Advanced Network Programming – Principles and Techniques*, Computer Communications and Networks,
DOI 10.1007/978-1-4471-5292-7_10, © Springer-Verlag London 2013

Fig. 10.1 Client–server network programming

communicating front-end servlet. However, there is no limitation in terms of any servlet invoking other servlets in their task execution process.

10.2 Remote Method Invocation

Most client–server communication approaches, including socket-bases solutions, rely on local method calls (both client and server calls are on the local machines). However, in distributed environments, often methods belonging to objects located on remote machines are called.

This is the principle behind Remote Method Invocation (RMI) paradigm which enables platform-independent remote method calls. Consequently, RMI is seen as a conceptual alternative to socket-based client–server communication. The latter exchanges data with the remote applications process in order to obtain results to be used locally. The former makes use of remote method calls to obtain results which are transferred to be used locally.

In order to better explain the basic principle of RMI, let us consider both a server and a client application. The server creates some objects, makes references to these objects accessible remotely, and waits for clients to call methods belonging to these objects. The client obtains a remote reference to a remote object on the server, calls its method(s), and uses the results.

The RMI architecture is presented in Fig. 10.2. Apparently, the remote object's method is called directly from the client object. However, from a development perspective, the client call uses a local place-holder for the remote object (Stub) to communicate with the server's interface (Skeleton), which has access to the remote object method implementation. In reality, the communication happens via a Remote Reference Layer (and transport layer) that serializes the parameters during the call and de-serializes resulting data (when the method returns a value or an object).

RMI involves several steps. First, the server creates the remote object. Then the server registers an interface with a naming service (e.g., registry) in order to make the object accessible to remote client programs. The interface (Skeleton) contains the signatures of those remote object methods the server wants to make accessible.

The client uses the same naming service to obtain reference to this interface. From this interface reference, the client Stub gets created as a local place-holder for the remote object.

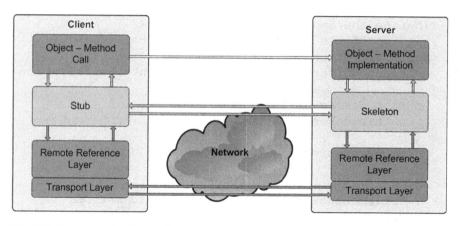

Fig. 10.2 Remote Method Invocation architecture

When the client invokes a method of the remote object, the local stub contacts the remote skeleton and forwards it the call and any required parameters. The Skeleton has access to the real object's method which is invoked. Any resulted value is passed to the Skeleton and then via the Stub is transmitted to the client local calling method.

Serialization and de-serialization of parameters and return value are also called marshalling and un-marshalling, respectively. The Remote Reference Layer hides all the details of the communication protocol between the Stub and the Skeleton. This layer uses transport services (e.g., TCP) provided by the Transport network layer for actual data transfer.

Next the RMI implementation steps are detailed:

- Step 1—Import three Java packages:

```
import java.rmi.*;
import java.rmi.server;
import java.rmi.registry;
```

- Step 2—Create the remote interface:

```
import java.rmi.*;
/*define the remote interface*/
public interface HelloWorld extends Remote {
/*define the method to be called remotely*/
  public String getHelloWorld()
      throws RemoteException;
}
/*Note: The interface must extend the
Remote interface which has no methods of her own*/
```

- Step 3—Define a class that implements the HelloWorld interface:

```
import java.rmi.*
import java.rmi.server.*
```

```
/*define the implementation interface*/
/*it implements the remote interface HelloWorld*/
public interface HelloWorldImpl
   extends UnicastRemoteObject implements HelloWorld
{
   public String HelloWorldImpl()
      throws RemoteException
   {
     /*constructor*/
   }

   /*implementation of the getHelloWorld method
    *exported by the remote interface*/
   public String getHelloWorld() throws RemoteException
   {
      return ("Hello World!");
   }
}
/*Note: The class must extend RemoteObject class
or one of its subclasses.*/
```

- Step 4—Create the server object and establish a connection between the object's name and its reference by registration:

```
import java.rmi.*;

/*implementation of the RMI server*/
/*the server creates the object to be exported*/
/*and publishes it*/
public class HelloWorldServer
{
/*server IP address or localhost if both
 *server and client run on the same physical machine
 *for experimental purposes*/
    private static final String HOST = "localhost";

/*main method is called when
 *starting the server application*/
  public static void main(String[] args)
          throws Exception
   {
     /*instantiates the HelloWorldImpl class*/
     HelloWorldImpl obj = new HelloWorldImpl();

     /*create the URL used to
      *publish the remote object*/
```

```
        String rmiRegName = "rmi://" + HOST +
                "/HelloWorld";

        /*publish the object*/
        Naming.rebind(rmiRegName, obj);

        System.out.println("Binding complete...\n");
    }
}
/*Note: the registration is performed using
the static method rebind of class Naming
that requires two parameters: a String that holds
the name of the remote object as URL with RMI
protocol and a reference to
the remote object (of type Remote).*/
```

- Step 5—Create the client process, obtain a reference to the remote object from the registry, and use it:

```
import java.rmi.*;

/*client implementation class*/
/*the client invokes the published method remotely*/
public class HelloWorldClient
{
/*server IP address or localhost if both
 *server and client run on the same physical machine
 *for experimental purposes*/
 private static final String HOST = "localhost";

/*main method is called when
 *starting the server application*/
 public static void main(String[] args) {
   try
   {
      /*retrieve a reference to the remote object*/
      HelloWorld obj=(HelloWorld)Naming.
        lookup("rmi://" +HOST+ "/HelloWorld");

      /*use remote server service
       *by invoking the method*/
      System.out.println
        ("Server output: " + obj.getHelloWorld());
   }
   catch (ConnectException conEx)    {
      System.out.println("Connection to server
```

```
      failed!");
      System.exit(1);
    }
    catch (Exception e)
    {
      e.printStackTrace();
      System.exit(1);
    }
  }
}
/*Note: The client obtains remote object's reference
using lookup method of class Naming.
The lookup method returns a Remote reference
which needs to be typecasted into HelloWorld*/
```

As in general many methods and objects are needed to be accessed remotely, there are two possible strategies that can be used for building complex applications.

The first strategy uses a separate class to hold all the instances of objects which have methods to be invoked remotely. The second strategy involves multiple references to separate instances of objects allowing the client to make use of them separately, if and when needed.

10.2.1 RMI Strategy A—Using a Common Class

Use a single instance of the implementation class to hold an instance (or more) of a class whose methods will be called remotely. Pass an instance of the latter class as arguments to the constructor of the implementation class. Such an implementation is presented as an example in the following paragraphs.

The interface and the implementation of the first RMI strategy are presented next:

```
/*define the remote interface*/
import java.rmi.*;
import java.rmi.server.*;
import java.util.*;
public interface Numbers extends Remote
{
  public Vector getSetOfNumbers()
    throws RemoteException;
}
/*define the implementation interface*/
public class NumbersImpl
```

Code Listing 10.1 Number.java & NumberImpl.java

```
    extends UnicastRemoteObject implements Numbers
{
  /*define a set of numbers as a vector*/
  private Vector setOfNumbers;

  /*constructor initializing the set of numbers*/
  public NumbersImpl(Vector setNum)
    throws RemoteException
  {
    setOfNumbers = setNum;
  }

  /*access method for the set of numbers*/
  public Vector getSetOfNumbers() throws
  RemoteException
  {
    return setOfNumbers;
  }
}
```

Code Listing 10.1   (Continued)

Implementation of the passed object:


```
/*define Operations class with serializable objects*/
public class Operations implements java.io.Serializable
{
  /*balance stores the account balance*/
  private int balance;

  /*constructor initializing the balance*/
  public Operations (int b)
  {
    balance = b;
  }

  /*implement Operations method*/
  public void addMoney (int sum)
  {
    balance = balance + sum;
  }
```

Code Listing 10.2   Operations.java

```
/*access method for the balance*/
public int getBalance()
{
  return balance;
}
}
```

Code Listing 10.2 (Continued)

Implementation of the server:

```
/*define the server class*/
public class NumbersServer
{
/*server IP address or localhost if
 *both server and client run on the same
 *physical machine for experimental purposes*/
  private static final String HOST = "localhost";

/*main method is called when starting
 *the server application*/
  public static void main(String[] args)
                    throws Exception
  {
    /*create an array of Operations objects*/
    Operations[] oper =
    {
        new Operations(0),
        new Operations(1000)};

    /*create a vector*/
    Vector vectNum = new Vector();
    /*load the array of Operation
     *objects into the vector*/
    for (int i=0; i<oper.length; i++)
      vectNum.addElement(oper[i]);

    /*create a NumbersImpl object
     *holding the vector of Operations*/
    NumbersImpl obj = new NumbersImpl(vectNum);
```

Code Listing 10.3 NumbersServer.java

```
     /*create the URI to publish the object*/
     String rmiRegName = "rmi://" + HOST + "/Numbers";

     /*publish the object*/
     Naming.rebind(rmiRegName, obj);
     System.out.println("Binding success.\n");
  }
}
```

Code Listing 10.3 (Continued)

Implementation of the client:

```
import java.rmi.*;
import java.util.*;

/*define the client class*/
public class NumbersClient
{
/*server IP address or localhost if both server and
 *client run on the same physical machine for testing*/
  private static final String HOST = "localhost";

/*main() is called when starting the server
 *application*/
  public static void main(String[] args)
  {
    try
    {
       /*get a reference to the remote object*/
       Numbers obj = (Numbers)Naming.lookup
                 ("rmi://"+HOST+ "/Numbers");

       /*get the vector of Operations*/
       Vector vectNum = obj.getSetOfNumbers();

       /*for each distinct object
        *perform the operations*/
       for (int i=0; i < vectNum.size(); i++)
```

Code Listing 10.4 NumbersClient.java

```
      {
        Operations oper =
            (Operations)vectNum.elementAt(i);
        oper.addMoney(1000);
        System.out.println
            ("Balance is: " + oper.getBalance());
      }
    }
    catch (ConnectException conEx)
    {
      System.exit(1);
    }
  catch (Exception e)
  {
      System.exit(1);
    }
  }
}
```

Code Listing 10.4　(Continued)

10.2.2 RMI Strategy B—Using Separate Instances

The second approach uses the implementation class to store directly required data and methods and creates instances of this class rather than using a separate class.

```
import java.rmi.*;
import java.rmi.server.*;
/*define the remote interface*/
public interface Numbers extends Remote
{
  /*define the methods to be published*/
  public void addMoney (int sum) throws
    RemoteException;
  public int getBalance() throws RemoteException;
}
```

Code Listing 10.5　Numbers.java

```
/*define the implementation interface*/
```

Code Listing 10.6　NumbersImpl.java

```
public interface NumbersImpl extends
    UnicastRemoteObject implements Numbers
{
  /*balance stores the account balance*/
  private int balance;

  /*constructor initializing the balance*/
  public NumbersImpl(int b) throws RemoteException
  {
    balance = b;
  }

  /*implement operation method*/
  public void addMoney (int sum) throws RemoteException
  {
    balance = balance + sum;
  }

  /*access method for the balance*/
  public int getBalance() throws RemoteException
  {
    return balance;
  }
}
```

Code Listing 10.6 (Continued)

Implementation of the server:

```
import java.rmi.*;
/*define the server class*/
public class NumbersServer
{
/*server IP address or localhost if both server and
 *client run on the same machine for testing purposes*/
  private static final String HOST = "localhost";

/*main() is called when starting the server
 *application*/
```

Code Listing 10.7 NumbersServer.java

```
public static void main(String[] args)
      throws Exception
{
  /*create and array of implementation objects*/
  NumbersImpl[] oper = {
      new NumbersImpl(0),
      new NumbersImpl(1000)};
  for (int i=0; i<oper.length; i++)
  {
    /*generate registration name
     by concatenating the position to URL*/
    String pos = new Integer(i).toString();
    /*generate the URL*/
    String rmiRegName = "rmi://" + HOST
              + "/Numbers" + pos;

    /*register every item of the
     *vector separately to publish it*/
    Naming.rebind(rmiRegName, oper[i]);

    System.out.println("Binding success.\n");
  }
}
}
```

Code Listing 10.7   (Continued)

Implementation of the client:

```
import java.rmi.*;
/*define the client implementation*/
public class NumbersClient
{
/*server IP address or localhost for testing*/
  private static final String HOST = "localhost";

/*define the number of remote objects*/
  private static final int no = 2;
```

Code Listing 10.8   NumbersClient.java

```
/*main method is called when starting
 *the client application*/
  public static void main(String[] args)
  {
    try
    {
      for (int i=0; i < no; i++)
      {
        /*obtain a reference to the
         *object from registry*/
        String pos = new Integer(i).toString();

        String rmiRegName = "rmi://" + HOST
              + "/Numbers" + pos;

        Numbers obj=(Numbers)Naming.lookup(rmiRegName);

        /*use remote server service*/
        obj.addMoney(1000);

        System.out.println("Balance:"
              + obj.getBalance());
      }
    }
    catch (ConnectException conEx)
    {
      System.exit(1);
    }
    catch (Exception e)
    {
      System.exit(1);
    }
  }
}
```

Code Listing 10.8 (Continued)

10.3 Applet–Servlet Communication

This section presents another mechanism to enable the client–server communication by making use of inter-communicating applets and servlets. However, unlike RMI and socket-based communications which exclude each other, the applet–servlet communication is complementary to the other methods. In fact, the applets and servlets can communicate using three distinct methods, including sockets, HTTP connections, and RMI. In the following sections, we will discuss and exemplify the applet–servlet communication using sockets and HTTP. The same steps as in any client–server RMI communications are involved when applets use RMI to access resources offered by the servlet.

Note that, as already mentioned when discussing applet security restrictions, the applets can create network connections to the host they originate from only. This restriction limits the servlet hosting machine to be the same with that which hosts the applet.

The applet–servlet HTTP and socket communication require several steps to be performed at the server and client side.

The applet first needs to get information about the server (IP address, port number) in order to initiate the connection. When the required information is available, it creates and opens a connection to the server. Once the connection is established, the applet sends to the server requests for data, and then it reads server responses. After the communication session finishes, the connection is closed. Various exceptions may be thrown during the communication session, and therefore the applet needs to catch and handle all potential exceptions.

A servlet listens for connection requests, reads, and processes incoming requests and sends responses to the requesting applet.

A simple applet which establishes communication with the servlet is presented next. The applet initiates the communication with the server and fetches the date returned by the servlet every time the *start()* method is called. The date is appended to a buffer which has its whole content displayed at each repainting of the applet display area.

The applet which communicates with the servlet is presented next. Please note that different implementations for the *getDateFrom Servlet()* method will be presented next, employing different communication mechanisms.

```
/*include the required packages*/
import java.applet.Applet;
import java.awt.Graphics;
public class ServCommApplet extends Applet
{
   /*default port to connect to the server*/
   static final int port = 8084;

   /*store messages from server*/
   StringBuffer buffer;

   /*override the start() method*/
   public void start()
   {
     buffer.append(getDateFromServlet());
   }
```

Code Listing 10.9 ServCommApplet.java

```
/*override the paint() method*/
public void paint(Graphics g)
{
  /*draw the string in the middle of the rectangle*/
  g.drawString(buffer.toString(),
     getWidth()/2, getHeight()/2);
}
}
```

Code Listing 10.9   (Continued)

The HTML document created to load the *ServCommApplet* applet which communicates with the *AppCommServlet* servlet is presented in the following code example.

```html
<html>
  <head>
    <meta http-equiv=
      "Content-Type" content="text/html;charset=UTF-8">
    <title>Applet-Servlet Communication Page</title>
  </head>

  <body>
    <h1>Applet-Servlet Communication Main Page</h1>
    <h2>Testing Servlet " AppCommServlet</h2>
    <a href="/servlet/AppCommServlet">AppCommServlet</a>

    <h2>Testing Applet - ServCommApplet</h2>
    <center>
      <applet code="ServCommApplet.class"
          width="300" height="180">
      </applet>
    </center>
  </body>
</html>
```

Code Listing 10.10   serv-comm.html

Servlets and applets may exchange data in the form of text messages or objects. When objects are exchanged, object serialization occurs. The applets and servlets exchange objects of type *Object*, and additional conversion of these objects to and from their original type is required. When applets and servlets exchange text, this is done in form of objects of type *String*. Conversion of data to and from type *String* is required.

Next these two situations are presented separately when the applet and the servlet communicate via text, and when they exchange objects, respectively. Sockets and HTTP connections are used in turn.

10.3.1 Applet–Servlet Communication—Exchanging Text

The following example shows the implementation of the *AppCommServlet* servlet which communicates with the *ServCommApplet* applet presented previously.

The next code snippet shows the implementation of the *doGet()* method of the servlet only. The *doGet()* method awaits applet connection request and responds by returning to the applet the current date.

```
protected void doGet(HttpServletRequest req,
        HttpServletResponse res)
            throws ServletException, IOException
{
  /*format response*/
  res.setContentType("text/html;charset=UTF-8");

  /*send current date in text format*/
  PrintWriter out = res.getWriter();
  out.println(getDate().toString());
  }
  /*close connection*/
  out.close();
}
```

Code Listing 10.11 ServCommApplet.java—doGet()

The following code shows the implementation of *ServCommApplet*'s *getDateFromServlet()* method which implements the communication between the applet and servlet using sockets and exchanging text.

```
/*method which reads data from socket as text*/
private String getDateFromServlet()
{
  /*declare input reader*/
  InputStream in = null;
  try
```

Code Listing 10.12 ServCommApplet.java—getDateFromServer() V1

```
    {
      /*create the socket*/
      /*get server IP address via getHost()*/
      Socket sock = new Socket(getCodeBase().getHost(),
               port);

      /*send an empty line (request text format)*/
      PrintStream out =
          new PrintStream(socket.getOutputStream());
      out.println();
      out.flush();

      /*read the response*/
      in = sock.getInputStream();
      DataInputStream res=
          new DataInputStream(new
                 BufferedInputStream(in));
      String date = res.readLine();

      /*return the retrieved string*/
      return date;
    }
    catch (Exception e)
    {
      e.printStackTrace();   return null;
    }
    finally
    {
      /*close the connection*/
      if (in != null)
      {
        try
        {
          in.close();
        }
        catch (IOException ignored)
        {
        }
      }
    }
}
```

Code Listing 10.12 (Continued)

The following code shows the implementation of *ServCommApplet*'s *getDate-FromServlet()* method which implements the communication between the applet and servlet using HTTP connections and exchanging text.

```
/*implement method which read data using HTTP as text*/
private String getDateFromServlet()
{
  /*declare input reader*/
  InputStream in = null;

  try
  {
    /*create and open URL connection to server*/
    URL url =
      new URL(getCodeBase(),
            "/servlet/AppCommServlet");
    URLConnection con = url.openConnection();
    con.setUseCaches(false);

    /*read response*/
    InputStream in = con.getInputStream();
    DataInputStream res =
      new DataInputStream(new BufferedInputStream(in));
    String date = res.readLine();

    /*return the retrieved string*/
    return date;
  }
  catch (Exception e)
  {
    e.printStackTrace();
    return null;
  }
}
```

Code Listing 10.13　ServCommApplet.java—getDateFromServer() V2

10.3.2 Applet–Servlet Communication—Exchanging Objects

Next the implementation of the *AppCommServlet* servlet's *doGet()* method which communicates with the *ServCommApplet* applet is presented.

The *doGet()* method awaits applet connection request and, if the applet's request is to exchange objects, the servlet responds by returning to the applet the current date as an object.

```java
protected void doGet(HttpServletRequest req,
        HttpServletResponse res)
            throws ServletException, IOException
{
  /*format response*/
  res.setContentType("text/html;charset=UTF-8");

  /*if "format=object" send current date in object
   *format*/
    if ("object".equals(req.getParameter("format")))
  {
    ObjectOutputStream out =
      new ObjectOutputStream(res.getOutputStream());
    out.writeObject(getDate());

    /*close connection*/
    out.close();
    }
}
```

Code Listing 10.14 ServCommApplet.java—doGet()

The following example shows the *ServCommApplet*'s *getDateFromServlet()* method which implements the communication between the applet and servlet using sockets and exchanging objects.

```java
/*implement method which read data from socket as
 *objects*/
private String getDateFromServlet()
{
  /*declare input reader*/
  InputStream in = null;
  try
  {
    /*create the socket*/
    /*get server IP address via getHost()*/
```

Code Listing 10.15 ServCommApplet.java—getDateFromServer() V1

```
      Socket sock = new Socket(getCodeBase().getHost(),
             port);
      /*send "object" (request an object)*/
      PrintStream out =
          new PrintStream(socket.getOutputStream());
      out.println("object");
      out.flush();
      /*read response*/
      ObjectInputStream res = new ObjectInputStream(
             new BufferedInputStream(in));
      /*read the object*/
       Object obj = res.readObject();
      /*perform conversion*/
      Date date = (Date)obj;
      return date.toString();
   }
   catch (Exception e)
   {
     e.printStackTrace();
     return null;
   }
   finally
   {
     /*close the connection*/
     if (in != null)
     {
       try
       {
         in.close();
       }
       catch (IOException ignored)
       {
       }
     }
   }
}
```

Code Listing 10.15 (Continued)

The following example shows the *ServCommApplet*'s *getDateFromServlet()* method which implements the communication between the applet and servlet using HTTP connections and exchanging objects.

```java
/*implement method which read data using HTTP as
 *objects*/
private String getDateFromServlet()
{
  /*declare input reader*/
  InputStream in = null;

  try
  {
    /*create and open URL connection to server*/
    URL url =
      new URL(getCodeBase(), "/servlet/AppCommServlet");
    URLConnection con = url.openConnection();
    con.setUseCaches(false);

    /*read the Date object from the stream*/
    InputStream in = con.getInputStream();
    DataInputStream res =
      new DataInputStream(new BufferedInputStream(in));
    Object obj = res.readObject();
    /*object type conversion*/
    Date date = (Date)obj;

    /*convert Date to String and return*/
    return date.toString();
  }
  catch (Exception e)
  {
    e.printStackTrace();
    return null;
  }
}
```

Code Listing 10.16   ServCommApplet.java—getDateFromServer() V2

More details about the applet–servlet communications can be found in [1].

10.4 Conclusion

This chapter has presented two client–server communication approaches which are different from the basic socket-based solution already presented. Remote Method Invocation (RMI) is an alternative solution to socket communications and involves servers making available some of their methods for remote calls and clients passing parameters, calling the remote shared methods, and collecting and making use of the results. RMI is introduced along with two examples and a step-by-step implementation guide. The applet–servlet communication is a solution complementary not only to socket-based communication, but also to RMI and HTTP-based solutions. This chapter presented examples of how applets and servlets can be employed for remote data exchange when sockets and HTTP connections are used in conjunction.

References

1. Hall M Java EE, Ajax, and Android training, tutorials, consulting, books, and resources. Online: www.coreservlets.com

Chapter 11
Conclusion

Abstract This chapters concludes the book, summarizing its content chapter by chapter.

The network application programming is a large and active area of interest. This book approached this field in a balanced manner, targeting the practical side of network programming, yet offering enough theoretical insight into network architectures, technologies, protocols, and techniques to best inform the readers.

The book starts by introducing theoretical aspects related to network topologies and network types. Existing network topologies such as ring, star, bus, and tree are discussed along with newer approaches such as mesh and ad-hoc.

Still on the theoretical side, network communication protocols and services are introduced. The layered protocol models are discussed next, while relevant layers for application programming such as transport and application layer are further detailed. The main communication-based services such as electronic mail, the World Wide Web, and multimedia delivery applications are then discussed.

The basic network programming paradigms and techniques are introduced first, before processes and threads are presented along with examples to show their use. Inter-thread and inter-process communications are also introduced as the basic principle of network programming.

Next, the basic elements of network programming communication, namely sockets, are detailed. Examples are presented for both socket communication solutions based on connection-less (UDP) and connection-oriented (TCP) transport protocols, respectively.

From an interaction point of view, the client–server communication paradigm is at the basis of any service provided over the Internet. The basic client–server programming techniques are introduced along with the corresponding examples. Unicast, multicast, and broadcast communication paradigms are presented along with implementation examples.

Having the basic network programming techniques introduced, communication-based services are discussed next. Network control and diagnostic services are presented along with more user-oriented services such as electronic mail and file transfer services. The support for Web content transfer services and database connectivity

B. Ciubotaru, G.-M. Muntean, *Advanced Network Programming – Principles and Techniques*, Computer Communications and Networks, DOI 10.1007/978-1-4471-5292-7_11, © Springer-Verlag London 2013

services is also introduced as well as that for multimedia delivery applications, as these are the most important application development avenues in the current context.

Furthermore, techniques and technologies used to develop applications and provided services residing at both ther server-side and client-side are presented. Among the server-side technologies, Java servlets and Java Server Pages are introduced as extremely powerful programming resources for building networking applications. Discussing client-side solutions, active documents based on JavaScript and more advanced application development based on applets are presented and exemplified. The book concludes with more advanced client–server network programming techniques to support Remote Method Invocation (RMI) and applet–servlet communication.

Index

B. Ciubotaru, G.-M. Muntean, *Advanced Network Programming – Principles and Techniques*, Computer Communications and Networks,
DOI 10.1007/978-1-4471-5292-7, © Springer-Verlag London 2013

Printed in the United States
By Bookmasters